# Making Semantics Pragmatic

**Current Research in the Semantics/Pragmatics Interface**
Series Editors:
**Klaus von Heusinger**, University of Stuttgart, Germany
**Ken Turner**, University of Brighton, UK

*Other titles in this series*:

# Making Semantics Pragmatic

EDITED BY

Ken Turner
University of Brighton, UK

United Kingdom – North America – Japan
India – Malaysia – China

Emerald Group Publishing Limited
Howard House, Wagon Lane, Bingley BD16 1WA, UK

First edition 2011

**British Library Cataloguing in Publication Data**
A catalogue record for this book is available from the British Library

ISBN: 978-0-85724-909-8
ISSN: 1472-7870 (Series)

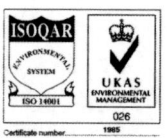

Emerald Group Publishing
Limited, Howard House,
Environmental Management
System has been certified by
ISOQAR to ISO 14001:2004
standards

Awarded in recognition of
Emerald's production
department's adherence to
quality systems and processes
when preparing scholarly
journals for print

INVESTOR IN PEOPLE

Current Research in the Semantics/Pragmatics Interface (CRiSPI)

Series Editors: Klaus von Heusinger, University of Stuttgart, Germany and Ken Turner, University of Brighton, UK

The aim of this series is to focus upon the relationship between semantic and pragmatic theories for a variety of natural language constructions. The boundary between semantics and pragmatics can be drawn in many various ways; the relative benefits of each gave rise to a vivid theoretical dispute in the literature in the last two decades. As a side effect, this variety has given rise to a degree of uncertainty and lack of purpose in the extant publications on the topic. This series provides a forum where the uncertainty within existing literature can be removed and the issues raised by different positions can be discussed with a renewed sense of purpose. The editors intend the contributions to this series to take further strides towards clarity and cautious consensus.

This is how philosophers should salute each other: "Take your time!"

Ludwig Wittgenstein
*Culture and Value*

# List of Contributors

Jay David Atlas
Department of Linguistics and Cognitive Science
Pomona College
Claremont, CA
USA

Alex Barber
Department of Philosophy
Open University
Milton Keynes
UK

Stephen Barker
Department of Philosophy
University of Nottingham
Nottingham, Nottinghamshire
UK

Gunnar Björnsson
Department of Culture and Communication
Linköping University
Sweden

Department of Philosophy
Linguistics and Theory of Science
University of Gothenburg
Sweden

Brendan S. Gillon
Department of Linguistics
McGill University
Montreal, QC
Canada

Marita Ljungqvist
Centre for Languages and Literature
Lund University
Lund
Sweden

Jaroslav Peregrin
Institute of Philosophy
Academy of Sciences of the Czech Republic, Prague &
Faculty of Philosophy
University of Hradec Králové
Czech Republic

Ian Ross
Formerly of University of Pennsylvania
USA

Ken Turner
School of Humanities
University of Brighton
Falmer, Brighton, East Sussex
UK

# Contents

# 1

# Introduction: Preliminary 'sketches of landscapes'

KEN TURNER

> What a Copernicus or a Darwin really achieved
> was not the discovery of a true theory but
> of a fertile new point of view.
> Wittgenstein (1980: 18e)

> The scientist who supposes that he is
> single-mindedly dedicated to the search for truth
> deceives himself. ... He as much decrees as discovers
> the laws he sets forth, as much designs as discerns
> the patterns he delineates.
> Goodman (1978: 18)

1. One dialect of the language game that is (relatively) mainstream academic philosophy can plausibly be said to constitute itself from any one of three principal points of view. From the first of these the questions that it asks, and the answers that it seeks, are metaphysical ones. For example:

1. What is truth?
2. What is justice?
3. What is beauty?

These are questions that have engaged the discourse of the discipline since Plato (if not before). Their answers are considered adequate when, for each question, a coherent and consistent set of necessary and sufficient conditions is provided. Rarely, if ever, have such answers been wholly

*Making Semantics Pragmatic*
Ken Turner (ed.).
Current Research in the Semantics/Pragmatics Interface, Vol. 24.
© 2011 by Emerald Group Publishing Limited. All rights reserved.

satisfactory.[1] From the second of these the questions that it asks, and the answers that it seeks, are semantic ones. For example:

4. What is the meaning of the word 'truth'?
5. What is the meaning of the word 'justice'?
6. What is the meaning of the word 'beauty'?

These are questions of a more recent vintage (as we shall see). Their answers are considered adequate when, for each question, a descriptively accurate and elegant set of correspondence conditions is provided. These sets, especially when conjoined with sets of truth conditions for declarative sentences, have sharpened analytic appreciation into the nature of (some parts of) natural language. And from the third of these the questions and the answers are pragmatic ones. For example:

7. How is the word 'truth' used?
8. How is the word 'justice' used?
9. How is the word 'beauty' used?

These questions are fashionable in present times, but it is not entirely clear what persuasive and convincing answers to them consists in. The 'vocabularies' of use are far from adequately developed.

2. There *may* be a natural, historical development in the appearance of these points of view. Recanati (e.g. 1994, 2004, 2005) certainly seems to think so.[2] Whilst he has relatively little to say about metaphysics, he is, in some of his work, quite confident that there is, and indeed should be, an historical, descriptive and theoretical evolution from semantic to pragmatic questions.[3]

---

[1] Or, somewhat more emphatically (to introduce someone whose work will be considered a little later): 'The pattern of attempted definition, counterexample, amended definition, further counterexample, ending with a whimper of failure, is repeated with variations throughout the Socratic and middle Platonic dialogues. Beauty, courage, virtue, friendship, love, temperance are put under the microscope, but no convincing definitions emerge. The only definitions Plato seems happy with are tendentious characterizations of what it is to be a sophist. He also gives a few trivial samples of correct definitions: of a triangle; of mud (earth and water)' (Davidson, 1996: 263).

[2] So, in some of his moods, does Davidson (e.g. Davidson, 1999: 42–43, 2006: 1067).

[3] Note for the post-preliminary sketch: Recanati (2005) makes a rather more interesting point than is acknowledged here in that he suggests that a focus be put on (the varieties of) semantic and pragmatic *answers*. Thus, to abbreviate too radically, he identifies such increasingly context-sensitive positions as 'proto-literalism', 'eternalism', 'conventionalism' and others, as attempts to provide the resources to answer the questions (4)–(6) above without the inquiry having to be 'tipped over' and faced with the questions (7)–(9). For the record, it is curious to note that, for Recanati (1994), Grice is a

2.1. Is, and indeed should be. If this proposal is plausible then Dummett can be recruited to locate the historical move from metaphysics to semantics. In 'the most pregnant philosophical paragraph ever written' (Dummett, 1991: 111) Frege argues:

> §62. How, then, are numbers to be given to us, if we cannot have any ideas or intuitions of them? Since it is only in the context of a proposition that words have any meaning, our problem becomes this: To define the sense of a proposition in which a number word occurs. That, obviously, leaves us still a very wide choice. But we have already settled that number words are to be understood as standing for self-subsistent objects. And that is enough to give us a class of propositions which must have a sense, namely those which express our recognition of a number as the same again. (Frege, 1953: 73e; originally 1884)

This, says Dummett, 'is the very first example of what has become known as the "linguistic turn" in philosophy. Frege's *Grundlagen* may justly be called the first work of analytic philosophy' (Dummett, 1991: 111). This suggestion has been robustly endorsed by Kenny (1995: 211).

2.1.1. But although endorsed in places, this suggestion has not, in other quarters, gone unchallenged. Hacker (1997) finds the transition in the *Tractatus* and this perspective is endorsed by Baldwin (2006). Others, or, at least, *an* other, prefer(s) to profile the Vienna Circle (e.g. Skorupski, 1997a, b). These, alternative, proposals, though not without a certain interest, are ultimately implausible. The Vienna Circle had views that were decidedly influenced by the contents of the *Tractatus*, and Wittgenstein first argued with and then countenanced Frege's work. In other words, and more explicitly, Frege's logicism provided the spark that put an end to the Dark Ages and began the intellectual illumination of the twentieth century. Neither Wittgenstein nor the Vienna Circle could have done what they did without Frege previously doing what he did. Not for the first time (cf. Turner, 1999: 3) the author of this Introduction stands four-square behind Dummett. (But historical periodicisation is never the most precise of sciences and any future

---

villain of the piece. He, Grice, says Recanati (1994: 160–161) launched a counter-attack on what he, Recanati, calls contextualism (the position interested in answering questions (7)–(9) above) but, concludes Recanati (1994: 161), 'the argument that Grice used in his counter-attack was either fallacious or did not constitute a refutation of contextualism'. This is an odd equivocation: Either it wasn't a valid argument or it *was* a valid argument, but not a refutation. Grice is not often, or even ever, lined up with the 'bad guys'. He is more often presented as the conciliator who brought peace in the arguments between the formal and ordinary language philosophers and, as a result, has since been canonised as the patron saint of the semantics–pragmatics interface.

sketch will profit from the careful study of Coffa (1991), Dummett (1994) and Losonsky (2006).)[4]

2.2. If Recanati's proposal continues to be plausible, then Brandom can be recruited to locate the historical move from semantics to pragmatics. He observes:

> ... the most significant conceptual development in this tradition (analytic philosophy, KT) – the biggest thing that ever happened to it – is the *pragmatist challenge* to it that was mounted during the middle years of the twentieth century. Generically, this movement of thought amounts to a displacement from the center of philosophical attention of the notion of <u>meaning</u> in favour of that of <u>use</u>: in suitably broad senses of those terms, replacing concern with semantics by concern with pragmatics. The towering figure behind this conceptual sea-change is, of course, Wittgenstein. (Brandom, 2008: 3)

The context makes it clear that of the several Wittgensteins now discernable (e.g. Stroll, 2000, 2002, but cf. Gerrard, 2002) it is the one which is standardly called the 'Later Wittgenstein' to which Brandom is here referring.

2.2.1. Brandom does not have Dummett's precision accuracy to pinpoint the 'pregnant philosophical paragraph' in which this second transformation might be said to have taken place. This is no doubt an inevitable consequence of the many challenges that face the Wittgenstein exegete (cf. any book or academic article with the word 'Wittgenstein' in the title). The 'Later Wittgenstein', on some accounts, seems to have been current, in different degrees of intensity, somewhere between 1930 and 1950. But although there is no paragraph, there is an event which may be employed for orientation. The story goes that Wittgenstein returned to philosophy and, on one occasion, explained his views to his colleague Piero Sraffa. In reply, Sraffa made 'a Neapolitan gesture' and asked (words to the effect) "What is the logical form of *that*?" This story is first mentioned in von Wright (1955/1958: 15) and has since become part of the folklore (cf. Monk, 1990: 260ff, 2005: 64; Heaton and Groves, 1994: 68; Baker and Hacker, 2005: 226–227; Schroeder, 2006: 116; McGuinness, 2008: 9). Malcolm (1958: 69) reports that Sraffa's question 'broke the hold ... of the conception that a proposition must literally be a "picture" of the reality that it describes' and Wittgenstein, in the Preface to the *Investigations*, himself

---

[4]Rorty (1967), too, should not go unmentioned. He provides a particularly clever and measured survey of the (strategic aspects of) the predicament.

acknowledges that he is 'indebted to *this* stimulus for the most consequential ideas of this book' (Wittgenstein, 1968: viii).[5]

2.3. But Recanati's proposal of linear, perhaps inevitable and deterministic, development of philosophical and linguistic inquiry is not the only model on the table. Stroll (2000: Chapter 1) proposes an alternative. He suggests that the processes employed in the manufacture of Sherry provide a suitable metaphor for the interanimation of philosophies (and philosophers). Quoting Lichine (1971: 492) he writes:

> The most interesting thing about Sherry ... is the peculiar system by which it is kept at its best. A very old, very fine Sherry has the power to educate and improve a younger one. Because of this, the old wines are kept in the oldest barrels of what the growers call *a solera*. This is a series of casks graduated by age. A series is made up of identical butts. The oldest class in a *solera* is the one called the Solera. The next oldest is the first Criadera, the next the second Criadera and so on. When the wine is drawn from the Solera, it is drawn in equal quantity from each butt. Then starts a progressive system by which the Solera is refilled by the first Criadera and that in turn by the second Criadera, etc. The magic result of this system is that the oldest casks remain eternally the same in quality. ... By this system, it is possible not only to preserve the same quality and character of wine over the years, but also, by constantly refreshing the Fino types with younger wine, to keep these from losing their freshness. (Stroll, 2000: 4)

Thus the Solera System is an alternative to the Linear System.[6] But it is doubtful that the metaphor is necessary.

2.3.1. 'One of the easiest, but more fallacious, ways of looking at the history of a subject or a branch of knowledge is that of unitary development. On this view, progress is essentially the gradual building up from the beginnings of the subject as it is envisaged, taught, and practiced at the time of writing'. Thus, the two first sentences of Robins (1976). He went on to consider aspects of the history of linguistics. But

---

[5]There is a small difference in the von Wright account with respect to the Malcolm account of this event (see Malcolm, 1958: 69fn1).

[6]There is some evidence that others already acknowledge something like the Solera System: 'we should treat those who are great but dead as if they were great and living, as persons who have something to say to us *now*; and, further, that in order to do this we should do our best to 'introject' ourselves into their shoes, into their ways of thinking; indeed to rethink their offerings as if it were ourselves who were the offerers; and then, perhaps, it may turn out that it *is* ourselves' (Grice, 1986: 66). And maybe: 'I believe that my originality (if that is the right word) is an originality belonging to the soil rather than to the seed. (Perhaps I have no seed of my own.) Sow a seed in my soil and it will grow differently than it would in any other soil' (Wittgenstein, 1980: 36e).

such observations can be applied to the history of philosophy in general and the philosophy of language in particular. One index of the absence of unitary development is that in spite of all the journals, the textbooks, the international organisations and conferences, all the institutional accoutrements in semantics and pragmatics of what Kuhn calls 'normal science', the metaphysical questions, for example, have not gone away.[7] Robins ends his discussion by quoting, apparently with approval, Fisher (1936: v): 'Men ... have discerned in history a plot, a rhythm, a predetermined pattern ... I see only one emergency following upon another as wave follows wave'.[8]

3. So much for the 'is'. Now for the 'should be'. One of the traditional sites for this discussion is that of the logical constants: what *do* they mean? The formal language 'side' (various) argues that the meaning of 'and' is representable by truth-functional '&', 'or' by truth-functional 'v', 'not' by truth-functional '¬' and 'if' by the material conditional '→'. The ordinary language 'side' (e.g. Strawson, 1952) deny this and counter-argue that the 'meaning' of each of these words is considerably more complicated than is recognised by the formalists' account.[9] Since Strawson, the relations between 'and' and '&', 'or' and

---

[7]See Soloman and Murphy (1990) and Schantz (2002) for just two examples. (Google will reveal more.)

[8]Or, to turn to a move in a different language game:

> You're searching, Joe,
> For things that don't exist; I mean beginnings.
> Ends and beginnings – there are no such things.
> There are only middles.
>
> Frost (1951: 141)

[9]In his 1969 Inaugural Lecture at the University of Oxford, entitled 'Meaning and truth' (published in Strawson, 1971: 170–189), Strawson rather lets rhetoric get the better of him and he makes reference to 'a Homeric struggle' between the theorists of formal semantics (the formal language side) and the theorists of communicative intention (the ordinary language side). Blackburn (1984: 127–130) recycles the label and the associated picture but Neale (2005: 177fn23) finds the expression and its implications 'bizarre'. It is difficult to disagree with this last judgement. In other work, Neale (2007a) replaces talk of a dichotomy with talk of a cline: there is 'heavy-handed semantics' and 'heavy-handed pragmatics' each with presumably numerous degrees of heaviness. And in other work again (Neale, 2007b), he expresses scepticism about the current fashion for analysing the meaning of 'know' in a very heavy-handed pragmatics. The original, contextualist, claim is that 'know' is an indexical. Neale argues that the hallmark of indexicality is perspectivity and that 'know' lacks this hallmark. (This is an argument that, in another context, deserves to be examined further, and compared with Bach's (2005, 2008) reservations about contextualism.)

'v' and 'not' and '¬' have been the focus of intense examination and it *may* be possible to now discern the emergence of a relatively stable consensus.[10] The relations between 'if' and ' → ' have always been, and still continue to be, much more troublesome.

3.1. Unlike the cases with the other connectives, where the truth-functional interpretations are yielding to arguments that purport to demonstrate that the natural equivalents of each of the formal operators has a more 'pragmatic' nature, there has been, and there continues to be, a concerted action to keep 'if' material.

3.1.1. Evidence.

> The question how well '$p \supset q$' conforms to the ordinary indicative 'if-then' is in any case one of linguistic analysis, and of little consequence for our purposes. What is important to note is that '$p \supset q$', the so-called material conditional, is to have precisely the meaning '$\neg(p \ . \ \neg q)$' (or '$\neg p$ v $q$'); and it will become evident enough ... how well adapted this concept is to purposes for which the idiom 'if-then' naturally suggests itself. In particular ... the material conditional is precisely what is wanted for the individual instances covered by a general conditional of the type (1) ( = 'If anything is a vertebrate, it has a heart'). (Quine, 1951/1974: 22)

3.1.2.

> Now one point we must make absolutely clear, at the risk of being tedious ... we have no intention of suggesting that 'If p then q' always means just 'p materially implies q'. In fact, in ordinary discourse, statements of the form 'If p then q' always (or almost always) mean *more* than 'p materially implies q'. But the important point is that they never mean *less*. Furthermore, material implication is the sort of notion which has a place in formal logic – it is a structurally based notion which we can deal with. ... But, you may say, 'If p then q' may never mean *less* than 'p materially implies q' – but does material implication catch *enough* of the meaning of 'If p then q'? ... The answer here is that regarding hypothetical propositions as expressing material implications does catch enough of their meaning *for our purposes*. We *can* get the results we seek by attending to just this element and ignoring the rest – and that is sufficient justification for doing so. (Hughes and Londey, 1965: 16–17; emphases in the original)

---

[10]On conjunction, see Carston (2002: Chapter 3), Blakemore and Carston (2005) and Txurruka (2003). On disjunction, see Simons (2000). On negation, see, of course, Horn (2001). For a general discussion, see Edgington (2006).

### 3.1.3.

Many intuitively valid inferences involving conditionals can be successfully analysed using the purely truth-functional →. In the light of this ... it may well be (I actually believe it to be) that the truth-functional conditional is *overall* the best coherent model of inferences involving indicative conditionals and that where our intuitions conflict with its deliverances those intuitions may simply not offer the best, or even good, guidance. There is nothing bizarre about this suggestion: intuitions are frequently, if reluctantly, ignored in the face of coherent theory which says that they are wrong. (Howson, 1997: 172; emphases added)

### 3.1.4.

The analysis of "if ... then ... " that is suggested by material implication is a truth functional one. That is to say A ⊃ B is true or false only because of the *truth values* of A and B. The sentence A ⊃ B does not imply that there is any causal link between A and B or anything like that. All that A ⊃ B states is that it happens not to be the case that both A is true and B is false. The question is: can this analysis be applied to natural language? *Despite its problems material implication* does *display many of the properties of the natural conditional.* We will assume the answer is "yes". Material implication is an excellent starting point for a logic of validity (among other things). (Gabbay, 2002: 67; emphases in the original)

### 3.1.5.

I'm inclined to think that English uses "if ... then ... " as a material conditional. (Keenan, 2005, 21 December, 5:37 pm).

3.2. An insufficiently appreciated fact is that Grice's Conversational Hypothesis has as one of its principal purposes to make the material analysis, at least for indicative conditionals, somewhat more palatable.[11] This Hypothesis appears to inoculate the analysis against the following paradoxes:

Paradox 1:  From any truth as premise one may infer the conditional composed of the negation of that truth as antecedent and any other proposition as consequent.

---

[11]Insufficiently appreciated but not entirely unappreciated (see Walker (1975: 133), Grandy (1989: 514), Prior (1962: 8) and Price (1986: 28) for relevant discussion). Hunter (1971: xiii) recommends that the different senses of 'if' be discriminated and considered in non-truth-conditional logics.

Symbolically:   From P, one may infer $\neg P \to Q$. More formally: $P \vdash$
                $\neg P \to Q$.

Colloquially:   'It is raining' therefore 'If it is not the case that it is raining
                then the Prime Minister is upbeat about the economy.

Paradox 2:      From any truth as premise one may infer the
                conditional composed of any proposition as antecedent
                and that original truth as consequent.

Symbolically:   From Q, one may infer $P \to Q$. More formally: $Q \vdash P \to Q$.

Colloquially:   'The Prime Minister is upbeat about the economy'
                therefore 'If it is raining the Prime Minister is upbeat
                about the economy'.

3.2.1. But there are inferences other than those classified as the paradoxes of material implication that are at least counter-intuitive and which fall outside the orbit of the conversational 'solution'. For example, the following is truth-functionally valid but intuitively invalid:

> If John comes from Brighton, then he is a southerner. Therefore, if
> John rides a bicycle to work he is a southerner, or, if he comes from
> Brighton, then he owns a Mercedes Benz.

whilst

> The meeting will be held in the Pavilion, or, if the weather is fine it
> will be held on the beach. Therefore, either the meeting will be held
> in the Pavilion or it will be held on the beach.

is truth-functionally invalid but intuitively valid.[12] These kinds of counterexamples do not find their way into the usual run of textbooks,

---

[12]Whatever the alleged merits of the Conversational Hypothesis, and whatever its impact on the paradoxes of material implication, the Hypothesis should be treated, ultimately, with caution. The maxims are vaguely formulated and uncoordinated, and it remains uncertain just how many there are ('And one might need others' (Grice, 1989: 27)); the definitions of 'saying' and 'implicating' are unorthodox; the classification of implicatures is arbitrary; the calculation of implicature is a puzzle; the justification for the assumption that 'it is more generally feasible to strengthen one's meaning by achieving a superimposed implicature, than to make a relaxed use of an expression' (Grice, 1989: 48) is not provided (Grice's next ten words are 'and I don't know how this assumption could be justified'); it is not clarified what the words 'beyond necessity' in the statement of Modified Occam's Razor – '*Senses are not to be multiplied beyond necessity*' (Grice, 1989: 47) – really mean; the scheme is restricted to 'maximally effective exchange[s] of information' (Grice, 1989: 28) and therefore needs 'to be generalized to allow for such general purposes as influencing or directing the actions of others' (Grice, 1989: 28); the

but their existence ought to shake the widespread confidence in the material analysis.

3.3. Consider, somewhat briefly, names. It used to be thought that names abbreviated certain properties and that knowledge of those properties ensured knowledge of the names' bearers and the proper use of the names. But the modal arguments removed the temptations in that picture and ushered in an alternative:

> Someone, let's say, a baby, is born; his parents *call* him by a certain name. They *talk* about him to their friends. Other people meet him. Through various *sorts of talk* the name is spread from link to link as if by a chain. ... a chain of *communication* [is] established, by virtue of ... membership in a community which passed the name on from link to link. (Kripke, 1980: 91; emphases added)

The baptismal account wears its pragmatic credentials confidently on its sleeve and is so natural and intuitive that, once stated, it is next to impossible to understand why the descriptivist account held sway for so long. The Description Theory of Names, in fact, is a perfect example of a picture holding captives.

3.4. Consider, next, knowledge attributions. The usual exhibit here is some version of the sceptical argument:

> I do not know that I am not an electro-chemically stimulated, formaldehyde sodden brain in a vat.

> If I do not know that I am not an electro-chemically stimulated, formaldehyde sodden brain in a vat, then I do not know that I have hands.

> Therefore, I do not know that I have hands.

This kind of argument has exercised the profession for centuries. The first premise is plausible and may be true. The second premise is true, but everybody will want to say that the conclusion is false. DeRose (e.g. 1992) with examples relating to his bank and Cohen (e.g. 1999) with examples relating to Chicago Airport both claim that the verb 'know' in the premise is not the same 'know' as that which appears

---

analysis of presupposition as implicature is unclear; the story about conditionals is, again in Grice's own words, 'rambling' and throws up a problem about which he is obliged to say 'I am afraid I do not yet see what defense (if any) can be put up against this objection' (Grice, 1989: 83); and the relationship between the theory of meaning and the theory of conversation is entirely mysterious. The various generations of neo-Gricean pragmatics have not, even on a sympathetic reading, firmed up much of this indeterminacy (and may well have introduced indeterminacies of their own). To repeat: The 'vocabularies' of use are far from adequately developed.

in the conclusion. The idea is this: speakers use knowledge attributions in at least two different kinds of contexts – High Stakes Contexts (HSCs) and Low Stakes Contexts (LSCs). In LSCs the consequences of being mistaken are negligible; in HSCs the consequences of being wrong are more serious. The sceptical paradox arises because the 'know' in the premise is being used in a HSC (where it might plausibly be said that we don't *really* know anything) and the 'know' in the conclusion is being used in an LSC (where it might plausibly be said that, for everyday purposes, we all know such mundane things). There is a further idea: it is that we spend, when we can, our conversational lives in the relative comfort of non-risky LSCs. There will come times, of course, when it is necessary to 'raise the stakes' (philosophy seminars, courts of law) but for the most part, at least with respect to knowledge attributions, LSCs are good enough. There may be here an association with vagueness: Lewis certainly seems to think so:

> ... for some reason raising of standards goes more smoothly than lowering. If the standards have been high, and something is said that is true enough only under lowered standards, and nobody objects, then indeed the standards are shifted down. But what is said, although true enough under the lowered standards, may still seem imperfectly acceptable. Raising of standards, on the other hand, manages to seem commendable even when we know that it interferes with our conversational purpose. Because of this asymmetry, a player of language games who is so inclined may get away with it if he tries to raise the standards of precision as high as possible – so, high, perhaps, that no material object whatever is hexagonal. (Lewis, 1979: 182)[13]

So, with this distinction between HSCs and LSCs speakers can now confidently assert that they know that they have hands.

3.4.1. DeRose and Cohen (and others) call their position epistemological contextualism. It is, currently, the most fashionable of the

---

[13]Schiffer would seem to agree with the association: 'The verb "to know", like virtually every expression, is vague, and there is a certain context variability inherent in vagueness. The penumbras of vague terms can dilate or constrict according to conversational purposes' (1996: 327). And Wittgenstein would seem to agree with the differences in standards and the consequences of those differences: 'When philosophers use a word – "knowledge" (other words deleted KPT) – and try to grasp the *essence* of the thing, one must always ask oneself: is the word ever actually used in this way in the language game which is its original home? What *we* do is to bring words back from their metaphysical to their everyday use' (1968: §116; emphasis in the original). The reference to hexagonal objects in the Lewis quote is, of course, to Austin's example 'France is hexagonal'.

'fertile point(s) of view' (cf. Stanley, 2005; DeRose, 2009). It can be anticipated that the contextualist strategy will be employed beyond epistemology.

3.5. Consider, finally, the strange case of truth-theoretic semantics.[14] This project starts with the claim that natural languages must be compositional because, if not, they would not be learnable. The project continues on the assumption that a 'Tarski-style theory of truth', slightly modified to attend to certain matters of context, is the preferred vehicle for modelling the compositionality.

3.5.1. So, with the suggested modification, T., below

> T.   $s$ is true if and only if $p$

(where '$s$' is, of course, a structurally described sentence in the object language and '$p$' a 'logical form'[15] expressed with the resources of an available meta-language) becomes (something like) T*. below

> T*.   $s$ is true relative to a speaker and a time if and only if $p$

3.5.2. It is freely acknowledged, however, that the contextualisation can be made even more sensitive:

> Convention T must be revised to make truth sensitive to *context* (Davidson, 1984: 58).

> ... it is necessary to relativize the theory of truth to times and speakers (*and possibly to some other things*). (Davidson, 1984: 149–150)

> If *a speaker's purpose* is to give information, or to make an honest assertion, then the speaker .... (Davidson, 1984: 161)

> ... it is the notion of truth, as applied to closed sentences, which must be connected with *human ends and activities* .... (Davidson, 1984: 222)

---

[14]The term is taken from Lepore and Ludwig (2007). The case is 'strange' because it seems that the centre of gravity of this paradigm is in pragmatics, rather than being within the orbit of truth (see the observation cited in Footnote 18 below).

[15]The scare quotes are there for a reason: 'the concept of logical form, as applied to natural languages, warrants much more attention than it has received. Many, including me, have been pretty cavalier in making claims about logical form when we have never tried very hard to define it' (Davidson, 2001: 301). Cf. Neale (1994); Jackson (2007) and especially Lepore and Ludwig (2001: 54) who add: 'Given its widespread use in philosophy and linguistics, it is rather surprising that the concept of logical form has not received more attention by philosophers than it has'.

And so, to conclude:

> Convention T, even when bent to fit *the awkward shapes of natural language*, points the way to a radical theory of interpretation. (Davidson, 1984: 75; emphases added in all cases)

'Context', 'and possibly ... some other things', 'a speaker's purpose', 'human ends and activities', 'the awkward shapes of natural language' all point the way to radical interpretation. But what *is* radical interpretation?

3.5.3. Radical interpretation is Brand Davidson's way of talking about pragmatics.[16] It involves a hearer making hypotheses about what a speaker 'holds true'. But radical interpretation is unlike all other varieties of pragmatic inquiry in that the hypotheses are arrived at not by principles of cooperation, relevance, politeness or rationality, or by maxims relating to Q, R, M or I but by 'wit, luck, and wisdom' (Davidson, 1986: 446), by 'the exercise of imagination' (Davidson, 2005: 110), by 'some degree of invention' (Davidson, 2005: 156) and by 'intuition ... and skill ... and taste and sympathy' (Davidson, 1984: 279). He concludes:

> ... all communication by speech assumes the interplay of *inventive* construction and *inventive* construal (Davidson, 1984: 245. Emphases added.) There is no more chance of regularizing, or teaching, this process than there is of regularizing or teaching the process of creating new theories to cope with new data in any field – for this is what this process involves. (Davidson, 1986: 446)[17]

---

[16]Or, perhaps more accurately, transcendental pragmatics. Radical interpretation is a rational reconstruction, and not an empirical account, of how one comes to understand another. Davidson has been pretty clear on the matter – 'I do not think I have ever conflated the (empirical) question how we actually go about understanding a speaker with the (philosophical) question what is necessary and sufficient for such understanding. I have focused on the latter question, not because I think it brings us close to the psychology of language learning and use, but because I think it brings out the philosophically important aspects of communication while the former tempts us to speculate about arcane empirical matters that neither philosophers nor psychologists know much about' (Davidson, 2005: 111–112) – but this has not prevented others making what Ramberg (1989: 74) has called the 'fatal' mistake of confusing the two. This may have been the source of many cross purpose discussions (cf. Fodor and Lepore, 1993; Sinclair, 2002) but the full ventilation of these details will be left for another day.

[17]'If you see a ketch sailing by and your companion says, "Look at that handsome yawl", you may be faced with a problem of interpretation. One natural possibility is that your friend has mistaken a ketch for a yawl, and has formed a false belief. But if his vision is good and his line of sight favourable it is even more plausible that he does not use the word "yawl" quite as you do, and has made no mistake at all about the position of the jigger on the passing yacht. We do this sort of *off the cuff interpretation* all the time,

Truth-theoretic semantics is, it is insufficiently recognised, thoroughly and constitutively pragmatic (cf. Child, 1987: 549).[18] On the spectrum of theoretical possibilities it is at the opposite end of those theories of pragmatics that acknowledge and employ propositions (and degrees of 'propositionality') which are essentially and constitutively semantic.

     4. What is your aim in pragmatics? – To shew the semanticist the way out of semantics.

# References

Bach, K. 2005. The Emperor's new 'knows'. In G. Preyer and G. Peter, eds., *Contextualism in Philosophy: Knowledge, Meaning, and Truth*, pp. 51–89. Oxford: Clarendon Press.

Bach, K. 2008. Applying pragmatics to epistemology. In E. Sosa and E. Villanueva, eds., *Interdisciplinary Core Philosophy*, (Philosophical Issues 18.), pp. 68–88. Oxford: Wiley-Blackwell.

Baker, G. P. and P. M. S. Hacker. 2005. *Wittgenstein: Understanding and meaning. Volume 1 of An Analytical Commentary on the Philosophical Investigations. Part II: Exegesis §§1-184.* (Second, extensively revised edition by P. M. S. Hacker.) Oxford: Blackwell Publishing.

Baldwin, T. 2006. Philosophy of language in the twentieth century. In E. Lepore and B. C. Smith, eds., *The Oxford Handbook of Philosophy of Language*, pp. 60–99. Oxford: Clarendon Press.

Blackburn, S. 1984. *Spreading the Word: Groundings in the Philosophy of Language.* Oxford: Clarendon Press.

Blakemore, D. and R. Carston. 2005. The pragmatics of sentential coordination with *and. Lingua* 115:569–589.

Brandom, R. 2008. *Between Saying and Doing: Towards an Analytic Pragmatism.* Oxford: Oxford University Press.

Carston, R. 2002. *Thoughts and Utterances: The Pragmatics of Explicit Communication.* Oxford: Blackwell.

Child, T. W. 1987. Critical notice: Truth and interpretation: Perspectives on the philosophy of Donald Davidson. Edited by Ernest Lepore. *Mind* 96:549–569.

---

deciding in favour of reinterpretation of words in order to preserve a reasonable theory of belief' (Davidson, 1984: 196; emphases added.)

[18]Insufficiently recognised, but not entirely unrecognised: 'Although, ... , the main part of Davidson's work in the philosophy of language appears to be, and is often taken to be, the elaboration of a theory of formal semantics, it becomes clear once one considers the question of how to apply a truth theory, that his real concern is with the interpretation of speakers of a language' (Evnine, 1991: 178).

Coffa, J. A. 1991. *The Semantic Tradition from Kant to Carnap: To the Vienna Station.* Cambridge: Cambridge University Press.

Cohen, S. 1999. Contextualism, scepticism, and the structure of reasons. *Philosophical Perspectives* 12:57–89.

Davidson, D. 1984. *Inquiries into Truth and Interpretation.* Oxford: Clarendon Press.

Davidson, D. 1986. A nice derangement of epitaphs. In E. Lepore, ed., *Truth and Interpretation: Perspectives on the Philosophy of Donald Davidson,* pp. 433–446. Oxford: Basil Blackwell.

Davidson, D. 1996. The folly of trying to define truth. *Journal of Philosophy* 93:263–278.

Davidson, D. 1999. Interpretation: Hard in theory, easy in practice. In M. de Caro, ed., *Interpretations and Causes: New Perspectives on Donald Davidson's Philosophy,* pp. 31–44. Dordrecht: Kluwer Academic Publishers.

Davidson, D. 2001. Comments on Karlovy Vary papers. In P. Kotatko, P. Pagin, and G. Segal, eds., *Interpreting Davidson,* pp. 285–307. Stanford: CSLI Publications.

Davidson, D. 2005. *Truth, Language, and History.* Oxford: Clarendon Press.

Davidson, D. 2006. The perils and pleasures of interpretation. In E. Lepore and B. C. Smith, eds., *The Oxford Handbook of Philosophy of Language,* pp. 1056–1068. Oxford: Clarendon Press.

DeRose, K. 1992. Contextualism and knowledge attributions. *Philosophy and Phenomenological Research* 52:913–929.

DeRose, K. 2009. *The Case for Contextualism: Knowledge, Skepticism, and Context,* Vol. 1. Oxford: Clarendon Press.

Dummett, M. 1991. *Frege: Philosophy of Mathematics.* London: Duckworth.

Dummett, M. 1994. *Origins of Analytical Philosophy.* Cambridge, MA: Harvard University Press.

Edgington, D. 2006. The pragmatics of the logical constants. In E. Lepore and B. C. Smith, eds., *The Oxford Handbook of Philosophy of Language,* pp. 768–793. Oxford: Clarendon Press.

Evnine, S. 1991. *Donald Davidson.* Cambridge: Polity Press.

Fisher, H. A. L. 1936. *A History of Europe.* London: Arnold.

Fodor, J. and E. Lepore. 1993. Is radical interpretation possible? In R. Stoecker, ed., *Reflecting Davidson: Donald Davidson Responding to an International Forum of Philosophers,* pp. 57–76. Berlin: Walter de Gruyter.

Frege, G. 1953. *The Foundations of Arithmetic: A Logico-Mathematical Inquiry into the Concept of Number,* English Translation by J. L. Austin. Oxford: Basil Blackwell. Second Revised Edition.

Frost, R. 1951. *Complete Poems.* London: Jonathan Cape.

Gabbay, M. 2002. *Logic with Added Reasoning.* Ontario: Broadview Press.

Gerrard, S. 2002. One Wittgenstein? In E. H. Reck, ed., *From Frege to Wittgenstein: Perspectives on Early Analytic Philosophy*, pp. 52–71. Oxford: Oxford University Press.

Goodman, N. 1978. *Ways of Worldmaking*. Hassocks: The Harvester Press.

Grandy, R. 1989. On Grice on language. *Journal of Philosophy* 86:514–525.

Grice, P. 1986. Reply to Richards. In R. E. Grandy and R. Warner, eds., *Philosophical Grounds of Rationality: Intentions, Categories, Ends*, pp. 45–106. Oxford: Clarendon Press.

Grice, P. 1989. *Studies in the Way of Words*. Cambridge, MA: Harvard University Press.

Hacker, P. M. S. 1997. The rise of twentieth century analytic philosophy. In H.-J. Glock, ed., *The Rise of Analytic Philosophy*, pp. 51–77. Oxford: Blackwell Publishers.

Heaton, J. and J. Groves. 1994. *Wittgenstein for Beginners*. Cambridge: Icon Books Ltd.

Horn, L. R. 2001. *A Natural History of Negation*. Stanford: CSLI Publications.

Howson, C. 1997. *Logic with Trees: An Introduction to Symbolic Logic*. London: Routledge.

Hughes, G. E. and D. G. Londey. 1965. *The Elements of Formal Logic*. London: Methuen.

Hunter, G. 1971. *Metalogic: An Introduction to the Metatheory of Standard First-Order Logic*. London: Macmillan and Co. Ltd.

Jackson, B. 2007. Beyond logical form. *Philosophical Studies* 132:347–380.

Keenan, E. 2005. How Much Logic Is Built into Natural Language? Talk given at the 15th Amsterdam Colloquium, Workshop on Semantic Universals. ILLC/Department of Philosophy, University of Amsterdam, 19th–21st December.

Kenny, A. 1995. *Frege*. Harmondsworth, Middlesex: Penguin Books.

Kripke, S. 1980. *Naming and Necessity*. Oxford: Blackwell.

Lepore, E. and K. Ludwig. 2001. What is logical form? In G. Preyer and G. Peter, eds., *Logical Form and Language*, pp. 54–90. Oxford: Clarendon Press.

Lepore, E. and K. Ludwig. 2007. *Donald Davidson's Truth-Theoretic Semantics*. Oxford: Clarendon Press.

Lewis, D. 1979. Scorekeeping in a language game. In R. Bäuerle, U. Egli, and A. von Stechow, eds., *Semantics from Different Points of View*, pp. 172–187. Berlin: Springer-Verlag.

Lichine, A. 1971. *Encyclopedia of Wines and Spirits*. New York: Knopf.

Losonsky, M. 2006. *Linguistic Turns in Modern Philosophy*. Cambridge: Cambridge University Press.

Malcolm, N. 1958. *Ludwig Wittgenstein: A Memoir. (With a Biographical Sketch by Georg Henrik von Wright.)* London: Oxford University Press.

McGuinness, B. (ed.). 2008. *Wittgenstein in Cambridge: Letters and Documents 1911–1951.* Oxford: Blackwell Publishing.

Monk, R. 1990. *Ludwig Wittgenstein: The Duty of Genius.* London: Vintage Books.

Monk, R. 2005. *How to Read Wittgenstein.* London: Granta Books.

Neale, S. 1994. What is *logical form?* In D. Prawitz and D. Westerståhl, eds., *Logic and Philosophy of Science in Uppsala: Papers from the 9th International Congress of Logic, Methodology and Philosophy of Science,* pp. 583–598. London: Kluwer Academic Publishers.

Neale, S. 2005. Pragmatism and binding. In Z. G. Szabó, ed., *Semantics vs. Pragmatics,* pp. 165–285. Oxford: Clarendon Press.

Neale, S. 2007a. Heavy hands, magic, and scene-reading traps. *European Journal of Analytic Philosophy* 3:77–132.

Neale, S. 2007b. On location. In M. O'Rourke and C. Washington, eds., *Situating Semantics: Essays on the Philosophy of John Perry,* pp. 251–393. London: MIT Press.

Price, H. 1986. Conditional credence. *Mind* 95:18–36.

Prior, A. N. 1962. *Formal Logic.* 2nd edn. Oxford: Clarendon Press.

Quine, W. V. O. 1951/1974. *Methods of Logic.* 3rd edn. London: Routledge & Kegan Paul.

Ramberg, B. T. 1989. *Donald Davidson's Philosophy of Language: An Introduction.* Oxford: Basil Blackwell.

Recanati, F. 1994. Contextualism and anti-contextualism in the philosophy of language. In S. L. Tsohatzidis, ed., *Foundations of Speech Act Theory: Philosophical and Linguistic Perspectives,* pp. 156–166. London: Routledge.

Recanati, F. 2004. Pragmatics and semantics. In L. R. Horn and G. Ward, eds., *The Handbook of Pragmatics,* pp. 442–462. Oxford: Blackwell Publishing.

Recanati, F. 2005. Literalism and contextualism: Some varieties. In G. Preyer and G. Peter, eds., *Contextualism in Philosophy: Knowledge, Meaning, and Truth,* pp. 171–196. Oxford: Clarendon Press.

Robins, R. H. 1976. Some continuities and discontinuities in the history of linguistics. In H. Parret, ed., *History of Linguistic Thought and Contemporary Linguistics,* pp. 13–31. Berlin: Walter de Gruyter.

Rorty, R. 1967. Introduction: Metaphilosophical difficulties of linguistic philosophy. In R. Rorty, ed., *The Linguistic Turn: Recent Essays in Philosophical Method,* pp. 1–39. Chicago: University of Chicago Press.

Schantz, R. (ed.). 2002. *What is Truth?* Berlin: Walter de Gruyter.

Schiffer, S. 1996. Contextualist solutions to scepticism. *Proceedings of the Aristotelian Society* XCVI:317–333.

Schroeder, S. 2006. *Wittgenstein: The Way Out of the Fly-Bottle.* Cambridge: Polity.

Simons, M. 2000. *Issues in the Semantics and Pragmatics of Disjunction.* London: Garland Publishing, Inc.

Sinclair, R. 2002. What is radical interpretation? Davidson, Fodor, and the naturalization of philosophy. *Inquiry* 45:161–184.

Skorupski, J. 1997a. Why did language matter to analytic philosophy? In H.-J. Glock, ed., *The Rise of Analytic Philosophy*, pp. 77–91. Oxford: Blackwell Publishing.

Skorupski, J. 1997b. Meaning, use, verification. In B. Hale and C. Wright, eds., *A Companion to the Philosophy of Language*, pp. 29–59. Oxford: Blackwell Publishers.

Soloman, R. C. and M. C. Murphy. (eds.). *What is Justice? Classic and Contemporary Readings*. Oxford: Oxford University Press.

Stanley, J. 2005. *Knowledge and Practical Interests*. Oxford: Clarendon Press.

Strawson, P. F. 1952. *Introduction to Logical Theory*. London: Methuen.

Strawson, P. F. 1971. *Logico-Linguistic Papers*. London: Methuen.

Stroll, A. 2000. *Twentieth-Century Analytic Philosophy*. New York: Columbia University Press.

Stroll, A. 2002. *Wittgenstein*. Oxford: Oneworld Publications.

Turner, K. 1999. Introduction – From a certain point of view (Seven inch version). In K. Turner, ed., *The Semantics/Pragmatics Interface from Different Points of View*, pp. 1–18. Oxford: Elsevier Science.

Txurruka, I. G. 2003. The natural language conjunction *and*. *Linguistics and Philosophy* 26:255–285.

Walker, R. 1975. Conversational implicatures. In S. Blackburn, ed., *Meaning, Reference and Necessity: New Studies in Semantics*, pp. 133–181. Cambridge: Cambridge University Press.

Wittgenstein, L. 1968. *Philosophical Investigations*. 3rd edn. Oxford: Basil Blackwell.

Wittgenstein, L. 1980. *Culture and Value*, Edited by G. H. von Wright in collaboration with Heikki Nyman, and translated by Peter Winch. Oxford: Basil Blackwell.

von Wright, G. H. 1955/1958. Biographical sketch. In N. Malcolm, ed., *Ludwig Wittgenstein: A Memoir*, pp. 1–22. London: Oxford University Press.

# 2

# Whatever Happened to Meaning? Remarks on Contextualisms and Propositionalisms ☆

JAY DAVID ATLAS

When I was a young philosophy student, my teacher Sir Michael Dummett talked about "understanding statements"; my teacher Donald Davidson talked about "truth-conditions of sentences in contexts"; my

☆ This chapter is an expanded, June 2007, version of my lecture, given at the International Pragmatics Association Conference, July 10–15, 2005, Riva del Garda, Italy, on the Panel "Making Semantics Pragmatic," Riva del Garda Congressi conference center, Sala Lido, 2:30 pm–3:00 pm, July 11, 2005. It was the subject of a Philosophy of Language Seminar/Workshop that I gave at the invitation of Professor E. Lepore, Department of Philosophy and Center for Cognitive Sciences, Rutgers University – the State University of New Jersey, New Brunswick, New Jersey, on April 26, 2010. It is a consideration of recent views of Cappelen and Lepore, Recanati, Borg, Bach, Bezuidenhout, Stanley, and others on "contextualism" from the point of view of the kind of "dual pragmatics," to use Emma Borg's term, that I helped to create in the 1970s (Atlas, 1974, 1975, 1977, 1978a, b, 1979; Atlas and Levinson, 1981; for historical remarks, see Ruth Kempson, 1988: 141, fn. 2, and Larry Horn, 1984, 1989: 433). I am indebted to David Wilkins, Pieter Seuren, Stephen Levinson, Penny Brown, and to the hospitality of the Max Planck Institute for Psycholinguistics, Nijmegen, The Netherlands, its Directors, and its staff, especially Edith Sjoerdsma, Nanjo Bogdanowicz, Karin Kastens, Anne Hoffman, Tobias van Valkenhoef, Ad Verbunt, Reiner Dirksmeyer, and Jan Achterberg. The original version of this lecture was given on Monday July 11, 2005, which had he lived would have been the 51st birthday of my brilliant pupil John Paul Egan III, B.A. in Philosophy, Pomona College, 1976, B.A. with First-class Honors in Philosophy, Politics, and Economics, University of Oxford (Magdalen College), 1978, and winner of the Henry Green Prize in Philosophy in Oxford University, 1978. This chapter is dedicated to his memory.

*Making Semantics Pragmatic*
Ken Turner (ed.).
Current Research in the Semantics/Pragmatics Interface, Vol. 24.

teacher Dana Scott talked about "propositional concepts," a logical notion of the set of functions from indices or "points of reference" to truth-values; my teacher Carl G. Hempel talked about "extensions" of predicates, sentences, and the denotations of singular terms; and though I, a properly raised Quinean student, never talked about "propositions," the rebellious among Quine's students like David K. Lewis and Saul Kripke eventually made talk of sets of possible worlds fashionable – but not linguistic meanings! The later Wittgenstein, and following him Paul Grice, talked about "what one said" or "what one implicated." What none of these people ever talked about, like the queer uncle in Chicago and the drunken aunt in the attic, were sentence-meanings – I mean real sentence-meanings.[1] So I began to talk about them, early, loudly and often. I even put the 'm' word into the title of my book *Logic, Meaning, and Conversation* (2005), a book about the debauched world of "dual pragmatics," as Emma Borg refers to it, a world that I in part created (Atlas, 1977, 1978a, b, 1979). Now that American philosophers, thirty years after Atlas and Levinson's (1981) revision of Grice's maxims of "logic and conversation," are in the middle of a *retrouvé* debate about context-sensitivity, indexicality, and pragmatic analyses of everything in sight, and a Thermidorean reaction has begun – see Emma Borg's *Minimal Semantics* (2004), François Recanati's *Literal Meaning* (2004), and Cappelen and Lepore's *Insensitive Semantics* (2005) – I still find that no one is willing to take word- and sentence-meanings seriously. Let me give you some contemporary philosophical examples. I begin the discussion with the influential views of Recanati.

## 1   Recanati's and Others' Differences with Paul Grice: Contextualism and Quasi-Contextualism

In the Conclusion, Chapter 10, of Recanati's book, he discusses the difference between his "Quasi-Contextualist" view and the view of Paul Grice. Besides the linguistic meaning of sentence-types, Grice has a view of "what is said" by the assertion of sentence-tokens. His view made the content of "what is said" a specification of the meaning of the sentence-token with values for the parameters of tense, indexical expressions, and demonstrative expressions – a notion of a "minimal" proposition expressed by the utterance. Any other differences between "what is said" and the utterance-interpretation of the speech-act were matters of context, of particularized and generalized conversational implicatures

---

[1]Notable exceptions to this rule were Paul Benacerraf and Jerry Katz.

derived from the semantic content of "what is said" and from an assessment of the speaker's intentions by the addressee. *Quasi-contextualism*, in Recanati's (2004: 86) sense, is the view that "minimal propositions [are] theoretically useless" entities, which play "no role in communication." Recanati remarks that he "has implicitly endorsed Quasi-Contextualism in arguing against the Syncretic View in Chapter 4." The latter View draws a distinction between "what is said" in an intuitive sense and "what is said" strictly and literally. These views are typical of the American philosophers Nathan Salmon, Scott Soames, and Kent Bach. Recanati himself had earlier held such a view, but he has since given up defending the notion of a minimal proposition, still defended by Cappelen and Lepore and Borg.

Sperber and Wilson (1998) are also Quasi-contextualists. As Recanati (2004: 97, fn. 33) describes them, "They accept that ordinary words have contents, in and by themselves, and that sentences containing them express propositions (once indexicals et al. have been assigned semantic values) – even though they take these contents and these propositions to be communicationally irrelevant." And Recanati quotes them (Sperber and Wilson, 1998: 185) as holding that "[m]any words seem to encode not a full-fledged concept but what might be called a pro-concept. ... As with pronouns, their semantic contribution *must* be contextually specified for the associated utterance to have a truth-value. ... All words behave *as if* they encoded pro-concepts: that is, whether or not a word encodes a full concept, the concept it is used to convey in a given utterance has to be contextually worked out." But Recanati contrasts this view with *genuine Contextualism*: "... a genuine contextualist denies that words have full-fledged contents or encode concepts. All words – or, cautiously, nearly all words – encode only 'pro-concepts' (semantic potentials) and serve as pointers to intended senses. In *Thoughts and Utterances* [2002], pp. 359–364, Robyn Carston tentatively amends relevance theory along those lines."

Recanati's Contextualists, like myself in my own "Meaning Dualism" – see Atlas (2007) – believe that the meanings of words are "modulated," the term used by Alan Cruse (1986: 50–53) and Ruhl (1989): the meaning of a word in an utterance is "affected by the meanings of other words in the same sentence." This is a view that Recanati attributes to James Ross (1981), Jonathan Cohen (1986), Ron Lahav (1989), and James Pustejovsky (1995), a view also to be found in Atlas (1983, 1989, 1990, 2005), especially my 1990 paper, discussed by Horn (1992: 175). Modulation results from "generation" of senses, not selection from among senses available from ambiguous expressions, an observation, Recanati (2004: 134, fn. 12) notes, that was made by Herb

Clark (1983, 1992), Clark and Gerrig (1983, 1992), Pustejovsky (1995), and Atlas (1989), as well as in Atlas (1975, 1977, 1978a, b, 1979, 1990, 2005).

In English sentences modulation is most obvious for words like 'red', 'get', and 'like' and other words whose polysemy is the result of the conventionalization of a modulated interpretation into a sense. It is important, as Recanati (2004: 136) recognizes, to distinguish modulation from indexicality, especially of the sort espoused by Stanley and Szabó (2000).[2] Recanati (2004: 136) writes, " ... modulation is a pragmatic process in the fullest possible sense: it is a *pragmatically controlled* pragmatic process, rather than a *linguistically controlled* pragmatic process (like saturation). Neither enrichment, nor loosening, nor transfer, nor any other of the mechanisms at work in modulation seems to require, on the side of the input, a 'slot' or gap in semantic structure demanding to be filled and triggering the search for an appropriate filler. In contrast to saturation, which proceeds from the bottom up, modulation seems to be fundamentally top-down." For Recanati (2004: 137) "modulation is a cover term for what ... [he has] called 'primary pragmatic processes of the optional variety'... " In examples like *She took out her key and opened the door* and *There is a big lion in the middle of the piazza*, the pragmatic processes that enrich the meanings of the sentences might not take place; they can suffer Gricean "cancellation." Then the contribution of the words to the utterance's truth-conditions is what Recanati calls "their bare linguistic senses."

Such a view assumes that some words have "bare linguistic senses" that can make an un-modulated contribution to a truth-condition that is the result of composition. My own view, like Ruhl's (1989), in Atlas (1975, 1977, 1979, 1989), was that some words are too abstract and schematic to have a determinate content (see Recanati (2004: 140, fn. 28)).[3] This is the view that Recanati calls "the Wrong Format view," i.e., the view that the meaning of a word is not represented by a format that specifies a determinate content. The result is that composition has a pragmatic character, a view familiar to us from Levinson's (1988, 2000)

---

[2]Recanati's Chapter 7 "Indexicalism and the Binding Fallacy" is a cogent and persuasive criticism of Jason Stanley and Zoltan Szabó's (2000) arguments in support of the Indexical, Saturation analysis of semantically incomplete sentences. On this, Recanati is in agreement with Cappelen and Lepore (2005). And I, in turn, with them.

[3]Recanati also cites Victorri and Fuchs (1996) and Gustave Guillaume (1929).

discussion of "pragmatic intrusion," to be found also in Katz (1972) and Walker (1975).[4]

As Recanati emphasizes, Classical Gricean views are anti-Contextualist, in that there is a sometimes contextually-relative but always determinate truth-conditional content to the assertion of a sentence, Grice's "what is said." Atlas's and Kempson's notion that even a logical particle in natural language, like 'not', much less 'and', which Grice takes to be semantically identical to the logical conjunction, is explicitly non-Gricean on this point. Kempson (1975) took the view, incorrectly, that 'not' was a logical disjunction of exclusion and choice negation, but Atlas (1974, 1975, 1977, 1978a, b, 1979) took the view that the meaning of 'not', as Recanati would have put it, has the Wrong Format to be a logical negation. In this regard I am a Contextualist in Recanati's sense.

Philosopher Emma Borg, deeply influenced by Lepore, and indirectly by Donald Davidson, has a somewhat different account of the problems of contextualism from Recanati's.

## 2 Borg's Minimal Semantics: Critique of Sperber, Wilson, Carston, Recanati, Bach

Emma Borg's book *Minimal Semantics* is a reply to Sperber and Wilson's (1986) Relevance Theory and François Recanati's (2004) "contextualism" (including contributions from Kent Bach's (1994a) views of "conversational implic*i*ture"). Borg wishes to defend a moderate form of formal semantics against the challenge of "covert contextualism" in sentences like the following, familiar examples (Borg, 2004: 34):

(1) a. Paracetamol is better [than aspirin]
    b. You won't die [from that cut]
    c. I've eaten [recently]
    d. It's raining [where the speaker is]
    e. Everybody [who came to the party] had a great time.
    f. Smith weighs 120 pounds [weighed before breakfast and undressed]
    g. The apple is green [on the outside]
    h. Holland is flat [for a country].

---

[4]Recanati also mentions Benveniste (1974), Rumelhart (1993), and Jackendoff (1997).

The bracketed material is inferred from the context of utterance in order to produce an interpretation of the sentence-token in the context that counts as "what is said." Borg calls these views "dual pragmatics," since she characterizes them as claiming essentially that pragmatic inferences are required not only to produce Gricean implicata from assertions or statements made but also to produce truth-conditional contents from sentence-meanings that do not generate truth-conditional contents from the sentence strings alone, even if there are no overt indexical or demonstrative terms in the sentence. For example (Borg, 2004: 38), (2a) is a sentence from which pragmatic inference produces a "complete" proposition (truth-evaluable content, "what is said") in (2b), from which in turn the speaker might have implicated (2c).

(2) a. Courtney will continue.
     b. Courtney will continue bowling.
     c. England's batsmen are in trouble.

Against a view like Borg's that claims that specification of literal meaning is restricted to what is presented by syntactic form and lexical content, and that context determines literal meaning only through "objective" features of context, which interpret tense, indexical elements, or demonstrative elements in the sentence, Borg (2004: 29) describes the "dual pragmatics" view as holding that the literal meaning of an utterance may result from "pragmatic intrusion" (Levinson, 1988, 2000) of information into the semantic content of the sentence, and that this information may be derived from the contents of a speaker's states of mind. About her notion of semantic content, Borg (2004: 33, fn. 25) is explicit; as she remarks, "... for something to count as *semantic* content for me it must reach the level of truth-evaluability. If it turns out that the only level of content which is recoverable on the basis of syntactic features alone fell below this level, then I would take it that formal semantics, as standardly conceived, was not possible." Thus, according to Borg (2004: 39), dual pragmatists make "the key claim ... [that] context-sensitive processes play a constitutive role in the determination of the semantic content of a sentence (i.e., to the truth-conditional content or the proposition expressed), as well as being relevant to the determination of implicatures." This key claim is what I have supported by arguments in Atlas (1974, 1975, 1977, 1978a, b, 1979, 1989, 2005).

## 3 The Conscious Awareness of Contents and Procedures: What is Said

It is part of Recanati's view that "bridging inferences" (see Clark and Haviland, 1977; Atlas and Levinson, 1981: 37) like the one from (3a) to (3b):

(3) a. Mary took out her key and opened the door.
    b. Mary took out her key and opened the door with it.

are subconscious processes; though the addressee hears (3a), he or she consciously understands only (3b). And Recanati takes (3a) to be sub-propositional. It is also part of Recanati's (2004: 16) view that "normal interpreters have intuitions concerning the truth-conditional content of utterances. ... [T]hose intuitions correspond to a certain 'level' in the comprehension process – a level that a proper theory of language understanding must capture. That is the level of 'what is said' (as opposed to e.g. what is implied)."

I have always found these claims about conscious and unconscious processing peculiar. Consider example (3c); according to Recanati I am supposed to hear (3c) and consciously understand only (3d), as I am supposed to do with (3e) and (3f). Allegedly I just subconsciously leap from hearing (3c) to understanding (3d). And (3c) is supposed to be sub-propositional. Why is that, do you suppose? I just don't find myself understanding (3c) as (3d) at the drop of a hat (or beret, either).

(3) c. Mary took out her car key and opened the door.
    d. Mary took out her car key and opened the door with it.
    e. Mary took out her car key and opened the car door.
    f. Mary took out her car key and opened the car door with it.

There is a large debate on issues of conscious awareness. How much linguistic knowledge does one have conscious access to? In his book Recanati assumes that there are conscious, explicit, occurrent judgments of "what is said," et al. His objection to minimal propositions is that their contents are not so judgeable.

In my work I have been notably silent on this controversy, for two reasons. First, I am averse to armchair psychologizing, and the few studies in empirical psychology on sentence-processing that seem relevant to the debate, like Raymond Gibbs's (1994) *The Poetics of the Mind*, or Rachel Giora's (2003) *On our Mind*, are ones that I am not knowledgeable enough to evaluate, and where I have been able to evaluate the experimental claims, e.g., some of those appealed to in

Sam Glucksberg (2001), I have found the empirical evidence in support of psycho-linguistic hypotheses to be far weaker than advertised. Second, the philosophical and linguistic discussion of "what is said" has proceeded as if there were clear, intuitive, reliable, consciously accessible notions of "what is said" and as if, if there were such clear notions, they mattered for purposes of theory-building. I have never believed either of those views. Paul Ziff (1972b) was right, I believe; there is nothing crisp denoted by 'what is said'. These debates are far too uncritical of the deliverances of intuitions about "what is said."

## 4   Borg's Defense of a Semantic Theory of Sentences

Borg wishes to claim, by contrast with Recanati's view, that there is a genuine account of semantic content for sentence-types (though relativized to a context in order to handle tense, indexicals, and demonstratives) that depends solely on formal features of the sentence. And there should be one, for it has the following advantages. First, it can explain the truth-conditional understanding of novel sentences by appeal to recursive rules of composition. By contrast, according to Borg (2004: 58), dual pragmatists must hold, that an addressee who fails to understand that an utterance of *Courtney will continue* means *Courtney will continue bowling* has failed to understand "what was said" in the utterance. Borg takes this to be a failure, from the dual pragmatists' point of view, of the addressee's knowledge of the language, and she finds that failure a peculiar claim for them to make. Second, a semantic theory of sentence-types can explain cancellation. If a speaker says, "I will get the washing in," and she does not do so before it rains, Borg notes that the speaker does not contradict herself if she says, "I just said that I'd get the washing in, not when I'd get it." There is, then, a notion of what one's words commit one to. Borg will, in order to provide truth-conditions for such sentences, adopt a familiar strategy: let the literal sense of the sentence be "For some time $t$, I will get the washing in by $t$." The form in which Borg (2004: 242) will put this, to accommodate indexicals and demonstratives, is a Davidsonian move to utterances, e.g., Borg's "If $u$ is an utterance of 'Jane can't continue' in a context $c$, then $u$ is true iff Jane can't continue something in $c$." Note the use of the existential quantifier in the truth-conditions on the right-hand-side of the biconditional. As Jonathan Dancy and Hanjo Glock emphasized to Borg (2004: 242, fn. 35), this existential quantification makes the sentence trivially, perhaps even necessarily, true (if the class of worlds is such that Jane exists in each of them and the necessity is, e.g., an S5 necessity). Borg's (2004: 243) defense of this consequence is as follows:

> ... the formal, modular semanticist at this point is in no way committed to claiming that liberal truth-conditions are what are communicated in these cases, nor even that the liberal truth-conditions are likely to be the subject of much interest to interlocutors in these cases. Rather the thought is simply that, if we are really interested in finding out what the words and sentences we use literally mean, then we have no need to look further than the meaning which can be recovered via sensitivity to formal features alone. Recall also that there is evidence that speakers *can* grasp this very liberal, literal meaning when they want to: children and philosophers, I often find, have a very acute sense of what they have literally committed themselves to by a given utterance and this fits entirely with the liberal truth-conditions specified above.

She continues (ibid.: 244):

> So the objection of triviality for very many analyses of the literal meaning of sentence-types relativized to contexts of utterance is not one I think we should be overly concerned with; it is really just an instance of the general claim made throughout this book, that knowledge of language is a good thing, but is far from the only thing worth having, and, abstracted from everything else that a competent agent knows, it may well look a very meager creature indeed. ... So, take the appropriate liberal truth-conditions for 'The apple is red', 'Mary can continue', 'It's not raining' or 'Paracetamol is better' ... [I]f the apple is not red in any respect, if Mary suddenly goes out of existence, if it's raining somewhere, or if Paracetamol is not better than anything, all of the relevant liberal truth-conditions will fail to be satisfied. ... [I]f it is held that the proposition expressed by 'Jane can't continue something' is necessary, then why should it be of any further concern to the advocate of liberal truth-conditions that the proposition expressed by 'Jane can't continue' is similarly necessary (especially since, in both cases, what will be communicated by an utterance of the sentence is likely to be a far richer, contextually salient proposition)?

Borg will say the same of 'Steel isn't strong enough' and 'Fido is bigger than John's dog', as in "If $u$ is an utterance of 'Steel isn't strong enough' in a context $c$, then $u$ is true iff steel isn't strong enough for something in $c$," and in "If $u$ is an utterance of 'Fido is bigger than John's dog, then $u$ is true iff Fido is bigger than the dog bearing some relation to John in $c$." This use of the existential quantifier was

Geoffrey Leech's (1974) strategy, and many others', including Recanati, at some time or another. No doubt Larry Horn will discover that some medieval logician also used it. (By the way, why does everyone think 'John's dog' entails uniqueness for Johannine dogginess, adopting the paraphrase '*the* dog bearing . . . '?)

The consequences of the view, and its formulation by Borg, are not as trivial as the apparent truth of the propositions expressed. Notice that in Borg's account in the quotation above, an utterance of 'Mary can continue' is falsified only by Mary's going out of existence. One might have thought that the truth of 'Mary cannot continue' would have sufficed for the falsification of 'Mary can continue'; but for Borg 'Mary cannot continue' expresses 'Mary cannot continue something'. On the predicate-negation interpretation of 'not' there is something that Mary cannot continue; on the sentence-negation interpretation there is nothing that Mary can continue (which will be true only if Mary does not exist). On the former interpretation, 'Mary can continue' and 'Mary cannot continue' are both true and so not contraries, much less contradictories, so the one cannot falsify the other. On the latter interpretation, 'Mary can continue' and 'Mary cannot continue' are contradictories. 'Mary can continue' is falsified only if there is nothing that Mary can continue, either because ($a$) Mary does not exist, or ($b$) she exists but can continue nothing. As for ($b$), if she exists, it is *trivially false* that there is nothing that she can continue (as Borg understands 'continue'). If she exists it is trivially true that Mary can continue. That leaves ($a$). So in order for 'Mary can continue' to be falsified, Mary must go out of existence, just as Borg suggested. But such a falsification condition arises only because Borg is assuming that 'x cannot F' means 'x cannot F something' and that negation can only be understood as a sentence and "exclusion" negation. Hence she has taken an implicit position on the semantics of 'not' in English. But surely hers is an incorrect account of 'not' in English. 'Not' is not only a sentence and "exclusion" negation (Atlas, 1974, 1975, 1977, 1989, 2005). But there are problems internal to her account in the passage as well.

In the quotation above she also claims that 'It's not raining' is not true if it is raining somewhere. So 'It's not raining' is true only if it is not the case that it is raining somewhere; i.e., 'It's not raining' is true only if it is not-raining everywhere (viz. raining nowhere). That means that one hardly ever utters a literal truth when one says 'It's not raining'. In fact, on Borg's view, the probabilities are that 'It's not raining' has never literally been true. Moreover, that construal of 'not' in 'It's not raining' is incompatible with the construal she gave of 'not' in 'Jane can't continue' as 'Jane can't continue something', also in the quotation above, instead of the parallel 'Jane can continue nothing' to the 'It's not raining' case. To claim, as she does, that 'Jane can't continue something' is a trivial or necessary truth, she must construe 'not' as having a narrow-scope Verb Phrase interpretation with respect to 'something', and so, if 'Jane can't continue something' gives the truth-conditions and logical form of 'Jane can't continue', 'not' in 'Jane can't continue' is also a narrow-scope, Verb Phrase "choice" negation. The sentence, as she claims, is also necessarily true (where the accessible worlds all contain Jane).

These examples are also complicated by the fact that Borg has chosen a modal verb 'can', which introduces scope problems of its own. But that aside, in the space of two pages Borg has claimed, in effect, that 'Mary can continue' is falsified only if 'not' is a wide-scope, sentence-negation and, since she admits that the negative sentence is trivially true, that 'not' in 'Jane can't continue' must be a narrow-scope, Verb Phrase negation. One must admit that this is an unsatisfactory semantic theory of the truth-conditions of 'not' sentences. One would at least like to avoid inconsistent semantic claims about 'not' in simple negative sentences. Negation is a difficult phenomenon, but if one is going to give a truth-conditional semantics for simple declarative sentences, the least one should do is decide what the relative scope of negation and one's covert existential quantifiers should be.

Borg goes on to diagnose why her opponents, like John Searle and Recanati, are "contextualists," who think that all there is to literal meaning is the speech-act contents of various utterances of sentences. She accuses them of confusing truth-conditions with verification-conditions, the conditions under which one decides in a particular context what the truth-value of an utterance is. I myself have emphasized making this distinction between truth and verification for similar reasons, in Atlas (1989: 62–64), which I called 'the Anscombe Point'; Miss Anscombe, in a famous paper (Anscombe, 1981), made the distinction forcefully. Borg believes that if one appreciates the Anscombe Point, one will not object to her truth-conditions making these sentences trivially true or trivially false. In this situation Borg needs help in explaining the intuition that many utterances of these trivially true or false sentences have non-trivial truth-conditions. So Grice's (1989) notion of implicature and Kent Bach's (1981, 1994a, b) notion of "non-literal" are sent to the rescue. Utterances whose truth-conditions are non-trivial are non-trivial utterances because they are non-literal uses of literal trivialities. Bach's (1981) cases are all cases where a sentence that is used non-literally is an elliptical version of a longer, more specific sentence for which the first sentence is used as a replacement. For example, in 'Ed doesn't look tired, he is tired', 'Ed doesn't look tired' is used non-literally in place of 'Ed doesn't merely look tired'. So, Borg suggests, 'It's raining' is used non-literally for 'It's raining here', and 'Jane can't continue' is used non-literally for 'Jane can't continue university education'. Since people like Recanati hold that what a semantic theory should explain are speakers' intuitions about the truth-conditions of utterances, and Borg wishes to preserve a truth-conditional theory of sentence-types, even if for her they are ultimately indexically sensitive sentence-tokens *à la* Davidson, massive non-literalness is, she believes, a small price to pay.

Myself, I think that this is a very high price. A sentence may be used to express a lot of different propositions, e.g., as 'I am here' does, but it does not follow that it expresses all of them non-literally. If one were Horn (1989) or Levinson (2000), one would think that 'Three boys dated five girls' literally means 'At least 3 boys dated at least 5 girls'. The meaning is hardly ever – and maybe never – expressed by an utterance of the sentence. But for them the sentence-meaning is a proposition, as it is for Borg, so the *natural* reason why the sentence-meaning might never be expressed by an utterance that *is* a proposition, viz. my view that the literal meaning of the sentence is *not* a proposition, cannot be appealed to. Horn and Levinson's position does not seem plausible to me anymore than similar views of Grice's (1989) did – see Atlas and Levinson (1981) and Atlas (1984a, 2005).

Borg's second diagnosis of "contextualism" is that Recanati et al. make what Cappelen and Lepore (2005) call 'The Mistaken Assumption' that literal meaning is identical to speech-act content (Borg, 2004: 252–254), because, again, she believes, the theorists ignore the difference between truth-conditions and verification-conditions. If one distinguishes sentence-meaning from speaker-meaning, she believes that one may give propositional contents to sentences that seem to "contextualists" to be syntactically and semantically "incomplete" while giving richer truth-conditions to "what is said" in utterances of the sentences. She writes, "To understand what is literally meant by 'It's raining' all we need to know, the (minimal) formal theorist claims, is the meaning of the syntactic parts of the sentence and their mode of combination; however to know what is communicated by an utterance of this sentence we need to know so much more" (Borg, 2004: 257). For the formal semanticist, "it precisely is the case that the truth-conditions for well-formed natural language sentences are recoverable on the basis of formal operations over syntactic features alone" (Borg, 2004: 261–262). On Borg's view, theories of "what is said" are properly pragmatic. "[W]hat is communicated by an utterance of a sentence semantically possessing such a liberal [existential-quantifier-laced] truth-condition is *always* [my emphasis] a much richer, pragmatically enhanced item," while "liberal truth-conditions [are] determined on the basis of syntactic features alone, churned out by the modular language faculty" (Borg, 2004: 262).

My objection to Borg's project is a diagnosis of why she has such trouble providing a consistent truth-conditional account of even simple negative sentences. She is not taking her own view seriously enough. If one thought that a semantic theory should theorize about the recursively generated sentence-strings of a language, with attention to their syntactic features, how in the world did Borg get her intuition that the sentence 'It's raining' permits the recovery of an existential quantifier quantifying over locations from its lexical content and its syntactical structure? I know that John Perry (1986) once said it had to be so, but was it? Is it? How does the syntactical analysis of 'It's raining' demand the occurrence of an existential quantifier over locations?

What do the following sentences in (4) indicate?

(4)  a.  It's raining in Palo Alto.
      b.  It's raining hard.
      c.  It's raining cats-and-dogs.
      d.  It's raining more than I can bear.
      e.  It's raining too much.
      f.  It's raining and raining.
      g.  It was raining this morning but not now.

According to Borg 'It's raining' can "non-literally" express any of these – well, maybe not the last one (4g), but which ones, and why? What are the literal truth-conditions for 'It's raining'? What domain shall we existentially quantify over? If you think that the syntax will answer this question, you have more insight into the semantic values of locative prepositional phrases, manner adverbials, compound verb phrases, and temporal adverbials than I do. Which value or values would you quantify over?

If one took Borg's project of Fodorean modularity seriously, one would have no reason to think that an existential quantifier is recoverable from the syntax and lexical content of these sentences. There is a relevant passage in Fodor's (1983) *Modularity of Mind* that has been far too little appreciated. Here is the passage (Fodor, 1983: 89–90):

> Is there, then, an encapsulated analyzer for logical and gramma-
> tical form? All the arguments are indirect; but, for what it's worth,
> it's rather hard to see how some of the processes that recognize
> logical and grammatical form could be anything but encapsulated.

Background information can be brought to bear in perceptual analysis only where the property that is recognized is, to some significant extent, redundant in the context of recognition. But, as we remarked above, there doesn't seem to be much redundancy between context variables and the *form* of an utterance, however much context may predict its *content*. Even if you know precisely what someone is going to say – in the sense of knowing precisely which proposition he is going to assert – the knowledge buys you very little in predicting the type/token relation for his utterance; there are simply too many linguistically different ways of saying the same thing.

It is not, therefore, surprising that the extreme proposals for context-driven language recognizers do *not* generally proceed by using contextual information to identify grammatical relations. Instead, they proceed whenever possible directly from a lexical analysis to a "conceptual" analysis – one which, in effect, collapses across synonymous tokens regardless of their linguistic type. It is unclear to me whether such models are proposed as serious candidates for the explanation of human communicative capacities, though sometimes I fear that they may be. (See, e.g., Schank and Abelson, 1975; for experimental evidence that linguistic form continues to have its effect as semantic integration increases, precisely as one would expect if the recovery of logical syntactic form is mandatory, see Forster and Olbrei, 1973.) To put the point in a nutshell: linguistic form recognition can't be context-driven because context doesn't determine form; if linguistic form is recognized at all, it must be by largely encapsulated processes.

So the present proposal is that the language-input system specifies, for any utterance in its domain, its linguistic and maybe its logical form. It is implicit in this proposal that it does no more than that[29] – e.g., that it doesn't recover speech-act potential (except, perhaps, insofar as speech-act potential may be correlated with properties of form, as in English interrogative word order).

I am interested in Fodor's footnote 29 to the remark that it "is implicit in this proposal that it does no more than that . . . ." This is the interesting footnote (Fodor, 1983: 135):

It may, indeed, do less. Hilary Putnam has the following poser. Lincoln said, "You can fool all of the people some of the time." Did he mean *there is a time at which you can fool all of the people* or did he mean *for each person there is a time at which you can fool him?* Putnam thinks that Lincoln's intentions may have been *indeterminate* as between these readings. This could, of course, be true only if the specification of quantifier scope is not mandatory in the internal representation of one's intended utterances. And *that* could be true only if such representations *do not* specify the logical form of the intended utterance. To put it another way, on Putnam's view, the internal representation of "You can fool all of the people some of the time," would be something like "You can fool all of the people some of the time," this latter being a *univocal* formula which happens to have disjoint truth conditions. Whether Putnam is right about all this remains to be seen; but if he is, then perhaps the specifically *linguistic* processes in the production/ perception of speech deploy representations that are *shallower* than logical forms.

It is important to notice that by 'disjoint truth conditions' Fodor (1983: 135) does not mean 'truth conditions expressed by a disjunction' (see Atlas, 1984b for discussion).[5] Also I had not only defended a position similar to Hilary Putnam's (Atlas, 1974, 1975, 1977, 1979, 1989, 2005), but I had gone farther than Putnam. I did not think that it was just a psychological matter of indeterminate intentions in a speaker. I had explicitly argued that negative *sentences* were scope-indeterminate, and so have no classical logical form, and that, like Putnam's view of utterance-intentions, a speaker's negative *thoughts* might be scope-indeterminate. That would not be the normal case, but it would be a theoretically possible case (Atlas, 1979). So not only might the language-*input* system fail to specify logical form, as Fodor and Putnam suggested, but the language-*output* system might be unable to specify a logical form for a sentence, even if the speaker's thoughts could be represented by a logical form, as Fodor admits in the last sentence of his footnote (see Atlas, 1989: 148–149). Nothing in encapsulation or modularity as Fodor understands it is inconsistent with Atlas-Kempson-style semantical underdeterminacy of sentences. I viewed it as a theoretical possibility for thoughts as well, but many philosophers have deep-seated intuitions about the nature of thoughts, more deep-seated than my own, largely because no one, including psychologists, knows enough about thoughts to contradict a philosopher's favorite view.

Moreover, nothing in Atlas-Kempson-style underdeterminacy undermines a theory of semantically valid arguments (e.g., classical first-order quantification theory), so long as the vehicles of truth are not merely sentence-types. Classical mathematicians never needed to

---

[5] Ruth Kempson (1975) used the expression 'disjunct truth-conditions' for 'disjoint truth-conditions', and then fallaciously inferred that disjoint truth-conditions could be expressed using a logical disjunction.

bother with the difference between sentence-types and sentence-tokens, so they didn't care whether the entailment relation had in its domain and co-domain sentence-types, utterance-types, or sentence-tokens. Even Fodor only worries about compositionality for *thoughts*, not for sentences. If one took Borg's Fodorean *reasons* for a minimal truth-conditional semantics as seriously as Fodor does, one could give up Borg's minimal truth-conditional semantics.

Maybe one should just confront the possibility that Chomsky was right, and Generative Semantics was wrong; syntax is autonomous, and Donald-Davidson-or-John-Perry-like semantic intuitions about the logical form of utterances are just seat-of-the-pants, philosophical-armchair inventions. Perry just thought that every time it rained, it rained in a place, i.e., somewhere. That common-sense notion about rain is not a syntactical generalization over all the grammatical strings of English that begin 'It is raining ...'. It is not a generalization over all the possible human utterances of grammatical strings that begin 'It is raining ...'. It is not a generalization over all the possible human thoughts that are expressible by a grammatical string that begins 'It is raining ...'. It is not a semantical claim about the lexical structure of the English word 'rains'. And so on and on. Frankly, I don't know what was in Perry's mind, except his (1993: 206) remark that in order to assign a truth-value to the statement *It's raining* he said, "I needed a place." Well, thank you, John, for that bit of autobiography about verifying your statement. As a result (?), a statement "It's raining at location $\ell$" is what for John Perry has a truth-value.

Even so, statements are not sentence-types; they are not merely sentence-tokens. Whatever Perry's theory of statements is, it is not a semantic theory of sentences. On this Borg and I agree. The difficulty that Borg faces is that she wants a sentence-semantics to be propositional, truth-conditional, logically form-ish. And she is a victim of a prejudice shared with Cappelen and Lepore: the proposition (that must be) expressed by 'It's raining' is the "least common denominator" of or an "abstraction" from all the speech-act contents of uttering grammatical sentences beginning with 'It's raining ...'. And, surely, there have to be locations referred to, directly or indirectly, in the contents of those speech-acts! Well, as American undergraduate "wits" – enthusiastic viewers of the comic movie *Airplane* – say, "Don't call me 'Shirley'." Borg believes that John Searle and Recanati are contextualists because they confuse verification-conditions with truth-conditions (like John Perry, perhaps?). Now it turns out that Borg is an existential-quantificationalist because she confuses verification-conditions with truth-conditions. Well, that's philosophical progress for you!

# 5   What is Context-Sensitivity?

A number of recent views in Anglo-American philosophy go by the name of 'contextualism'. Somewhat late in their critique of "context-sensitivity" in their book *Insensitive Semantics*, Cappelen and Lepore (2005: 146) clarify what they mean by an expression *e* of a language being "context sensitive." For them it means two things: first, (*a*) *e* is context sensitive if and only if "its contribution to the *propositions expressed* by utterances of sentences containing *e* varies from context to context;" the paradigm case of context-variability for them is the contribution of the first-person, singular pronoun 'I' to the proposition "semantically expressed" by utterance *u*, viz. the speaker of *u* himself. Second, (*b*) *e* is context sensitive if and only if "its contribution to the truth conditions of utterances *u* of a sentence S containing *e* (in some way or other) references various aspects of the context of *u*." For example, the truth conditions of an utterance of a sentence containing 'I' refer to the speaker of the sentence; 'I am F' is true in English at a point of reference *i* ($i = \langle w,t,p,a,\ldots \rangle$, where *w* is a possible world, *t* is a time, *p* is a three-dimensional position in space, *a* is a speaker or agent, etc. (Scott, 1970: 149) if and only if at *i* the speaker of the sentence 'I am F' is F.

These are distinct notions of "context-sensitivity," even though Cappelen and Lepore illustrate both notions by use of the indexical expression 'I'. The second notion (*b*) is the one we associate with "indexical semantics," in the work of Richard Montague, Dana Scott, Richmond Thomason, David Kaplan, and, more recently, in applications of the ideas of indexical semantics by Jason Stanley, Kent Bach, David Lewis, Stephen Neale, Zoltán Szabó, John Perry, and Mark Crimmins to epistemology, philosophy of language, philosophy of mind, and metaphysics. The first notion (*a*), though the example given is also the first-person singular pronoun in English, is interestingly different in character. It talks of "propositions," "utterances," and "sentences," and it says that utterances of 'I' contribute the speaker of 'I' to the proposition – a Russellian-Kaplanian singular proposition containing the speaker himself. That this is their picture of propositions is confirmed by Cappelen and Lepore's (2005: 145) example of the proposition "semantically expressed" by an utterance of the sentence 'She's happy', which turns out to be the ordered 3-tuple $\langle b,t,happy \rangle$, where the contextually salient reference of 'she' in the utterance is *b*, the time of utterance is *t*, and the semantic value of 'happy' is *happy*. Let's refer to the notion sketched in (*a*) as the "context-variability" of what utterances "express." For Cappelen and Lepore what is expressed are singular propositions, but their notion of a singular proposition is not essential to their notion of the context-variability of the interpretations of utterances. The linguists and philosophers associated by Cappelen and Lepore with the context-variability of utterance-interpretation are Speech Act Theorists John Searle, Charles Travis, Kent Bach, Anne Bezuidenhout, and François Recanati, and the London-Paris School of Relevance Theorists Deirdre Wilson, Daniel Sperber, and Robyn Carston.

What kind of context-variability do these philosophers have in mind? Cappelen and Lepore (2005: 44) make much of an example of Anne Bezuidenhout's (2002) in which her son says, "Here's a red one." He is picking through a barrel of apples at a county fair. Bezuidenhout (2002: 107; quoted in Cappelen and Lepore, 2005: 44) writes:

> But what counts as being red in this context? For apples, being red generally means having a red skin, which is different from what we normally mean by calling a watermelon, or a leaf, or a star, or hair, red. But even when it is an apple that is in question, other understandings of what it is to call it 'red' are possible, given suitable circumstances. For instance, suppose now that we're sorting through a barrel of apples to find those that have been afflicted with a horrible fungal disease. This fungus grows out from the core and stains the flesh of the apple red. My son slices each apple open and puts the good ones in a cooking pot. The bad ones he hands to me. Cutting open an apple he remarks: 'Here's a red one'. What he says is true if the apple has red flesh, even if it also happens to be a Granny Smith apple.

One utterance about a healthy McIntosh apple is true because of its red skin; one utterance about a sick, green-skinned Granny Smith apple is also true. If 'red' just meant in the utterances 'red-skinned', one utterance would be true, the other would be false. But they are both true utterances. 'Red' in one utterance is understood to mean 'red-skinned'; in the other utterance 'red' is understood to mean 'red-fleshed'. But the utterance-type "Here's a red one" is the same. Thus 'red' is a context-sensitive expression. Utterances of this *unambiguous* sentence have utterance-interpretations that depend on context. "What is said (asserted)" differs in each context. The phenomenon of context-shifting Cappelen and Lepore see as the first step to viewing language as "fully" context-sensitive.

The next step is "semantical incompleteness," as illustrated by Kent Bach's (1994b: 269) example *Steel isn't strong enough* and his (1997: 228) example *Fred is ready*. These examples are characterized by Bach as being "semantically or conceptually incomplete, in the sense that something must be added to the sentence for it to *express a complete and determinate proposition*." With *Steel isn't strong enough* "we need to know strong enough for what (it does not express the weak proposition that steel is strong enough for something or other) ... " The sentence is "semantically underdeterminate, [so] understanding its utterance requires a process of *completion* to produce a full proposition (Bach, 1994a: 125)." Bach (1997: 228) says that *Fred is ready* has "a missing argument," e.g., *Fred is ready for X*.

Remarks made by Sperber and Wilson (1986: 188) about the genitive Noun Phrase *Peter's bat* in *Peter's bat is gray*, where utterances of the possessive may be interpreted as 'owned by Peter', 'chosen by Peter', et al., were understood by Cappelen and Lepore to treat *Peter's bat* as a Bach "incompleteness" case. Unlike Bach, Sperber and Wilson contrast "semantic incompleteness" with the ambiguity of the sentence, not with a Bachian determinate, truth-valued proposition expressed by an utterance.[6] Though I (Atlas, 1974, 1975, 1977, 1978a, b, 1979) made a claim about negative sentences similar to Sperber and Wilson's (1986) about genitive NPs, I do not contrast incompleteness with ambiguity; I contrast semantical non-specificity of sentences (*aka* semantical generality of sentences) with sense-ambiguity of sentences. To call it 'incompleteness' confuses the cause with the effect. The sentence is only "incomplete" by contrast with its various, more semantically specific, utterance-interpretations, but it is open to various specifications in its utterance-interpretations because it is a sentence that is semantically univocal and sense-nonspecific with respect to basic semantical properties that allow various specifications of utterance-meaning (and disallow others) in any literal use of the sentence.

Sperber and Wilson and Bach used the term 'incompleteness', which led Cappelen and Lepore to think that the phenomena of the genitive NP and of *strong enough* and *is ready* were the same. Not so. Instead, Sperber and Wilson's sentence 'Peter's bat is gray' is like Bezuidenhout's sentence 'Here's a red one'; they are not ambiguous just because in varying contexts sentence-tokens may be used to express varying interpretations 'red-skinned' and 'red-fleshed' or express varying interpretations 'owned by' and 'chosen by'. 'Red' is not polysemous between 'red-skinned' and 'red-fleshed'; neither is 'John's bat' polysemous (ambiguous). What Sperber and Wilson call 'incompleteness' is just Bezuidenhout's context-variability. The genitive NP is not like Bach's 'ready' and 'strong enough', which beg for "completions" like 'for battle' and 'to stop a uranium-tipped shell'. Bach thinks that these

---

[6]See the discussion of *the girl with the flowers* in Atlas (1989) and in Atlas (2005: 31–32) and the possessive in Atlas (2005: 19, 36, 85).

"completions" are required by the semantic properties of the sentences, the surface structures of which fail to provide a phrase as a value for the underlying meta-variable attached, syntactically or in a semantic interpretation, to 'ready' and 'strong enough'. Bach thinks that 'ready' and 'strong enough' are like 'big', 'short', and, I would add on his behalf, 'tall'. The natural "completions" are expressions like 'big for a first-grader', 'short for a NBA center', or 'tall for a Dutchman'.

## 6   Semantic Non-Specificity, Underdeterminacy, Semantic Solipsism, and Skepticism: Cappelen and Lepore's Reaction to Contextualisms

So far, then, we have the context-variability of the interpretations of utterances of a sentence and the Bachian "semantical or conceptual incompleteness" of sentences.[7] But none of this is linguistically or logically surprising. What is surprising are the claims about nonambiguity, in fact semantical non-specificity, of certain sentences, like the negative ones discussed by Atlas (1974ff.), which are not discussed by Bezuidenhout, Sperber and Wilson, or by Bach in recent work (but see his 1982, 1987). What is also surprising are claims about the genitive NP, mentioned by Sperber and Wilson (1986) and by Atlas (2005). So why should sentiments as old as J. L. Austin's (1962: 110–111) remark, "Sentences are not *as such* either true or false," suddenly take on for Cappelen and Lepore the opprobrium of a slogan of Friedrich Engels or Osama bin Laden? What gets under Cappelen and Lepore's (2005: 38) skins are comments like this from Relevance Theorists like Robyn Carston (2002: 29):

> Underdeterminacy is an essential feature of the relation between linguistic expressions and the propositions (thoughts) they are used to express; generally, for any given proposition/thought, there is

---

[7]It is unfortunate that Bach fudged by saying 'semantical or conceptual', since it matters which. Semanticality is a property of sentences; conceptuality is an attribute of mental contents or propositions. Cappelen and Lepore note the similarity of Bachian "incompleteness" to John Perry's (1986, 1993), Mark Crimmins's (1992), and Ken Taylor's (2001) observations about how a sentence like 'It's raining' receives a truth-value in a context. They believe that the sentence contains a syntactically unrealized argument taking places or locations as values. Thus the underlying structure of the sentence is 'It's raining (at) X'. Of course there is also the usual question of tense, and so an argument for a time $t$ as well: 'It is $\langle t \rangle$ raining (at) X'. So when I utter the sentence, one utterance-interpretation is "It is now raining here."

> no sentence which *fully* [my emphasis – JDA] encodes it ....
> Underdeterminacy is universal and no sentence ever *fully* [my
> emphasis – JDA] encodes the thought or proposition it is used to
> express.[8]

Of course, if sentences do not express propositions, the contents of
thoughts and the bearers of truth-values, then what do we need a
semantic theory of sentences for? And if no sentence, tokens of which are
uttered by speakers to addressees, ever *fully* expresses a thought,
semantical solipsism looms: you might really be alone with your
thoughts, or at least some of them, despite having a language. For
utterance-interpretation might be too weak a reed to support communication between speaker and addressee: too unreliable as a process to
ever produce "full" knowledge of what the speaker was thinking or meant
by his utterance of the sentence. And then J. L. Austin was right, along
with Wittgenstein. The vehicles of meaning are not sentences, *pace*
Frege, but are utterances, speech-acts, discourses, or even – how to stop
the dread slide? – language-games! Then John Searle and "Levinstein"
(Levinson, 1979/Wittgenstein, 2009) were right: a theory of meaning is
just a theory of speech-acts or of language-games. But on Cappelen and
Lepore's view that takes you directly to "contextualism," and then to
semantic *solipsism*, semantic *skepticism*, semantic *relativism* (Cappelen
and Lepore, 2005: 152–153).[9] Either defend an account in which
sentences, not just utterances, express propositions, or sink into the
philosophical abyss! So Cappelen and Lepore mount their white chargers
and ride out to do battle with the forces of darkness. Refute J. L. Austin,
and all his shadowy progeny, or succumb to contextualism: the unholy

---

[8]I made remarks superficially like this in Atlas (1997) and Atlas (2005: 17–30), but I
avoided the word 'fully', which gives away Carston's 19th century Hegelian game – back
to F. H. Bradley's sentences expressing all of Reality in order to be true or false: the whole
truth is assumed to be the only truth. Carston's language also presupposes that there is a
useful notion of a sentence expressing approximately the content of a thought, as if we
were translating from a Fodorean Language of Thought into English with a greater or
lesser degree of success in squeezing all the information out of the bedraggled little
thought. But who knows? Maybe the mind operates the way Fodor (1975) says. I don't
think there are any arguments in *The Language of Thought* to show that, however, but
that is a discussion for another day. There certainly is no scientific evidence of any kind.
But if not, then Carston's model of the relationship of language to thought has no
purchase, and Cappelen and Lepore may relax.

[9]Cappelen and Lepore (2005: 154) also believe that their view will avoid an internalist
doctrine of a speaker's Original Sinn for speech-act contents and will separate questions of
semantics from questions of metaphysics, thus allowing for a "pure" philosophy of
language (in Richard Rorty's (1979) sense, describing the work of Donald Davidson).

trinity of solipsism, skepticism, and relativism! Cappelen and Lepore (2005: 6) summarize the Radical Contextualist view that they oppose as follows:

> No English sentence S ever semantically expresses a proposition.[10]
> Any semantic value that Semantic Minimalists [like Lepore] assign to S can be no more than a *propositional fragment* (or *radical*), where the hallmark of a propositional fragment (or radical) is that it does not determine a set of truth conditions, and hence, cannot take a truth value.[11]
> Context-sensitivity is ubiquitous . . . [12]
>
> Only an utterance can semantically express a complete proposition, have a truth condition, and so, take a truth value.[13]

Cappelen and Lepore believe that these claims are all highly implausible, but they acknowledge that there are views not as radical, which they label 'moderate contextualism'. Their strategy is to show that the arguments that, they believe, are typically used to support the more moderate position, if they are plausible, make the radical position just as plausible. On their view one cannot be a moderate contextualist like Kent Bach without being logically forced into being a radical contextualist like Charles Travis. About sentences like 'Steel isn't strong enough' or 'Fred is ready' Kent Bach (1994a: 125) claims that they have a "missing

---

[10]See Cappelen and Lepore (2005: 63–64) citing Travis (1985: 197). The crucial phrase here is 'no sentence'.

[11]Cappelen and Lepore cite Carston (1988: 167; 2002), Sperber and Wilson (1986), Recanati (1993, 2004), Bach (1994a, 1994b: 128ff.), Taylor (2001). The earliest locus for this view is Atlas (1974, 1975, 1977, 1979), with specific application to negative definite description sentences, e.g., 'The king of France is not bald', not to all sentences. See also Atlas (1989, 2004a, 2005). I do not make this claim for all English sentences, and so I am not a Radical Contextualist like Charles Travis. Propositional fragments or radicals are described by Bach (1994b) as what is expressed by the ' . . . is ready' sentences.

[12]This is Robyn Carston (2002) and friends.

[13]Again, the crucial phrase here is 'only an utterance'. The same cast of characters, including Atlas, J. L. Austin, Strawson (1950), Davidson (1968/1984), and Kaplan (1989) at moments have taken the view that only utterances *of certain types of sentences* carry truth values. What distinguishes Atlas from Strawson and Davidson and from some of the others is a semantical thesis about the univocality, the lack of scope-ambiguity, of negative sentences and my commitment to a sentence-semantics. I am not a semantical minimalist about propositions like Cappelen and Lepore. I am about as enthusiastic about propositions as Quine was. I argue elsewhere (Atlas, 2007) that all the work that Cappelen and Lepore want their minimalist propositions to do can be done by sentence-meanings (and both Chomsky and Frege will thank me). I show how to be a conservative contextualist and a sentence-semanticist at the same time – what I call "Meaning Dualism." (Actually I have already shown how to do that, in Atlas (1977, 1979, 1989, 1997, 2005), but these ideas are worth re-examining in light of the current debate over contextualism.)

argument" and so do "not by virtue of linguistic meaning express a complete proposition."

## 7 How can Moderate Contextualists Avoid Semantic Solipsism and Skepticism?

Suggested completions for sentences like 'Fred is ready' are 'Fred is ready for the exam', 'Fred is ready to leave for the party'. Cappelen and Lepore (2005: 62–63) suggest that the content of Bach's and others' intuitions about such completions is that they are required in order to answer 'would it be true' questions about the sentences; e.g., 'Is ready for what?' has to be answered if truth or falsity is to be ascribed to the sentence. Bach's intuition is supposedly that one cannot answer the question 'Under what circumstances would it be true that Fred is ready?' Cappelen and Lepore point out that one can ask the same question again about the new sentence, e.g., 'Is ready for the exam when?'. The completion would then be: Fred is ready for the exam today. But can we ascribe truth or falsity if we can ask, "How ready for the exam today?" So then: Fred is completely ready for the exam today. And so on.[14]

Then Cappelen and Lepore point out that if this sort of argument justifies Bach's claims for incompleteness, then almost no sentence of English is complete, and one must become a Radical Contextualist like Charles Travis. Cappelen and Lepore (2005: 68) have a similar argument against Bezuidenhout's example 'Here's a red one'. If the object is an apple, then where is it red? On its skin, or inside? Red in what kind of light? Red because it is painted red? Again, they observe, these questions can be raised about almost every English sentence. So if one is impressed by context-variability for Bezuidenhout's example and by incompleteness for Bach's example, the argument should be applicable to almost any example of English.

They consider two possible replies to their objection that context-sensitivity is "unbounded." The first is what they call 'a psychological reply'. Speakers who assert 'Fred is ready' intend to communicate that Fred is ready for so-and-so, with 'so-and-so' filled in for a particular speech context. Speakers do not "typically" or "usually" intend to communicate that Fred is ready for so-and-so today, or that Fred is completely ready for so-and-so today. Their answer to this reply is

---

[14]What looks to Cappelen and Lepore like a *reductio ad absurdum* infinite "progress" argument was to a 19th century Hegelian like F. H. Bradley just obviously correct metaphysical reasoning.

philosophically striking (Cappelen and Lepore, 2005: 65): "an incompleteness claim, as we have construed it, is a metaphysical claim. ... it is not a claim about what speakers usually do. It is a claim about what propositions exist. It is, for example, the claim that there is no such thing as the proposition" *that Fred is ready*.

It is certainly true that Bach is committed to saying that whatever 'Fred is ready' expresses, it is a propositional fragment or propositional radical, not something that is a "complete thought" as it stands. So the issue boils down to a battle of the metaphysicians: Are there propositions expressed by *that Fred is ready* and by *the apple is red*? I react by asking, Does one even understand that question?[15]

Cappelen and Lepore (2005: 66–67) also consider an objection by Ken Taylor (2001: 60). Taylor pins Bach's incompleteness on lexical structure; in Taylor's case the example was 'It's raining', and the missing piece from what would be "expressed determinately in a full proposition" is where it is raining. In order for the utterance of the sentence to have a truth-value, a location must be provided by the context of utterance, e.g., "It's raining in Palo Alto." But Taylor formulates his defense in terms of our "felt inability" to assign a truth-value in the absence of information about a location and the source of this feeling in our cognizing the missing semantic location argument in the verb 'rain'. By talking about our "felt inability" Taylor opens himself up to the same objection that he is arguing psychology not semantics. Thus in order to argue against Cappelen and Lepore's unboundedness interpretation of Bach's incompleteness, Cappelen and Lepore claim that their opponent must argue that there is not the same "felt inability" to assign a truth value to 'It's raining hard in Palo Alto', or 'It's raining intermittently in Palo Alto'. And then Cappelen and Lepore simply ask, "Why does one's 'felt inability' bear on the question whether there exists a complete proposition for the sentence to express?"

## 8   Semantics is Not Psychology; Meaning is Not Merely Truth-Conditions; Meaning is Not Reference

Taylor's rhetoric laid him open to this objection and allowed Cappelen and Lepore to ignore his semantic argument. That argument was an appeal to the structure of the lexicon of English expressions. What kind

---

[15]I say, "A pox on both your houses." Bertrand Russell and F. H. Bradley deserved each other; see Atlas (2004b: 354–358).

of word is 'ready'? What kind of verb is 'rains'? Unfortunately for Taylor, I doubt that 'rains' really does have a semantic argument for locations. But I do not doubt that 'ready' is semantically more complex than the surface string 'Fred is ready' suggests, e.g., 'ready TO VERB', 'ready FOR NOUN'. These linguistic questions about meaning are not questions about the psychology of speakers, but they are also not questions about the precise specifications of the verification conditions or of descriptions of the facts that would make an utterance of the sentence true. Even if, as Cappelen and Lepore point out, we can elaborate the descriptions of the facts that might verify the sentence *ad nauseum*, why should the possibility of such elaborations have any bearing on whether the original sentence has a linguistic meaning of a particular sort – and one should not assume, as in Cappelen and Lepore's construal, that the meaning would be of the sort by virtue of which the sentence with that meaning describes completely each or all or any of these facts. What is involved in Bach's incompleteness is not whether a sentence like 'Fred is ready' describes a Total Fact, or Reality as a whole. If the psychology of utterers of a sentence is beside the point, so is whether a sentence is a total description of reality.

Cappelen and Lepore's construal of Bach's argument is a mistaken construal. Taylor had it more or less right: it is a matter of lexical semantics, whether of 'ready' or 'red'. That is to say, it is a matter of meaning, not of facts, truth-conditions, or total descriptions, and not what it is even for Taylor, a matter of a "fully determinate proposition." If instead it is a matter of linguistic meaning, there is no slippery slope from moderate to radical contextualism, even if there is a slippery slope in metaphysics from one description of a fact to a longer description of a bigger fact until one gets to the Biggest Fact of them all.

'Ready' does require a completion of meaning, 'ready TO VERB' or 'ready FOR NOUN'. 'Rains' actually does not require a completion of meaning 'rains LOCATION'. Taylor chose a poor example, as did Perry (1986: 206) and Crimmins (1992: 17). By the way, if you are still a Situation Semanticist, you will have to say that in 'It is raining', 'It' is a referring term, and it denotes Reality, or the World, which has the property of "raining," however that is managed. And then the LOCATION parameter gets a little dicey. 'Palo Alto' seems a poor description of where Reality is. Now what about 'the apple is red'? Is 'red' semantically parameterized for 'red *on the inside*' and 'red *on the outside*'? 'On the inside' and 'on the outside' may describe facts about the apple by virtue of which 'the apple is red' when asserted turns out to be true or false, but the meaning of 'red' is not lexically incomplete the way 'ready' is. Cappelen and Lepore (2005: 68) mistakenly assimilate the two cases. If they had paid more attention to lexical meaning, Cappelen and Lepore could have avoided their misconstrual of Kent Bach's argument caused by their focus on truth-conditions or "propositions."

My conclusions are these: (*a*) Don't substitute truth conditions for linguistic meanings and think that you have not changed the subject. (*b*) Don't use the word 'proposition' when you talk about what sentences express, as contrasted with what utterances express; "complete sentence meanings" will make sense in the case of sentences; "full propositions" make no sense even in the case of utterances (Bach, 1994a: 125); "fully determinate propositions" are really creatures of darkness. These notions do not make things better – and you not only know what I mean by 'better', you know what the word 'better' means.

# References

Anscombe, G. E. M.   1981. Before and after. In G. E. M. Anscombe, ed., *Metaphysics and the Philosophy of Mind: Collected Philosophical Papers, Volume II*, pp. 180–195. Minneapolis, MN: University of Minnesota Press.

Atlas, J. D. 1974. Presupposition, Ambiguity, and Generality: A Coda to the Russell-Strawson Debate on Referring. TS. Department of Philosophy, Pomona College, Claremont, CA.

Atlas, J. D.  1975. Frege's polymorphous concept of presupposition and its role in a theory of meaning. *Semantikos* 1:29–44.

Atlas, J. D.  1977. Negation, ambiguity, and presupposition. *Linguistics and Philosophy* 1:321–336.

Atlas, J. D. 1978a. Presupposition and Grice's pragmatics. *Colloquium Lecture*, Department of Phonetics and Linguistics, University College, London, May 1978.

Atlas, J. D.  1978b. On presupposing. *Mind* 87:396–411.

Atlas, J. D.  1979. How linguistics matters to philosophy: Presupposition, truth, and meaning. In D. Dinneen and C. K. Oh, eds., *Syntax and Semantics 11: Presupposition*, pp. 265–281. New York: Academic Press.

Atlas, J. D.  1983. Comments on 'Metalinguistic Negation and Pragmatic Ambiguity' by Larry Horn, Yale University, June 1983. TS. The Institute for Advanced Study, Princeton, NJ, December 1983.

Atlas, J. D.   1984a. Comparative adjectives and adverbials of degree: An introduction to radically radical pragmatics. *Linguistics and Philosophy* 7:347–377.

Atlas, J. D.  1984b. Grammatical non-specification: The mistaken disjunction theory. *Linguistics and Philosophy* 7:433–443.

Atlas, J. D.  1989. *Philosophy Without Ambiguity*. Oxford: Clarendon Press.

Atlas, J. D. 1990. Implicature and logical form: The semantics-pragmatics interface. Five lectures, 6 August–10 August 1990. *Second European Summer School in Language, Logic, and Information.* Leuven, Belgium: Katholieke Universiteit.

Atlas, J. D. 1997. On the modularity of sentence processing: Semantical generality and the language of thought. In J. Nuyts and E. Pederson, eds., *Language and Conceptualization,* pp. 213–228. Cambridge: Cambridge University Press.

Atlas, J. D. 2004a. Presupposition. In L. R. Horn and G. Ward, eds., *The Handbook of Pragmatics,* pp. 29–52. Oxford: Blackwell.

Atlas, J. D. 2004b. Descriptions, linguistic topic/comment, and negative existentials: A case study in the application of linguistic theory to problems in the philosophy of language. In M. Reimer and A. Bezuidenhout, eds., *Descriptions and Beyond,* pp. 342–360. Oxford: Clarendon Press.

Atlas, J. D. 2005. *Logic, Meaning, and Conversation: Semantical Underdeterminacy, Implicature and Their Interface.* New York: Oxford University Press.

Atlas, J. D. 2007. Meanings, propositions, context, semantical underdeterminacy. In G. Preyer and G. Peter, eds., *Context-Sensitivity and Semantic Minimalism,* pp. 217–239. Oxford: Clarendon Press.

Atlas, J. D. and S. C. Levinson. 1981. *It*-clefts, informativeness, and logical form: An introduction to radically radical pragmatics. In P. Cole, ed., *Radical Pragmatics,* pp. 1–61. New York: Academic Press.

Austin, J. L. 1962. *How to Do Things With Words.* Oxford: Clarendon Press.

Bach, K. 1981. Referential/attributive. *Synthese* 49:219–244.

Bach, K. 1982. Semantic non-specificity and mixed quantifiers. *Linguistics and Philosophy* 4:593–605.

Bach, K. 1987. *Thought and Reference.* Oxford: Clarendon Press.

Bach, K. 1994a. Conversational impliciture. *Mind and Language* 9:124–162.

Bach, K. 1994b. Semantic slack. In S. Tsohatzidis, ed., *Foundations of Speech Act Theory,* pp. 267–291. London: Routledge.

Bach, K. 1997. Do belief reports report beliefs? *Pacific Philosophical Quarterly* 78:215–241.

Benveniste, E. 1974. La Forme et le Sens dans le Langage. In E. Benveniste, ed., *Problèmes de Linguistique Générale II,* pp. 215–238. Paris: Gallimard.

Bezuidenhout, A. 2002. Truth-conditional pragmatics. *Philosophical Perspectives* 16:105–134.

Borg, E. 2004. *Minimal Semantics.* Oxford: Clarendon Press.

Cappelen, H. and E. Lepore. 2005. *Insensitive Semantics: A Defense of Semantic Minimalism and Speech Act Pluralism.* Oxford: Blackwell.

Carston, R. 1988. Implicature, explicature, and truth-theoretic semantics. In R. Kempson, ed., *Mental Representations: The Interface Between Language and Reality,* pp. 155–181. Cambridge: Cambridge University Press.

Carston, R. 2002. *Thoughts and Utterances: The Pragmatics of Explicit Communication*. Oxford: Blackwell.

Clark, H. 1983. Making sense of nonce sense. In G. B. Flores d'Arcais and R. J. Jarvella, eds., *The Process of Language Understanding*, pp. 297–331. London: Wiley.

Clark, H. 1992. *Arenas of Language Use*. Chicago and Palo Alto: University of Chicago Press and Center for the Study of Language and Information.

Clark, H. and R. J. Gerrig. 1983. Understanding old words with new meanings. *Journal of Verbal Learning and Verbal Behavior* 22:591–608.

Clark, H. and S. E. Haviland. 1977. Comprehension and the given-new contract. In R. Freedle, ed., *Discourse Production and Comprehension*, pp. 1–40. Hillsdale, NJ: Lawrence Erlbaum.

Cohen, J. 1986. How is conceptual innovation possible? *Erkenntnis* 25:221–238.

Crimmins, M. 1992. *Talk about Beliefs*. Cambridge, MA: MIT Press.

Cruse, D. A. 1986. *Lexical Semantics*. Cambridge: Cambridge University Press.

Davidson, D. 1968/1984. On saying that. In D. Davidson, *Inquiries into Truth and Interpretation*, pp. 93–108. Oxford: Clarendon Press.

Fodor, J. A. 1975. *The Language of Thought*. New York: Thomas Y. Crowell.

Fodor, J. A. 1983. *The Modularity of Mind*. Cambridge, MA: MIT Press.

Forster, K. and I. Olbrei. 1973. Semantic heuristics and syntactic analysis. *Cognition* 2:319–347.

Gibbs, R. 1994. *The Poetics of Mind: Figurative Thought, Language, and Understanding*. Cambridge: Cambridge University Press.

Giora, R. 2003. *On Our Mind: Salience, Context, and Figurative Language*. New York: Oxford University Press.

Glucksberg, S. 2001. *Understanding Figurative Language: From Metaphors to Idioms*. New York: Oxford University Press.

Grice, H. P. 1989. *Studies in the Way of Words*. Cambridge, MA: Harvard University Press.

Guillaume, G. 1929. *Temps and Verbe*. Paris: Champion.

Horn, L. R. 1984. Toward a new taxonomy for pragmatic inference: Q-based and R-based implicature. In D. Schiffrin, ed., *Georgetown University Round Table on Languages and Linguistics 1984. Meaning, Form and Use in Context: Linguistic Applications*, pp. 11–42. Washington, DC: Georgetown University Press.

Horn, L. R. 1989. *A Natural History of Negation*. Chicago: University of Chicago Press.

Horn, L. R. 1992. The said and the unsaid. *SALT II: Proceedings of the Second Conference on Semantics and Linguistic Theory*, pp. 163–192. Columbus, OH: Ohio State University Linguistics Department.

Jackendoff, R. 1997. *Architecture of the Language Faculty*. Cambridge, MA: MIT Press.

Kaplan, D. 1989. Afterthoughts. In J. Almog, J. Perry, and H. Wettstein, eds., *Themes from Kaplan*, pp. 565–614. New York: Oxford University Press.

Katz, J. J. 1972. *Semantic Theory*. New York: Harper Row.

Kempson, R. 1975. *Presupposition and the Delimitation of Semantics*. Cambridge: Cambridge University Press.

Kempson, R. 1988. Grammar and conversational principles. In F. J. Newmeyer, ed., *Linguistics: The Cambridge Survey. Vol. 2. Linguistic Theory: Extensions and Implications*, pp. 139–163. Cambridge: Cambridge University Press.

Lahav, R. 1989. Against compositionality: The case of adjectives. *Philosophical Studies* 57:261–279.

Leech, G. N. 1974. *Semantics*. London: Penguin.

Levinson, S. C. 1979. Activity types and language. *Linguistics* 17:356–399.

Levinson, S. C. 1988. Generalized Conversational Implicatures and the Semantics/Pragmatics Interface. TS. Department of Linguistics, Stanford University, Stanford, CA.

Levinson, S. C. 2000. *Presumptive Meanings: The Theory of Generalized Conversational Implicature*. Cambridge, MA: MIT Press.

Perry, J. 1986. Thought without representation. *Proceedings of the Aristotelian Society*, Suppl. Vol. 60: 263–283; reprinted in Perry, J. (1993, pp. 205–225); reprinted in Perry, J. (2000, pp. 171–188).

Perry, J. 1993. *The Problem of the Essential Indexical and Other Essays*. New York: Oxford University Press.

Perry, J. 2000. *The Problem of the Essential Indexical and Other Essays*. Stanford, CA: CSLI Publications.

Pustejovsky, J. 1995. *The Generative Lexicon*. Cambridge, MA: MIT Press.

Recanati, R. 1993. *Direct Reference: From Language to Thought*. Oxford: Blackwell.

Recanati, F. 2004. *Literal Meaning*. Cambridge, MA: Cambridge University Press.

Rorty, R. 1979. *Philosophy and the Mirror of Nature*. Princeton, NJ: Princeton University Press.

Ross, J. 1981. *Portraying Analogy*. Cambridge: Cambridge University Press.

Ruhl, C. 1989. *On Monosemy: A Study in Linguistic Semantics*. Albany, NY: State University of New York Press.

Rumelhart, D. 1993. Some problems with the notion of literal meaning. In A. Ortony, ed., *Metaphor and Thought*. 2nd edn, pp. 71–82. Cambridge: Cambridge University Press.

Schank, R. and R. Abelson. 1975. Scripts, plans and knowledge. In P. Johnson-Laird and P. Wason, eds., *Proceedings of the Fourth International Joint Conference on Artificial Intelligence*, Tblisi; reprinted in *Thinking*, Cambridge, Cambridge University Press, 1977.

Scott, D. S. 1970. Advice on modal logic. In K. Lambert, ed., *Philosophical Problems in Logic: Some Recent Developments*, pp. 143–173. Dordrecht: Reidel.

Sperber, D. and D. Wilson. 1986. *Relevance*. Oxford: Blackwell.

Sperber, D. and D. Wilson. 1998. The mapping between the mental and public lexicon. In P. Carruthers and J. Bouchers, eds., *Language and Thought: Interdisciplinary Themes*, pp. 184–200. Cambridge: Cambridge University Press.

Stanley, J. and Z. Szabó. 2000. On quantifier domain restriction. *Mind and Language* 15:219–261.

Strawson, P. F. 1950. On referring. *Mind* 59:320–344.

Taylor, K. 2001. Sex, breakfast, and descriptus interruptus. *Synthese* 128:45–61.

Travis, C. 1985. On what is strictly speaking true. *Canadian Journal of Philosophy* 15:187–229.

Victorri, B. and C. Fuchs. 1996. *La Polysémie*. Paris: Hermès.

Walker, R. 1975. Conversational implicatures. In S. Blackburn, ed., *Meaning, Reference, and Necessity*, pp. 133–181. Cambridge: Cambridge University Press.

Wittgenstein, L. 2009, *Philosophical Investigations*. Rev. 4th edn. Chichester: Wiley-BlackWell.

Ziff, P. 1972a. *Understanding Understanding*. Ithaca, NY: Cornell University Press.

Ziff, P. 1972b. What is said. In Ziff (1972a, pp. 21–38).

**3**

# What Refers? How?

ALEX BARBER

## 1 Introduction: What Refers?

*Guns don't kill people, people kill people.* This National Rifle Association slogan has a popular analogue in the philosophy of language: *Words don't refer, people refer.* Thus we have Peter Strawson asserting, in his reply to Bertrand Russell, that:

> 'referring' ... is not something an expression does; it is something that someone can use an expression to do. (Strawson, 1950: 326)

Echoing him, Leonard Linsky writes:

> Of the first importance [in discussions of the reference relation] is the consideration that it is the users of language who refer ... and not, except in a derivative sense, the expression which they use in so doing. (Linsky, 1963: 74)

Noam Chomsky cites Strawson in support of a similar-sounding view:

> The question, "to what does the word X refer?," has no clear sense .... In general, a word, even of the simplest kind, does not pick out an entity of the world, or of our "belief space" .... (Chomsky, 2000: 181)

James McGilvray, too, criticizes those who:

> ... think of reference as a conventional relationship between word and world, or perhaps even look for a "natural" relationship in a realist construal of information theory; in either case, they apparently ignore the fact that people use words (and they use

*Making Semantics Pragmatic*
Ken Turner (ed.).
Current Research in the Semantics/Pragmatics Interface, Vol. 24.
© 2011 by Emerald Group Publishing Limited. All rights reserved.

them in many ways) to refer to things. (McGilvray, 2005: 15; see
also McGilvray, 1998)

But just as campaigners for gun control persist in talking of the
lethal properties of guns, many philosophers of language, including
W. V. Quine and Nathan Salmon, continue to talk of the referential
properties of words, conceding only that the identity of these properties
must sometimes be relativized to a context of utterance.

> One thinks of reference, first and foremost, as relating names and
> other singular terms to their objects. (Quine, 1990: 27)

> [T]he semantic attributes of expressions are not conceptually
> derivative of the speech acts performed by their utterers, and
> are [instead] intrinsic to the expressions themselves, or to the
> expressions *as* expressions of a particular language and as occurring
> in a particular context. (Salmon, 2004: 238)

And of course, formal semantics, even when cognitivist in orientation, involves the ascription of referential properties to expressions:

> 26 a.　　*Rabbit* refers to rabbits.
> ....
> Proper nouns like *Jill* ... are analysed as having persons as their
> semantic values, that is, as referring to those individuals:
> 9 a.　　Val($x$, *Jill*) iff $x$ = Jill. (Larson and Segal, 1995: 41, 118)

So what refers, words or people? Perhaps both do. Many,
including Saul Kripke and Kent Bach, have insisted on the
dissociability of two distinct notions of reference:

> The speaker's referent is the thing the speaker referred to by the
> designator, though it may not be the referent of the designator, in
> his idiolect. (Kripke, 1977: 238)

> Failing to distinguish speaker reference from linguistic reference .
> .. inevitably leads to theoretical confusion. (Bach, 1987: 6)

Completing the logical space, a fourth possibility is that neither words
nor people refer.

Rather than launching into an investigation of which of these four
possible views is correct, it would be as well to ask whether and why it
matters how we fill the subject position when using the verb 'to refer'. I
take this question up in Section 2. The rest of the chapter uncovers then
tackles a specific puzzle about the relation between speaker reference
and word reference. The ingredients of the puzzle are entirely familiar,
having to do with the apparent intentionality (in senses loosely
associated with Brentano) of speaker reference, a trait that word

reference seems to lack. In view of this apparent contrast, how could both speakers and words refer? The puzzle is introduced in Section 3 and firmed up in Sections 4–8, with a solution offered in Section 9. Part of the firming up process involves explaining how some standard views on speaker reference and word reference seem to have led to the puzzle being either overlooked or dismissed.

## 2  What Turns on What Refers?

The question of whether it is speakers or words or both or neither that refer could be – and clearly often is, tacitly at least – approached naïvely, as a question about proper usage of the verb 'to refer'. But why should we care about the folk's view on what refers? Folk views sometimes constitute useful if crude proto-theories, platforms from which to develop more rigorous proposals. That does not seem to be the case here. But in any case, the folk's opinion is unclear. Asking explicitly yields no helpful answer, since the folk are vague in their views and easily led away from their initial answer no matter what it may have been. Notice in addition that acceptability judgements vary from one linguistic culture to another. As readily as English speakers allow that universities educate students, French speakers allow that lawnmowers mow lawns, even though this latter is unacceptable to most English ears. Unless we aspire only to a parochial theory of reference, there is little to be gained from asking English speakers which, if any, "sounds better" out of the views of Quine and Strawson, quoted above.[1]

Rather than addressing a semi-interesting question about ordinary usage with no clear answer, I will attempt to raise a genuine puzzle about reference by coming at the topic of opacity from an unfamiliar angle. Others have had reasons of their own for taking a view on whether it is words or speakers that refer. I will summarize two such reasons briefly, below, not because anything I say bears directly on them or because there are no other reasons a person could have,[2] but

---

[1]Davis (2005) seems to take seriously what it is 'natural' to say about what a person has referred to; and Chomsky (2003: 272), citing Strawson, writes that whereas talk of speakers referring is 'normal in English (with counterparts in other languages)', talk of words referring is 'a technical innovation that remains obscure and unexplained', and infers from this that '[t]hose who believe that some notion of "word-thing reference"' has an explanatory role 'have to explain what they mean, and provide the evidence'.

[2]Thus, Kripke's distinction is designed to call into question Donnellan's criticism of Russell's account of definite descriptions, while Quine's claim is driven, presumably, by a concern with logical relations whose study has traditionally involved the interpretation of the elements of formal languages.

because they impinge, obliquely, on what I have to say about the puzzle that is my more immediate concern.

The essence of Strawson's point is that if we treat referring as something people can do with words, Russell's theory of descriptions and its corollary, his theory of ordinary names, have no purpose. Whenever a person attempts to refer using a definite description (perhaps disguised as a name), they make, or affect to make, certain presuppositions – that there is a unique contextually salient satisfier of the description, for example. They succeed in referring only if these presuppositions are met. Russell's mistake is to confuse the presupposition relation, which holds between a *speaker* and some condition, for an entailment relation, i.e. one that holds between the *expression used* and this same condition. His theory of the logical form of descriptions explains this entailment, but if Strawson is right, no such explanation is needed. One can utter a definite description in an attempt to refer but fail to refer because nothing uniquely satisfies the description. This is no more mysterious than the fact that one can, for example, swerve in an attempt to avoid an obstacle but fail because there was no obstacle to avoid. Neither calls for a semantic explanation.[3]

If referring is indeed something people do with words and not a standing characteristic of words, a more general moral one might draw is that attempts to deliver a systematic theory of the referential properties of the expressions of a language are misconceived. Referring would be an aspect of the use of language rather than of a stable body of knowledge codified in the language faculty – an aspect of performance rather than competence as Chomsky would once have put it. Ambitions to provide a theory of this use would be as hopeless as behaviourist attempts to capture our dispositions to produce particular sounds. Intuitions about reference may feed into the explanation of systematic, relatively contained phenomena, such as binding relations. But according to Chomsky, McGilvray and others (e.g. Pietroski, 2003), attempting to construct a theory of reference as philosophers of language tend to use this phrase, in which word-world relations entail a compositional theory of truth for the sentences of a language, is the wrong way to set about developing a natural science of language.

---

[3]Compare Strawson (1950: 333). One might accept this point but still see in Russell's theory the seeds of a useful explanation of our capacity to *think* about non-existent objects. In that case, his theory of descriptions would feed into a theory of mental content, not linguistic content, and be relevant to attempts to refer (or to avoid) that fail through the lack of an object.

I will remain as neutral as I can on both Strawson's and Chomsky's concerns, which are broader than my own. But both are connected, tangentially, to the puzzle to which I now turn.

## 3 A Puzzle About Reference

I am interested in the ramifications of an apparent contrast between the characteristics of word reference, assuming there is such a thing, and the characteristics of speaker reference, again assuming there is such a thing. Given assumptions I will come to, speaker reference is arguably intentional in the Brentano sense. That is to say, facts about speaker reference seem to respect neither of two logical laws, the law of existential generalization and the law of identity. Were it a fact that someone had touched Santa Claus, it would follow that Santa Claus existed; and from the fact that Hesperus is a planet it would follow that Phosphorus is a planet. But from the fact that a person has referred to Santa Claus it does not follow that Santa Claus exists; and from the fact that a person has referred to Hesperus it does not follow that they have referred to Phosphorus. Word reference, by contrast, and once again given assumptions I will come to, is arguably intentional in neither respect: a word cannot refer to Santa Claus given that no such person exists, and if a word refers to Hesperus it refers equally to Phosphorus.

To keep things manageable I will focus exclusively on the failure of the law of identity until Section 9, at which point I will show that a solution to the version of the puzzle thrown up by substitution failure works to solve the version of the puzzle thrown up by failure of existential generalization. In the meantime, and in the form of it that I will be focussing on, the puzzle arises out of a tension between two claims, I and II below.

I. Speaker reference is substitution unfriendly.
II. Word reference is substitution friendly.

A property is substitution friendly if and only if it always respects the law of identity, so that if some object has that property then anything identical with the object also has the property. I and II, then, make contrasting claims about whether being referred to is among those properties that respect the law of identity: if it is a speaker doing the referring, the law is not respected; if it is an expression doing the referring, the law is respected. If Jane refers to Hesperus she has, according to I, not necessarily referred to Phosphorus, despite their being one and the same planet. By contrast, if 'Venus' refers to Hesperus, then according to II it must also refer to Phosphorus.

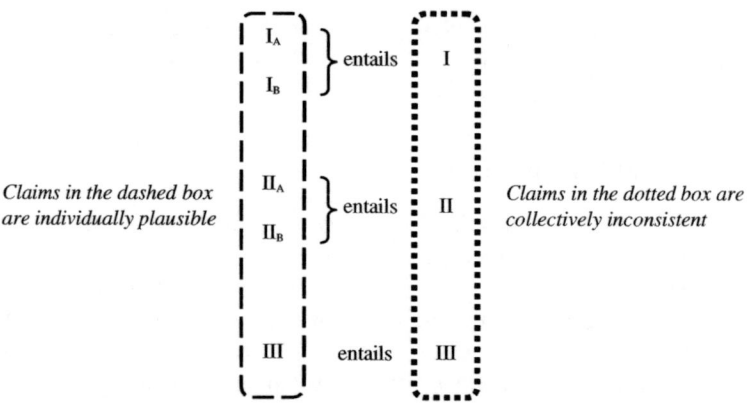

FIGURE 1    The structure of the puzzle.

Let me stress that the puzzle is *not* simply that I and II are immediately plausible but inconsistent with one another. Rather, it is that further claims, which are plausible, collectively entail I and II; and that another claim, also plausible, is provably inconsistent with I and II. Programmatically, the dialectic is as in Figure 1.

The puzzle comes to this: five plausible claims – $I_A$, $I_B$, $II_A$, $II_B$ and III, none yet stated – cannot all be true. I and II merely play a central role in demonstrating that the five claims are inconsistent with one another.

In Section 3 I will be concerned only with the entailment of I by $I_A$ and $I_B$ and the entailment of II by $II_A$ and $II_B$ (and of course with saying what $I_A$ through to $II_B$ are). Only in the sections that follow will I be concerned with the alleged inconsistency – arguing for its seriousness, and suggesting a solution.

Assumption $I_A$ is that what a speaker refers to in uttering a word is constitutively determined by that speaker's intention in performing the utterance. There are various forms the relevant intention could take. In what follows, I will take $I_A$ to be the schematic generalization[4] of which the following is an instance:

> Jane uses 'Venus' to refer to Hesperus if and only if her intention in
> uttering the word is that her audience should think of her doing so
> as a reference to Hesperus.

---

[4]I will follow a policy throughout of illustrating $I_A$, etc., using instances rather than expressing them as generalizations. Generalizations would need to be expressed schematically rather than using objectual quantification into the complement clause of psychological operators, and using schematic generalization does not illuminate anything.

The precise formulation of the intention is not critical. I have adopted this one rather than, say, ' . . . her intention in uttering the word is to refer to Hesperus' because intentions, in general, must be liable to being acted on unsuccessfully.[5] Jane could easily fail in her intention to be thought of as referring to Hesperus, but if the intention that constituted her referring to Hesperus was the intention to refer to Hesperus, her intention would be self-fulfilling. For all that, there is an unusual connection between the success condition for her intention and her intention's content: to succeed in bringing about what she intends, it is both necessary and sufficient that her intention be recognized. In this respect, referring can be grouped along with promising, asking, insinuating, and other meaningful acts like depicting, and distinguished from other kinds of non-meaningful acts such as kicking or finding. Arguably it is a mark of meaningful acts that they belong to some kind $k$ such that one counts as having $k$ed if and only if one has acted with the intention of being thought of as having $k$ed (where additional characteristics are needed to distinguish meaningful act types from one another). $I_A$ merely combines this thought about what it is to be meaningful with the platitude that for a person to refer is for them to perform a meaningful act.

$I_B$ is a claim about all intentions, not only semantic ones. Suppose Jane intended to pat Rex. It does not follow that she intended to pat Fido, even if Rex and Fido are one and the same dog. It may be that she had no idea that Rex and Fido were the same dog. $I_B$, the generalization of this, is the claim that intending is substitution unfriendly. Of course, not everyone agrees that psychological attitudes are substitution unfriendly. I discuss their views in Section 8. At this stage I am merely attempting to flesh out the dialectic of Figure 1, and it is enough that many would find $I_B$ plausible. If we apply $I_B$ to the intentions found in $I_A$, I follows: speaker reference is substitution unfriendly. This result is not peculiar to my idiosyncratic formulation of the intention that constitutes someone having referred to something. The same conclusion is invited by any formulation instances of which name or idiosyncratically describe the referent inside the scope of 'intends' or some other psychological operator on the right-hand side of the 'iff'. This or something approaching it appears to be a commitment of many existing definitions of speaker reference or related notions (see, e.g. Kripke, 1977: 238; Evans, 1982: 318–320; Bach, 1987: 52; Barker, 2004: 113; Davis, 2005: 162, 202–203; see also Searle, 1969: 94 and the penultimate note of this chapter).

---

[5]The reasons for this are similar to the reasons for why beliefs must not be true merely because they are held – something I argue for explicitly in Section 7.

What about II? Before searching for plausible claims that entail it, it is important to distinguish it from a similar sounding but more familiar thesis. Let II' be the claim that licences any inference with the same pattern as the following:

'Hesperus' refers to Venus.
'Phosphorus' refers to Venus.
∴ ' ... Hesperus ... ' is true if and only if ' ... Phosphorus ... '.

In other words, according to II', co-referring expressions of the object language can always be substituted *salva veritate* within sentences of the object language. (There are, of course, some widely debated apparent exceptions to this pattern, including attitude reports.) By contrast, the inference licensed by II is:

'Venus' refers to Hesperus.
Hesperus is Phosphorus.
∴ 'Venus' refers to Phosphorus.

II' insists that substitution of one object-language expression for another co-referring object-language expression does not affect the truth of the object-language sentence within which the substitution is made. II concerns the choice between two co-referring expressions of the metalanguage. The two claims are related since II asserts, in effect, that constructing sentences using '"Venus" refers to ... ' does not generate exceptions to II'; but II and II' are distinct for all that.

That word reference is substitution friendly follows from $II_A$ and $II_B$. $II_A$ is the claim that the truth-conditional properties of sentences lacking opaque operators are substitution friendly. Given that Hesperus is Phosphorus, for example, if 'Venus is wet' is true if and only if Hesperus is wet, then it is true if and only if Phosphorus is wet. $II_B$ is the converse of compositionality. Compositionality (in the sense I am using the expression here) is the thesis that there is a function from the referential properties of simple expressions onto the referential properties of the complex expressions built out of them. As a special case of this, if, for each word within a sentence, the condition is set for an arbitrary entity being that word's referent, then there is no room for manoeuvre on what it would take for that sentence to be true. The converse of this, $II_B$, is that once the condition for a particular sentence being true is set, there is no room for manoeuvre on the condition for any expression within it to refer to something: change the requirement an object must meet for it to be the referent of any word in a given sentence and you will change the range of circumstances in which that sentence is true. For example, if a name 'Nelson' referred not to Nelson but to Churchill, the circumstances under which 'Nelson was British' is true would change.

The proof of II from $II_A$ and $II_B$, summarized below, is essentially a matter of showing that the substitution friendliness of reference conditions follows from the substitution friendliness of truth conditions, given the converse of compositionality.

$II_A$. If Hesperus is Phosphorus then the biconditional, that 'Venus is wet' is true-iff-Hesperus is wet iff 'Venus is wet' is true-iff-Phosphorus is wet, holds.

$II_B$. The biconditional, that 'Venus is wet' is true-iff-Hesperus is wet iff it is also true-iff-Phosphorus is wet, requires the biconditional, that 'Venus' refers to Hesperus iff it refers to Phosphorus.

∴  If Hesperus is Phosphorus then 'Venus' refers to Hesperus iff it refers to Phosphorus.

The conclusion, here, is but an instance of II, but the proof clearly generalizes.[6]

Against this supposed demonstration of II one might ask whether the condition for the truth of 'Venus is wet' really can be expressed using 'Phosphorus' in place of 'Hesperus' (assuming use of the latter were acceptable). After all, the resulting expression of the condition differs in meaning, or cognitive significance, from the original one. I will reject this response in detail in a later section. At present I am concerned only with making a prima facie case for the existence of a puzzle. All the same I will make two related points even here. First, if a

---

[6]The version of the proof below, though still informal, is detailed enough to reveal how the contribution of $II_A$ distributes out into uncontroversial uses of Hypothetical Syllogism and the Law of Identity (see main text). Moreover, the contribution of $II_B$ dissolves into the re-use of the background semantics for the rest of the sentence (i.e. P2, as used in going from SC3 to Conc.).

| | |
|---|---|
| P1. | 'Venus' refers Hesperus. |
| P2. | [Semantics for 'Venus is wet' minus P1] |
| SC1. | 'Venus is wet' is true iff Hesperus is wet. (From P1, P2) |
| P3. | Hesperus is Phosphorus. |
| SC2. | Hesperus is wet iff Phosphorus is wet. (From P3 using the Law of Identity uncontroversially.) |
| SC3. | 'Venus is wet' is true iff Phosphorus is wet. (From SC1 & SC2, in an uncontroversial use of HS ) |
| Conc. | 'Venus' refers to Phosphorus. (From SC3, P2) |

good case can be made for thinking that meaning, or cognitive significance, is substitution unfriendly, then that does not necessarily represent a problem for the view that truth conditions are substitution friendly, which is all that $II_A$ demands. It might equally be interpreted as a challenge for the simple identification of meaning with truth conditions. While meaning and truth conditions are intimately related, their relation is not well captured by the slogan that the meaning of a sentence *is* its truth condition. Second, there is good reason to think that the condition for a sentence's being true is substitution friendly. Were it not, we would be forced to re-evaluate our endorsement of the law of identity and the hypothetical syllogism in contexts that seem entirely benign, such as the two inferences below:

Hesperus is Phosphorus
∴ Hesperus is wet iff Phosphorus is wet

$p$ iff Hesperus is wet
Hesperus is wet iff Phosphorus is wet
∴ $p$ iff Phosphorus is wet

But if these inferences are legitimate – assuming any grammatical replacement of '$p$' in the second inference – they can be concatenated to legitimize our illustrative instance of $II_A$ (as the more detailed proof in the previous note makes clear):

'Venus is wet' is true iff Hesperus is wet
Hesperus = Phosphorus
∴ 'Venus is wet' is true iff Phosphorus is wet

Unhappiness with this concatenation is likely to spring from claims about what attributions of truth conditions are meant to achieve. It may be that they achieve this using 'Hesperus' but not 'Phosphorus'. This unhappiness, which springs from a desire to maintain a tight connection between truth conditions and meaning, is taken up in Section 7.

## 4   Interlude: Summary So Far and Sketch of What Follows

I have shown that two claims, I and II, which are in tension though not inconsistent with one another, are entailed by four other claims, $I_A$, $I_B$, $II_A$ and $II_B$, all of which have some claim to plausibility. I will now consider some different ways in which one might be underwhelmed by this tension. Each way corresponds to some stance one might take to the question of whether it is words or speakers that refer. All the stances I look at give rise either to resistance to my suggestion that there is something to worry about in the alleged tension between I and II or to a failure even to acknowledge this tension.

First, a person may agree that there are two notions but insist that, for this very reason, there is no tension. I call this position *dualism*. By not conflating the two kinds of reference, e.g. by abandoning the ambiguous expression 'reference' entirely and replacing it with two terms, one for word reference and another for speaker reference, the so-called tension evaporates. Or so dualists will claim. In Section 5 I argue against dualism by showing how a third claim, the 'III' of Figure 1, generates an inconsistency between I and II even if one keeps the two notions of reference distinct.

In contrast, *monists* maintain that there is in fact only one notion of reference, the existence of distinct notions being a readily explicable illusion. If there is only one notion of reference, there cannot be a tension between the "two" notions. I respond to monism in Section 6, first by arguing for its implausibility, and second by showing how the inconsistency arises even for monists, albeit in a different form.

A third stance, *cognitivism*, is the topic of Section 7. Cognitivists assume that attributing referential properties to words is best construed as describing an aspect of a speaker's psychology. If word reference is psychological in this way, it could be as substitution unfriendly as speaker reference, and for the same reason.

The final source of hostility to seeing anything worth labelling a "puzzle" in the tension between I and II takes the form of a disjunctive dilemma. Names refer either directly or indirectly. If they refer directly, the tension can be explained by rejecting $I_B$, the claim that psychological attitudes are substitution unfriendly. If they refer indirectly, via a description that is associated somehow with the name, then other aspects of the argument for the inconsistency become vulnerable. So while we may not know which of the two theories of names is correct, the tension is a problem for no one. I consider this disjunctive response in Section 8.

If I am right that these attempts to trivialize the puzzle all fail, the five propositions are inconsistent and we must abandon at least one of them. In Section 9 I explore the possibility that the source of the problem lies with intention-based accounts of speaker reference. I do not deny that an acceptable intention-based account of reference is available, but its form must be such as to allow that speaker reference is substitution friendly even if intentions are not. I go on to suggest such a form.

# 5   Dualism About Reference: Two Notions, Not One?

I and II taken together sound vaguely paradoxical, but could equally
serve as a further reminder of the importance Kripke, Bach and others
attach to the distinction between speaker reference and word reference.
An effective way of maintaining the distinction would be to introduce
different terms, such as 'picking out' for what speakers do and
'designating' for what words do. This distinction is a real one in at least
this: speaker reference (or picking out) and word reference (or
designating) are dissociable. I may refer to an overbearing sub-Dean as
'Napoleon', using a word that designates a dead French military leader to
pick out a living British civilian. Or I may accidentally refer to someone
using the name of someone else who I had been thinking about moments
earlier.

The two notions may be distinct, but a puzzle arises anyway if the
two notions coincide in what I will call normal circumstances. (I will say
much more about "normality" shortly.) That is, I and II are
inconsistent if taken together with III, which is the claim that there
is normally a symmetry between speaker reference and word reference.

III.   *"The symmetry principle"*: In normal circumstances, a speaker
       refers to whatever the word she or he uses refers to.

In other words, for a speaker to refer to something, it is normally
both enough and required that the word used refers to that thing. If
I use the name 'The Admiral Lord Nelson', for example, then barring
performance error, irony, massive ignorance of early 19th century
European history and other arguably abnormal factors, I will have
referred, not to Napoleon, but to Nelson. It is both enough and
necessary for me to refer to Nelson that I use a word that refers to
Nelson. This symmetry is inconsistent with the conjunction of I and II:

> *The inconsistency of I, II, and III*
>
> Suppose Jane uses 'Venus' to refer to Hesperus in what, let us
> suppose, are normal circumstances. Did she refer to Phosphorus?
> The symmetry principle (in one direction) tells us that the word
> she used refers to Hesperus, and hence, by II, that it refers to
> Phosphorus, and hence, by the symmetry principle (in the other
> direction), that Jane did indeed refer to Phosphorus. This shows us
> that, in normal circumstances anyway, speaker reference is
> substitution friendly, *pace* I.

Whatever the merits of this argument against dualism, it survives
the replacement of 'Jane refers' and '"Venus" refers' by 'Jane picks

out' and '"Venus" designates'. Reservations are likely to turn, rather, on the qualification in III: 'In normal circumstances, ... '.

The most immediate concern is that the inconsistency shown above is not between II, III, and I, but between II, III, and the claim that substitution failure in speaker reference can occur in normal circumstances. This leaves open the possibility that speaker reference is substitution unfriendly, but only in abnormal circumstances. Were that so, the tension Hesperus-Phosphorus cases give rise to could be assimilated to the class of cases in which it is known that speaker reference and word reference fail to ride in tandem.

Two ways of responding to scepticism about the 'in normal circumstances' qualification in the anti-dualist argument are available. The first, and probably more promising, would be to formulate the demonstration of an inconsistency without using the qualification, perhaps by replacing III with something else. I do precisely this in the next section, in the course of looking at monism. The second would be to impose more robust constraints on the qualification instead of leaving it so vague. These constraints would need to be tight enough to render the use of 'Napoleon' to refer to a sub-Dean abnormal but liberal enough for Hesperus-Phosphorus cases to be classified as normal.

Swift's *Gulliver's Travels* contains a clue to how this second option might be pursued. Gulliver's host during his visit to the Grand Academy of Lagado parades before him what are in fact parodies of various 18th century scientific and philosophical innovations. Among them is a progressive new language, innovative for its lack of words. Gulliver is informed in its defence that:

> [s]ince Words are only names for Things, it would be more convenient for all Men to carry about them, such Things as were necessary to express the particular business they are to discourse on. (Swift, 1726: 76)

'Speakers' of this language are weighed down with the objects they wish to 'talk' about with their colleagues in silent 'conversations'. The moral of Swift's satire is that language's value depends on its enabling us to share thoughts about a thing without being contextually tied to that thing. By using a word in a thing's stead we need not carry the thing itself around – and need not rely on other heavily contextual cues to enable our interlocutor to figure out what we are referring to. Of course, we *can* still communicate in a way that does rely on heavily contextual cues (including presentation of the referent as a limiting case). When this happens, or when the audience must diagnose a performance error in order to identify the referent, a speaker may use a word to refer to something other than what the word refers to. But the use of a word to refer is normal to the extent that exploiting heavily contextual cues and diagnosing performance error are not necessary for the audience to identify the referent. In these circumstances, the choice of word does the trick, which is in effect what III is claiming. Jane's using 'Venus' to refer to Hesperus in the course of asserting that Hesperus is wet appears to be normal in this (loose but tighter) sense.

A lingering worry, here, is that no reason has been given to think that III works in both directions. Suppose Jane uses 'Venus' to refer to Hesperus, in a situation normal enough that 'Venus' refers to Hesperus. By II, 'Venus' then also refers to Phosphorus. At this point someone could dig their heels in. Perhaps the situation counts as fully normal only if Jane knows that Hesperus is Phosphorus, and because she does not, she has not referred to Phosphorus. In less than fully normal circumstances the most we could say is that the word Jane uses refers to Phosphorus only if there is something identical to Phosphorus that she has referred to.

This possibility is hard to reconcile with any plausible account of word reference, without which dualism would lack plausibility in any case. I will say more about what the options are in the next section, but on a conventionalist account, for example, a word refers to that which people regularly use it to refer to. It must be possible for it to be used on different occasions and by different people to refer to the same thing known in different ways without sabotaging the potential for a convention. If $S_1$ uses W to refer to $O_1$ and $O_2$ without realising that $O_1$ and $O_2$ are $O_3$, $S_2$ uses W to refer to $O_2$ and $O_3$ without realising that $O_2$ and $O_3$ are $O_1$, and $S_3$ uses W to refer to $O_3$ and $O_1$ without realising that $O_3$ and $O_1$ are $O_2$, that could count as the community of $S_1 \ldots S_3$ using W in a common enough way for the convention to establish itself. It would be peculiar for the convention itself to discriminate in favour of one particular speaker's perspective on the object. All objects admit of a multiplicity of perspectives, but why should one particular perspective be definitive of *the* use defining the convention. More plausible (in so far as conventionalism is plausible) would be that all uses from which word reference is extrapolated should be thought of as some person or other's use of the word to refer to the object that is taken up as the referent of the word.[7]

---

[7]The fallback position I am urging against here is more clearly problematic in the version of the puzzle that figures in Section 6. It is difficult to see how a speaker could use a word referringly without using it to refer to what the mental representation they thereby invoke refers. (See the next section for a definition of 'invoke'.)

To begin, then, why is the view that only speakers refer implausible? The answer springs out of an intention-based account of speaker reference along the lines of $I_A$ plus two plausible psychological assumptions. If what a person refers to is a matter of what they intend to be thought of as referring to, they can refer only if they can form the relevant intention. But forming intentions requires an expectation of success. Right now, for example, I am not in a position to leap to the moon, and because I know this I cannot even form the intention to leap to the moon. To form that intention, I would need to believe that leaping to the moon is possible. I cannot simply choose to believe this, since belief formation is itself subject to a psychological requirement: that one have some evidence in favour of the proposition to be believed. These two principles – expectation of success as a requirement on intention formation and evidence as a requirement on belief formation – taken together with $I_A$ mean that I can only refer if I have some reason to think that I will be recognized as having referred. In some circumstances this condition will be met even in the absence of any stable relation between word and referent. (That performance errors do not always sabotage communication is proof of this – for instance, someone may refer to someone called Paul using 'Peter' without the audience being misled as to who was referred to, perhaps because they can see the speaker looking straight at a known Paul, or because, even when this Paul is absent from the conversational arena, the speaker attributes to the person she calls 'Peter' a number of properties that could only plausibly be ascribed to the Paul.) But in other circumstances, those I hesitatingly labelled 'normal' in the previous section, more is required. What this move comes to can be left open here, since any spelling out is likely to yield a notion of word reference that is distinct from speaker reference. A traditional understanding of the extra requirement is that of a convention relating the word's sound to the speaker's referent. The existence of such a convention would, in that case, constitute the word's having the referent it does. Others, sceptical of the explanatory potential of conventions, assume instead merely a stable association in the speaker's psychology between the word they use and the object they refer to (see Laurence, 1996; Mercier, 2003). What constitutes a word's referring to what it does refer to will, in that case, be defined in terms of such stable associations. Conventionalism and cognitivism (as I will call the second view) both require that, in normal contexts at least, speakers can refer only if words refer, contrary to monism

A critic of this argument could point to live controversy surrounding both psychological assumptions. Against the expectation requirement on intention formation, for example, it does not seem implausible that many First World War soldiers who fired their decrepit rifles across no-man's-land could have done so with the intention of hitting someone, despite their having little reason to expect success. Structurally similar cases involving lottery tickets have given rise to the so-called lottery paradox. There are linguistic instances, too: addressing people in English while travelling outside English-speaking countries can have a vanishingly small chance of success, but one often attempts it before resorting to arm-waving. On the other hand there does seem to be a psychological block to forming the intention to jump to the moon, and an obvious sense in which such a block would be adaptive. There is also a clear selective advantage to forming only beliefs for which one has evidence.[10] This has not prevented some – doxastic voluntarists – from rejecting the second psychological assumption used in the argument above. Here is no place to try to settle these disputes. I will therefore only reiterate that both are highly plausible for many cases and have clear selective advantages, and express the hope that troublesome cases can be assimilated in a way that does not threaten their use in the argument against monism.[11]

A second line of response to the anti-monist argument springs from the thought that word reference is ultimately definable in terms of established usage, or beliefs about established usage or potential usability or something along those lines. If some such definition is available, so that the notion of word reference can be reduced to that of speaker reference, can't we say that there is only one notion after all? The difficulty with this response is that, even if the inconsistency does not threaten the very prospects for a reduction, the fact that there is only one *fundamental* notion of reference – in the sense that all other relevant notions of reference reduce to it – does not mean there is only one notion of reference. Average height in a population can be defined in terms of, and hence reduces to, the notion of the actual height of an individual. It does not follow that they are the same notion. Likewise, that word reference could be defined in terms of speaker reference would not show that word reference has speaker reference's characteristics. It would still be possible

---

[10]One line to take with a voluntarist about belief is to challenge them to form the belief that there is a human-sized pigeon behind them; if they claim to have met the challenge, bet them €1,000 that there is no such pigeon. By refusing they will be implicitly conceding the argument. Were they to accept, you would at least end up a little wealthier. In an evolutionary context, the latter outcome would be equivalent to them being at a reproductive disadvantage.

[11]For more on constraints on intention formation, see Bratman (1987); for more on doxastic anti-voluntarism see Ginet (2001).

in principle for that latter to be substitution friendly while the former is not.

A final reservation over the argument calls for a more serious response. Someone could insist that a motley conglomeration of mental states underpins our semantic abilities, including knowledge of the world, syntactic competence and ad hoc on-the-hoof reactions to specific utterances. Nowhere in this *mélange* should we expect to find knowledge of, or belief in, a stable association between words and things. No contribution is made to the explanation of linguistic practice by such an association. On such a view, semantics as traditionally conceived – a substantial discipline sitting between syntax and pragmatics and dedicated to tracing word–world relations – withers away, along with the notion of word reference that is essential to the generation of the puzzle in the previous section. This is the view highlighted at the end of Section 2 and associated with Chomsky among others (e.g. McGilvray, 1998: 228). For those sympathetic to this view, and indeed to anyone unhappy with the anti-monist argument just given, what follows is a monist-friendly version of the puzzle.

Even if words do not refer (in a sense that is even moderately invariant over contexts), allowing that speakers can use words to refer commits one to the mental equivalent of referring words. Following tradition, call these entities *mental representations*. The inconsistency reached in Section 5 can be generated in a different form, couched in terms of the characteristics of the referential properties of mental representations rather than of words.

In expressing an opinion about something on a particular occasion I may use a word to refer to it. I may never have used, and never again use, this same word to this same referential end, and it may be that no one else uses this word to refer to this thing, either. Still, I will be able to do this only if I have a mental representation of the entity I have referred to. My utterance of the word *invokes* this mental representation, which is to say that the mental representation is tokened as part of the intention that constitutes the speaker's having referred using the word. This mental representation has referential properties of its own, a fact that is intimately connected to my ability to refer when I use a word that invokes it. This intimate connection can be captured in III$^*$, a modified version of III.

III$^*$. *"The symmetry principle$^*$"*: When a speaker refers using a word, she refers to whatever is referred to by the mental representation invoked by her utterance of that word.

That is, for a speaker to refer to something, it is enough and it is required that the word used invokes a mental representation referring to that thing. Using this to reach an inconsistency between speaker reference and mental-representation reference, requires updating II into $II^*$:

$II^*$. Mental-representation reference is substitution-friendly.

In other words, if Jane's mental representation refers to Hesperus, then it also refers to Phosphorus given that Hesperus is Phosphorus – whether Jane realizes this or not.

$II^*$ follows from suitably modified versions of $II_A$ and $II_B$. $II_A$ held that the truth conditions of sentences are substitution friendly. $II_A^*$ holds that complex mental representations with truth conditions are substitution friendly. Given that Hesperus is Phosphorus, if $p$, a mental representation, is true iff Hesperus is wet, then it is also true iff Phosphorus is wet. Denial of this would be hard to reconcile with the congruence of satisfaction conditions across a wide range of attitudes, including believing, desiring and intending. It may be possible to hold the belief that polenta is yellow without holding the belief that cornmeal is yellow, but given that polenta *is* cornmeal, the belief that polenta is yellow will be correct if and only if the belief that cornmeal is yellow is correct. Similarly, while it may be possible to intend to pat Fido without intending to pat Rex, the fact that Rex is Fido means that any intention to pat Fido will be successfully acted upon if, and only if, the intention to pat Rex is successfully acted upon. Finally, while it may be possible to desire that Superman takes you out on a date without desiring that Clark Kent takes you out on a date, the fact that Clark Kent is Superman means that the desire to be taken out on a date by Superman will be met when, and only when, the desire to be taken out on a date by Clark Kent is met.

$II_B$ held that a difference in the reference conditions for a word gives rise to a difference in the truth conditions of any sentence in which the word appears. $II_B^*$ holds that a difference in the referential properties of a mental representation gives rise to a difference in the truth conditions of complex mental representations containing the first mental representation. This is highly plausible. For example, if mental representation C referred to Napoleon not Nelson, a belief containing C would be correct according to whether something was true of Napoleon, not according to whether it was true of Nelson. The proof of $II^*$ from $II_A^*$ and $II_B^*$ is essentially the same as the one set out in Section 3.

Now, finally, we are in a position to prove the inconsistency:

*The inconsistency of I, II$^*$, and III$^*$*

Suppose that Jane uses 'Venus' to refer to Hesperus. Using II$^*$ and III$^*$, it is possible to show, contrary to I (given the arbitrariness of the example), that she referred to Phosphorus. For in referring using 'Venus' she will have invoked a mental representation, call it $V$, that (by III$^*$) refers to Hesperus. But from this and II$^*$ (and the fact that Hesperus is Phosphorus) it follows that $V$ refers to Phosphorus. By III$^*$ (again) she has, therefore, referred to Phosphorus.

Jane may well have two mental representations, both of which refer to Hesperus/Phosphorus but only one of which is invoked by her utterance of 'Venus'. But this is irrelevant to the demonstration of an inconsistency. It challenges neither the premises nor any step of the argument based on them.

This new version of the puzzle improves on the old one in several respects. For a start, it makes no assumption that words refer. This was the initial motive for developing it. In addition, because it uses III$^*$ in place of III, the symmetry it presupposes is not confined, perhaps dubiously, to "normal circumstances". But then, the new version also introduces what some would see as weaknesses. In particular it assumes some version of the representational theory of mind. How robust or extensive its commitments are in this respect is hard to say, but it is only right to acknowledge in passing that a persistent and significant minority reject the representationalist vision.[12] Which version of the puzzle one finds more compelling will therefore vary according to one's broader theoretical commitments.

# 7  Cognitivism: Word Reference as a Feature of Speaker Psychology?

I have looked at two takes on the relation between speaker reference and word reference – monism and dualism – and at how they disguise the very existence of the puzzle I am interested in. The third stance I wish to consider is really a view on word reference alone, but it, too, has the effect of hiding the puzzle. Contrary to II it appears to offer a route

---

[12]It is not clear, for example, whether the anti-monist argument requires an information-theoretic theory of content of the kind criticized by McGilvray (echoing Chomsky) in the quotation in Section 1 rather than, say, a more interpretationist semantics such as that apparently endorsed in Chomsky (2000: 160), and more familiarly associated with Daniel Dennett.

to treating word reference as substitution unfriendly, just as, according to I, speaker reference is.

According to cognitivists about word reference, claims about what a word refers to is properly to be thought of as an explicit statement of something known or believed by an individual speaker or group of speakers – or perhaps tacitly known or tacitly believed, since the knowledge may differ in one way or another from regular knowledge or belief. Abstracting from internecine controversies that are here unimportant, let us fix on 'tacit belief' as the label for the relevant cognitive relation, whatever its nature. On the cognitivist picture, overlap in what a group of language users tacitly believe about the referential properties of words, such as it is, contributes to the capacity each has to understand the others, such as it is. Talk of words referring *simpliciter* is loose, say cognitivists. It needs to be embedded in a psychological context. What words refer to independently of their being tacitly believed to refer, in so far as that makes any sense, is explanatorily otiose.

If word reference were substitution friendly in the same way that intentions are, the discrepancy between I and II, on which the puzzle trades, would evaporate. On the present construal of the ascription to words of referential properties, this promises to be the case. Suppose that Jane could tacitly believe the content of (1) without tacitly believing the content of (2). That is, suppose that (3) could hold without (4) holding.

(1) 'Venus' refers to Hesperus.
(2) 'Venus' refers to Phosphorus.
(3) Jane tacitly believes that 'Venus' refers to Hesperus.
(4) Jane tacitly believes that 'Venus' refers to Phosphorus.

Since claims like (1) and (2) are, strictly speaking, properly to be thought of as code for something like (3) and (4), substitution unfriendliness of tacit belief transposes into substitution unfriendliness of word reference.

This inference from cognitivism to the substitution unfriendliness of word reference is not so smooth as it seems. Even if an ascription of referential properties to words is code for a claim about some individual's idiolect, the latter constituted out of the content of their tacit beliefs, it does not follow that word reference inherits the substitution unfriendliness of tacit belief. An analogy helps to see the *non sequitur*. Suppose psychologists working on the human visual system were to assert, casually, that lines fanning out from each end of a line make that line longer, while lines arrowing out from its ends make it shorter. This would be their loose way of saying that the human visual system perceives its environment in this way. It does not follow from this that the length property of lines is as substitution unfriendly as the perception-as relation. Patently it does not: the Müller-Lyer is an illusion.

Perhaps a word's referential properties lack the objectivity of a line's geometrical properties. The length of a line is an objective feature of the world. There is more to being 15 cm long than being perceived to be 15 cm long. In contrast, it may be that there is nothing to a word's referring *other than* its being believed to refer. For this reason the analogy between word reference and line length just used to defeat the inference from cognitivism about word reference to the substitution unfriendliness of word reference could be unfair.

To rescue the cognitivist argument for the substitution unfriendliness of word reference in this way requires commitment either to extreme subjectivism about reference or to the believability of nonsense, even though neither is tenable. It requires both that individual speakers are capable of (tacitly) believing that a given word refers to such-and-such and either that it is meaningless to describe a word as referring *simpliciter* or that no distinction can be drawn between a word's referring and a word's being tacitly believed to refer. But belief states can be individuated from one another only if they make distinct demands on the world. If a belief's content was nonsensical, or if a belief's being held correctly amounted to no more than its being held, it would not be distinct from other beliefs with the same trait. All putative beliefs about reference would collapse into one another.[13] What the objectivity of word reference amounts to, for those who think tacit beliefs about word reference are possible and must be objective, is a further matter. It could be a threshold likelihood that the word is or can be or will be used by particular speakers to refer in some way, or it could be a convention. Whatever answer is preferred, the strengthened form of cognitivist argument against II (and hence against $II_A$ and $II_B$) seems flawed.[14]

---

[13]Similarly, states of intending are distinct only if acting on them successfully requires distinct outcomes. This is why referring cannot be a matter of intending to refer to it. See Section 3 and the discussion of $I_B$.

[14]For an explicit if slightly dated exchange on the believability of nonsense, see the exchange between Avrum Stroll (1953, 1955) and W. W. Mellor (1954). François Recanati (1997) allows that nonsense can be believed, but predicates this possibility on the believer hearing and deferring to a speaker without realizing that the words coming out of the latter's mouth have no content. Whatever its merits, applying this explanation in the present context would mean treating all tacit belief about reference as parasitic on explicit talk about reference. This would fail to explain how people sheltered from such explicit talk may nevertheless be linguistically competent.

Though it is only debatably classified as cognitivist in orientation, Jerry Fodor's account of linguistic competence provides another platform for arguing that the "puzzle" is but a phantasm, and an opportunity to review some of the counter-arguments already offered. According to Fodor (1976, Chapter 3), hearing a familiar word triggers, by default, a particular mental representation, and with luck it triggers one that is appropriate to the occasion, i.e. one with the same content as that invoked by the word's utterance. This view is often associated with the rejection of cognitivism about truth-conditional semantics for natural language, and indeed with the rejection of truth-conditional semantics for natural language *tout court.* But it does not have to be. On adopting this model of linguistic understanding one can either abandon the thought that speakers know a compositional truth theory or, alternatively, view the model as an implementation of that very thought (see Matthews, 2003 for discussion). The Fodorian model seems to offer a quick way with our puzzle no matter how it is classified. If it is a refutation of word reference (as opposed to speaker reference), including cognitivism about word reference, the puzzle disappears instantly: no word reference means no tension or inconsistency between the characteristics of word reference and the characteristic of speaker reference. If it is an implementation of cognitivism about word reference, in specifying what a word refers to we had better use words in our metalanguage that reflect the content of the mental representation associated with (i.e. habitually triggered or invoked by) the word. So if 'Venus' triggers tokenings in Jane of (her mental representation) HESPERUS rather than of (her mental representation) PHOSPHORUS, we should say that in her idiolect it refers to Hesperus, and not that it refers to Phosphorus. In that case, word reference would be substitution unfriendly.

Responses to both strategies are implicit in what has already been said. The 'refutation' line is, in effect, a form of monism. For that reason it is susceptible to the second form of the puzzle, set out in Section 6. The 'implementation' line is also susceptible to that form of the puzzle (since it presupposes the representationalist theory of mind) but is, in addition, vulnerable to the criticisms of cognitivism presented in this section. A word presumably inherits its referential properties from the referential properties of the mental representation with which it is associated. Jane may not tacitly believe that 'Venus' refers to Phosphorus (even if she does tacitly believe that it refers to Hesperus), but there is no way of blocking the claim that 'Venus' *in fact* refers to Phosphorus without denying either that a word refers to whatever the mental representation it is associated with refers to or that the mental representation associated with 'Hesperus' refers to what the mental representation associated with 'Phosphorus' refers to. Neither option is attractive. By generalizing from this instance, II follows: what a word refers to, even relative to an idiolect, is substitution friendly.

## 8   Direct versus Indirect Theories of Reference: A Disjunctive Solution?

I have been considering why a puzzle, or what I claim is a puzzle, has not been raised or taken seriously in this form. A fourth explanation of this phenomenon arises out of a long-standing debate over whether names are disguised definite descriptions, as Russell held, and so refer, if at all, indirectly; or whether instead they refer, if at all, directly, i.e. without the mediation of a description somehow associated with the name. Both sides in that debate face familiar and yet to be negotiated hurdles. Descriptivists need to meet the various objections set out in or adapted from Kripke (1980). Direct reference theorists, who often accept a commitment to denying substitution failure in attitude reports, need to explain away our contrary intuitions more convincingly than they have done so to date. All the same, the puzzle set out in various versions in Sections 3–6, above, arguably dissolves once one accepts that at least one of the two sides is, in some form, correct.

How promising is this disjunctive stance? Arguing against it is not easy. The descriptivist/anti-descriptivist debate has spawned logically connected but self-sustaining disputes concerning attitude reports, modality, quotation, referential and attributive uses of definite descriptions, internalism versus externalism about both linguistic and mental content, information-theoretic versus conceptual-role semantics in the philosophy of mind and so on. Inevitably this has given rise to a dense spectrum of views in place of the simple dichotomy of lore. A further question is pressing in the present context: which positions are addressing the question of how words refer (i.e. directly or indirectly), and which are addressing the question of how speakers refer? Taking each view in turn and seeing if and how it circumvents the puzzle would be an unrealistic goal in this chapter. The simplest way of accommodating the profusion of theories would be for me to hand the puzzle over to you, the reader, by asking you to choose for yourself which from among the five assumptions that give rise to the inconsistency in Section 5 you would like to reject, given your theoretical commitments in this area, and then to ask you to repeat the performance for the asterisked version of the inconsistency in Section 6. Rather than washing my hands entirely, though, I will persist with the pretence and offer some reasons to think that, in fact, neither of the two dominant views generates an uncomplicated solution to the puzzle.

Many direct reference theorists will look askance at $I_B$. Their view is associated with attempts to show, precisely, that if Lois Lane believes that Superman can fly then, appearances notwithstanding, she believes that Clark Kent can fly. What goes for believing goes for intending, with the result that if Jane, in uttering 'Venus', intends in so doing to be taken as referring to Hesperus, she also intends in so doing to be taken as referring to Phosphorus. The hope is that the contrary appearance can be explained away as a pragmatic effect.

There is something dialectically peculiar about direct reference theorists appealing to the substitution friendliness of the attitudes to see off the puzzle that is my main concern in this chapter. Substitution friendliness is not a felicitous corollary of the direct reference perspective. Rather, it is a controversial lemma that needs to be argued for if one particular strategy for coping with a serious embarrassment for the perspective is to succeed. To see this, notice that unhappiness with descriptivism (for independent reasons such as those in Kripke, 1980) does not make the reasons people were initially attracted to descriptivism go away. Among these reasons is the ease with which descriptivists seem able to cope with the apparent substitution unfriendliness of the attitudes. Direct reference theorists need to show either that the appearance of substitution failure is deceptive (so that descriptivist accounts of substitution failure, even if they work, are redundant), that directness of reference is in fact compatible with substitution unfriendliness (so that descriptivists are not the only ones able to account for it) or that substitution unfriendliness is a problem that arises independently of any commitment to directness of reference (so that both direct and indirect reference theorists are on an equal footing – see, e.g. Kripke, 1979). The second and third strategies, for all that they succeed in the dispute between direct and indirect theorists of reference, can be pursued without rejecting $I_B$. Only the first strategy calls for rejection of $I_B$. But its rejection is a burden, not a part of the theory. Against this background, rejecting $I_B$ because one has a direct-reference badge on one's lapel would be like appealing the possibility of causal overdetermination because one is a Cartesian dualist. Cartesians should worry about causal over-determination, not make free appeal to it. Certainly, eye-rolling at the obviousness of the proper solution to the puzzle would be premature before the falsehood of $I_B$ is established on a more secure independent footing than it has been.[15]

A further complication is that taking psychological attitudes to be substitution friendly with a view to making speaker reference substitution friendly may have unwelcome side-effects. In the definition of speaker reference, the name for the referent is doubly embedded within attitude verbs. For speaker reference to be substitution friendly, both 'intends' and 'think' need to be substitution friendly. But now suppose that Lois Lane's friend, Mandy, utters 'Clark Kent is a superhero' to her. Mandy is fully aware of the identity, but she assumes that Lois is ignorant. In performing this utterance, she is in no way intent on letting Lois in on Clark's secret. She wishes merely to suggest that Lois should stop being so demanding of potential suitors, and to induce in her a belief that Clark is a superhero in, so to speak, a metrosexual kind of a way. To make sense of Mandy's utterance it is hard to avoid supposing that in uttering 'Clark Kent' she intends her action to be thought of as a reference to Clark Kent but that she does not intend her action to be thought of as a reference to Superman. Making intending and judging substitution friendly in order to make speaker reference substitution friendly sabotages this appealing description of Mandy's psychological profile.

What about indirect theories of reference? The nature of the descriptivist response to the puzzle will vary according to the nature of the descriptivism. Let us say that all forms of descriptivism treat an ordinary name, 'Venus' for example, as a definite description in disguise – 'the V', say, for some predicate 'V'. Sentences containing 'Venus' will therefore be true if, and only if, there is exactly one salient satisfier of 'V' and that satisfier meets the condition imposed by the semantics for the rest of the sentence. Strong descriptivists go further in saying, with Russell, that the definite description – and hence the name – lacks meaning in isolation. Russell's thought, here, is that, although the

---

[15]As it happens, the first strategy, when it has been followed, has led to a theory that resembles the solution offered to the puzzle in Section 9, even though this latter does not involve rejecting $I_B$. According to Salmon (1986), the belief relation, which is a two place relation, is derivative of a three-place relation, $BEL(\ldots)$, which holds between a person, a Russellian proposition, and one of that proposition's guises. $S$ believes that $p$ if and only if $\exists x(BEL(S, p, x))$. *Believes* is therefore insensitive to the choice among distinct but co-referring terms to pick out its relata, but the choice of word pragmatically implicates a particular guise. Whether this use of (what I will call) an extensionalizing existential succeeds is a moot point, but it is possible to use a similar sounding strategy to make speaker reference substitution friendly without rejecting $I_B$ (and without quantifying over guises).

function of a name (and, indeed, of an explicit definite description) appears to be that of referring to an object in order that some property may then be attributed to that object by predication, the appearance is misleading. Since names do not refer, the "puzzle" of Section 3 evaporates.

Weak descriptivists agree with strong descriptivists that names and definite descriptions fail to refer to simple entities in the world, but allow that they refer to something, for example to generalized quantifiers. Once again the puzzle disappears. 'Venus' refers, not to a planet, but to a complex abstract object. Moreover, generalized quantifiers can be discriminated as finely as the properties expressible in a description, so replacing 'V' in 'the V' with co-extensive 'V$^*$' would change the referent. As a result, no name can have a referent that the speaker fails to appreciate is its referent, and no contradiction along the lines of the proof in Section 5 will be possible.

While the puzzle about speaker reference and word reference gets no grip here, a simple variation on it is easy to construct, based on the notion of denotation in place of reference. An object $a$ is denoted by a definite description 'the A', or by a name that disguises such a definite description, if and only if there is exactly one entity with the property expressed by 'A', and $a$ is it, i.e. if and only if 'the A' refers to a generalized quantifier that determines $a$. Word denotation is substitution friendly. Speaker denotation seems not to be. Suppose Jane, in uttering 'Venus', denotes Hesperus. Does it follow that she has denoted Phosphorus? It does not, if denotation is defined in the illocutionary fashion (so that what a speaker denotes is a matter of what she intends to be thought of as having denoted – see Section 3). Speaker denotation is a difficult notion for descriptivists, weak or strong, to do without, since they must appeal to it in accounting for the appearance of a distinction between referential and attributive uses of definite descriptions. But admitting it threatens to re-introduce the puzzle by the back door.

## 9   The Puzzle Solved

I have been arguing for the existence of, and explaining the failure to take seriously or even notice, a puzzle facing anyone who accepts a number of assumptions. The assumptions are that speaker reference is determined by the speaker's intention (perhaps those of the form of $I_A$), that psychological attitudes permit substitution failure ($I_B$), that a change in the referential properties of a word alters the truth conditions of all sentences in which it appears ($II_B$), that truth conditions are substitution friendly ($II_A$) and that, normally, to refer to something it is necessary and sufficient to use a word that refers to that thing (III) – or else the asterisked versions of $II_A$, $II_B$ and III for those who are sceptical of word reference but not of mental-representation reference. The challenge has been to show that a puzzle exists. Once it is acknowledged, a solution invites itself: change $I_A$. More specifically, introduce an existential quantifier – an *extensionalizing existential* – into the formulation of the intention that constitutes a speaker's referring.

Let $I_A$' be the generalization of which the following is a particular instance:

> Jane uses 'Venus' to refer to Hesperus if and only if $\exists x(x = $ Hesperus & Jane's intention in uttering the word is that her audience should think of her doing so as a reference to $x$).

This modification (the quantifier plus the identity-conjunct) renders the choice of metalinguistic term used to identify the referent less demanding, and so solves the puzzles instantly: speaker reference is no longer substitution unfriendly, notwithstanding intending's substitution unfriendliness. The proof of this, below, is long but straightforward – apart, perhaps, from the step to SC6. It shows how, given $I_A$' and the identity of Hesperus with Phosphorus, if Jane is referring to Hesperus when she uses 'Venus', she must equally be referring to Phosphorus.

P1    Jane uses 'Venus' to refer to Hesperus.

P2    Jane uses 'Venus' to refer to Hesperus iff $\exists x(x = $ Hesperus & her intention in uttering 'Venus' is that her audience should think of her doing so as a reference to $x$). [Instance of $I_A$']

SC1   $\exists x(x = $ Hesperus & Jane's intention in uttering 'Venus' is that her audience should think of her doing so as a reference to $x$). [From P1, P2]

P3    $c = $ Hesperus & Jane's intention in uttering 'Venus' is that her audience should think of her doing so as a reference to $c$. [Assumption, discharged at SC7]

SC2   $c = $ Hesperus. [From P3]

P4    Hesperus = Phosphorus.

SC3   $c = $ Phosphorus. [From SC2, P4]

SC4   Jane's intention in uttering 'Venus' is that her audience should think of her doing so as a reference to $c$. [From P3]

SC5   $c = $ Phosphorus & Jane's intention in uttering 'Venus' is that her audience should think of her doing so as a reference to $c$. [From SC3, SC4]

SC6 $\exists x(x =$ Phosphorus & Jane's intention in uttering 'Venus' is that her audience should think of her doing so as a reference to $x$). [From SC5]

SC7 $\exists x(x =$ Phosphorus & Jane's intention in uttering 'Venus' is that her audience should think of her doing so as a reference to $x$). [From SC1, P3, and SC6 by $\exists$E]

P5 Jane uses 'Venus' to refer to Phosphorus iff $\exists x(x =$ Phosphorus & Jane's intention in uttering 'Venus' is that her audience should think of her doing so as a reference to $x$). [Instance of $I_A$']

C Jane uses 'Venus' to refer to Phosphorus. [From SC7, P5]

SC6 uses existential generalization on a term that lies inside the scope of a psychological attitude verb. The worry is that this is no less objectionable than substituting within such a context. But the existential generalization at SC6 is immunized against the opacity of 'intends' by the identity claim in SC5, in which '$c$' occurs in a non-opaque context.[16]

This points to a different objection to $I_A$, sidelined since my decision at the beginning of Section 3 to focus on just one half of the notion of intentionality. The right-hand side of $I_A$ does not contain a commitment to the existence of the referent but its left-hand side does. A puzzle similar to the one I have been concentrating on can be mounted on the following contrast:

$I_{\exists}$: Speaker reference is not existentially committed.

$II_{\exists}$: Word reference is existentially committed.

That speaker reference is existentially non-committed follows from $I_A$ and $I_{\exists B}$, a cousin of $I_B$.

---

[16]In earlier versions of the chapter I experimented with using substitutional quantification to avoid the worry. I now think that on balance an objectual treatment is adequate, and avoids the need to confront anxieties about both substitutional quantification *per se* (see Kripke, 1976) and 'metalinguistic' approaches to opacity (see Saul, 1996). Worth noting is that Searle (1969) includes a substitutionally interpreted existential quantifier in his 'rules of reference' (pp. 94–96; the interpretation of the quantifier is discussed on p. 94). This seems designed to block existential failure (to be discussed below in the main text) rather than substitutional failure, as his rules lack anything equivalent to the '$x =$ Hesperus', and remarks on pp. 89–90 indicate reluctance to include one. Indeed, he steers around the puzzle by defining (the equivalent of) 'Jane refers' rather than 'Jane refers to Hesperus'. In the preliminaries to the rules, he assimilates puzzles about substitution to what I earlier called II' (pp. 79, 90–1) and an 'axiom of identification' (p. 80). Of course, his account could be adapted. My emphasis has been on failure to spot the puzzle, not on the difficulty of making changes to cope with it once it is spotted.

$I_{\exists B}$:  Intending is not existentially committed (e.g. someone could intend to touch Santa Claus).

That word reference is existentially committed follows from acceptance of logical inferences such as existential generalization even in benign contexts:

'John is tall' is true
∴ 'Something is tall' is true

This puzzle vanishes once $I_A'$ is adopted in place of $I_A$. $I_A'$, unlike $I_A$, requires the referent to exist. It is simply not possible for a person to refer to a non-existent. A person can still *attempt to* refer to Santa Claus, of course. To attempt to refer to Santa Claus is to attempt to bring it about that there is some entity, $x$, such that $x$ is Santa Claus and one's audience recognizes one's utterance of the word 'Santa' as a reference to $x$. Attempting's lack of existential import makes Santa's non-existence harmless. When we say of someone, colloquially, that they referred to Santa Claus (or any other non-existent being, fictional or otherwise), we are really saying that they attempted, or perhaps feigned to attempt, to refer to Santa Claus.

I conclude, then, that accounts of speaker reference can remain intention-based without our having either to make word-reference substitution unfriendly or to give up on the intentionality of the attitudes. Showing this has not been hard. It required only the introduction of what I called an extensionalizing existential. Most of the work in this chapter has been directed at showing that it needed to be shown.

### Acknowledgements

This chapter has evolved out of talks with the same title at (in chronological order) the *Proper Names* workshop at the Humboldt Institute in Berlin, the philosophy departments of Sussex University, Birmingham University, and the Open University, the *Pragmatics* conference in Riva del Garda, the *Canadian Philosophical Association* at the University of Western Ontario, the *Joint Session of the Aristotelian Society and Mind Association* in Southampton and the *Philosophy of Linguistics* workshop at the Inter-University Centre in Dubrovnik. My thanks in particular to John Collins, Michael Devitt, Christopher Gauker, David Hunter, Guy Longworth, Paul Pietroski, Ben Shaer, Ken Turner and Barry Smith.

# References

Bach, K. 1987. *Thought and Reference.* Oxford: Clarendon Press.

Barker, S. J. 2004. *Renewing Meaning: A Speech-Act Theoretic Approach.* Oxford: Clarendon Press.

Bratman, M. E. 1987. *Intention, Plans, and Practical Reason.* Cambridge, MA: Harvard University Press.

Chomsky, N. 2000. *New Horizons in the Study of Language and Mind.* Cambridge, UK: Cambridge University Press.

Chomsky, N. 2003. Reply to Egan. In L. Antony and N. Hornstein, eds., *Chomsky and His Critics,* pp. 268–274. Oxford: Blackwell.

Davis, W. A. 2005. *Nondescriptive Meaning and Reference: An Ideational Semantics.* Oxford: Clarendon Press.

Evans, G. 1982. *The Varieties of Reference.* Oxford: Clarendon Press.

Fodor, J. A. 1976. *The Language of Thought.* Hassocks, UK: Harvester Press.

Ginet, C. 2001. Deciding to believe. In M. Steup, ed., *Knowledge, Truth, and Duty.* Oxford: Oxford University Press.

Kripke, S. 1976. Is there a problem about substitutional quantification?. In G. Evans and J. McDowell, eds., *Truth and Meaning: Essays in Semantics,* pp. 325–419. Oxford: Clarendon Press.

Kripke, S. 1977. Speaker's reference and semantic reference. *Midwest Studies in Philosophy* 2: 255–276. Page references are to the reprint in G. Ostertag, 1998. *Definite Descriptions: A Reader,* pp. 225–256. Cambridge, MA: MIT Press.

Kripke, S. A. 1979. A puzzle about belief. In A. Margalit, ed., *Meaning and Use,* pp. 239–283. Dordrecht: Reidel.

Kripke, S. A. 1980. *Naming and Necessity.* Cambridge, MA: Harvard University Press.

Larson, R. K. and G. Segal. 1995. *Knowledge of Meaning: An Introduction to Semantics.* Cambridge, MA: MIT Press.

Laurence, S. 1996. A Chomskian alternative to convention-based semantics. *Mind* 105(418):269–301.

Linsky, L. 1963. Reference and referents. In C. E. Caton, ed., *Philosophy and Ordinary Language,* pp. 74–89. Urbana, IL: University of Illinois Press.

Matthews, R. J. 2003. Does linguistic competence require knowledge of language?. In A. Barber, ed., *Epistemology of Language,* pp. 187–213. Oxford: Oxford University Press.

McGilvray, J. 1998. Meanings are syntactically individuated and found in the head. *Mind and Language* 13(2):225–280.

McGilvray, J. (ed.). 2005. *The Cambridge Companion to Chomsky.* Cambridge: Cambridge University Press.

Mellor, W. W. 1954. Believing the meaningless. *Analysis* 15:41–43.

Mercier, A. 2003. Are language conventions philosophically explanatory? (Or: "It's Shirt-Buttoning All the Way Down, Ruth!"). *Croatian Journal of Philosophy* 3(8):111–124.

Pietroski, P. M. 2003. The character of natural language semantics. In A. Barber, ed., *Epistemology of Language*, pp. 217–256. Oxford: Oxford University Press.

Quine, W. V. 1990. *Pursuit of Truth*. Cambridge, MA: Harvard University Press.

Recanati, F. 1997. Can we believe what we do not understand?. *Mind and Language* 12(1):84–100.

Salmon, N. 1986. *Frege's Puzzle*. Cambridge, MA: MIT Press.

Salmon, N. 2004. The good, the bad, and the ugly. In M. Reimer and A. Bezuidenhout, eds., *Descriptions and Beyond*, pp. 230–260. Oxford: Clarendon Press.

Saul, J. M. 1996. What's wrong with metalinguistic views. *Acta Analytica* 16/17:81–94.

Searle, J. R. 1969. *Speech Acts: An Essay in the Philosophy of Language*. London: Cambridge University Press.

Strawson, P. F. 1950. On referring. *Mind* 59:320–344.

Stroll, A. 1953. A problem concerning the analysis of belief sentences. *Analysis* 14:15–19.

Stroll, A. 1955. Believing the meaningless: A reply to Mr Mellor. *Analysis* 16(2):45–48.

Swift, J. (ed.). 1726. *A voyage to Laputa, Balnibarbi, Glubbdubdrib, Luggnag and Japan*. Book III of Volume 2 of *Travels into Several Remote Nations of the World. By Captain Lemeul Gulliver*. London: Benjamin Motte.

# 4

# Bearers of Truth and the Unsaid

Stephen Barker

The standard view about the bearers of truth – the entities that are the ultimate objects of predication of truth or falsity – is that they are propositions or sentences semantically correlated with propositions. Propositions are meant to be the contents of assertions, objects of thought or judgement, and so are ontologically distinct from assertions or acts of thought or judgement. So understood propositions are meant to be things like possible states of affairs or sets of possible worlds – entities that are clearly not acts of judgement. Let us say that a sentence $S$ *encodes* a proposition «P» when linguistic rules (plus context) correlate «P» with $S$ in a manner that does not depend upon whether $S$ is asserted or appears embedded in a logical compound. The orthodox conception of truth-bearers then can be expressed in two forms:

> **TB1**: The primary truth-bearers are propositions.
> **TB2**: The primary truth-bearers are sentences that *encode* a
> proposition «P».

I use the term *primary truth-bearers*, since orthodoxy allows that assertions or judgements, etc., can be truth-bearers, it is just that they are derivatively so; their being truth-apt depends on other things being truth-apt. Some orthodox theorists prefer **TB1** – Stalnaker (1972) – some prefer **TB2** – Richard (1990). We need not concern ourselves with the reasons for their preferences here. Rather, our concern shall be this: why accept orthodoxy at all in either form: **TB1** or **TB2**?

There is without doubt a strong general reason to accept the propositional view. Reflection on the conditions required for a sentence

*Making Semantics Pragmatic*
Ken Turner (ed.).
Current Research in the Semantics/Pragmatics Interface, Vol. 24.
© 2011 by Emerald Group Publishing Limited. All rights reserved.

to be *truth-apt* seem to show that orthodoxy is right. A sentence $S$ is truth-apt if and only if it is a candidate for truth or falsity. To be truth-apt $S$ must be contentful in some minimal sense. It seems reasonable to hold that the content $S$ requires to be truth-apt does not depend on its being asserted, or conceived of as being performed potentially in an assertion or judgement. Two facts suggest this is right:

F1:   Truth-apt sentences can be embedded in logical compounds, but sentences embedded in logical compounds are unasserted.

F2:   Appeal to assertion seems to do little work in explaining truth-aptness. Indeed we might appeal to truth to explain assertion.

Thus $S$'s truth-aptness depends on $S$'s possessing content fixed independently of facts about assertion. But what is the content $S$ possesses independently of assertion? Here orthodoxy steps in with the answer: the proposition «P» encoded by $S$. Thus a truth-apt sentence is just a sentence encoding a proposition, and $S$'s truth, it seems, just resides in that proposition obtaining. That means that the primary truth-bearer just is «P» or $S$ encoding «P».

This is a nice argument, but it cannot be right, since the conclusion, I shall argue is false. Truth-bearers cannot be understood in terms of propositions. Several independent paths of argumentation converge on this conclusion. This chapter concentrates on one path. That path focuses on the semantic status of conventional implicatures.

Conventional implicatures are meanings introduced by conventional-implicature operators like *even, but, nevertheless, therefore,* etc. Conventional-implicature operators introduce non-truth-conditional contents to sentences. The orthodox view is that conventional implicatures, as part of non-truth-conditional meaning, are not elements of semantic content in the sense of content that can embed in sentential compounds and can enter into logical arguments. But that is wrong. In Barker (2003), I argue that conventional implicatures are components of semantic content. This fact has significant implications: (*a*) We need to give up the thesis of semantic *content monism* according to which semantic content only has one form – truth-conditional content. (*b*) The T-schema cannot generally be valid. (*c*) We must abandon the idea that the primary truth-bearers are propositions, thought of as extra-linguistic entities. Truth-bearers must be capable of having not only truth and falsity, but also *felicity* and *infelicity*, where the latter are the kinds of evaluative properties that sentences bearing conventional implicatures can have. That means, as I shall show below, that **TB1** is false.

Such are the conclusions of Barker (2003). But now I want to push these implications further. In relation to truth-bearers, the conclusions of Barker (2003) are conservative; I understated the threat facing the orthodox view. Admitting the presence of conventional implicatures as semantic contents really means that both **TB2** and **TB1** need to be abandoned. In short, purely non-pragmatic views of said-content cannot be right. Having argued for this negative claim, I offer a positive pragmatic account of said-content and of conventional implicature.

# 1   Conventional Implicature, the T-Schema and Content Monism

Sentences featuring conventional-implicature operators are sentences like *Even Granny danced, She is poor but nice, Therefore, we are finished*, etc.[1] I shall treat conventional-implicature operators as sentential operators. So an implicature-bearing sentence can generally be represented as a sentence $N[..S_j..]$, which comprises a sequence of sentences $S_1$, $S_2$,... combined with an implicature operator $N$. The sentence $N[..S_j..]$ has dual content, possessing a truth-conditional content, which determines application of the truth-predicate, and an implicature content. To illustrate this idea, take (1):

(1)  Even Granny got drunk,

(1) has the truth-conditional content $\varepsilon$ and the implicature contents $\iota_1$ and $\iota_2$: that

$\varepsilon$:   Granny got drunk.
$\iota_1$:   Granny is a particularly surprising instance of drunkness relative to the class of individuals C. (C is fixed by context.)
$\iota_2$:   Other individuals in C got drunk.

Thus if Granny was a notorious boozer (1) would be odd. If Granny was the sole person to get drunk, then (1) would be odd. But in neither case would (1) be false. Neither $\iota_1$ nor $\iota_2$ contributes to truth-conditions. Rather, as I argue in Barker (2003), (1) is true iff $\varepsilon$ is the case, and *felicitous* if and only if $\varepsilon$ is the case and both $\iota_1$ and $\iota_2$ hold, where *felicity* is a kind of correctness that incorporates both truth and implicature content satisfaction.

---

[1]The most philosophically interesting implicature operator is 'if'. Though, it is controversial that it is an implicature operator – see Barker (2004) and Jackson (1987). Given the controversy I will not include it in my class here.

This portrayal of implicature needs an important refinement. The implicature component $\iota_1$ of (1) involves probability. The probability is subjective and not objective. We are not concerned with the objective chance of Granny's getting drunk, compared with others, but with an epistemic matter. It is surprising for us, given what we expect, that Granny got drunk. Thus the implicature $\iota_1$ relates to subjective-probability, which is a personal matter. But note: the implicature $\iota_1$ is not that the speaker has a certain subjective-probability. In judging (1) right, an audience does not determine if the utterer U has a certain subjective-probability state. Rather H judges utterance of (1) right, if and only if, she has a subjective-probability state of a certain kind, and accepts the other elements $\varepsilon$ and $\iota_2$. This means that $\iota_1$ is not so much associated with a condition in the sense of a state of affairs, but with a property: the mental property of having a certain subjective-probability state. An audience judges (1) to be felicitous if and only if she accepts that Granny got drunk, and defends the subjective-probability state and the belief that other (relevant) people were drunk. I argue in Barker (2003) that this shows, generally speaking, that it is better to conceptualise conventional implicatures in terms of mental properties, like subjective-probability states and belief-states, rather than propositions.

To get a clear representation of this, let us generalise. Let $\varepsilon$ be a proposition, and $\iota$ a mental property, which may be quite complex. If so an implicature-bearing sentence $N[..S_j..]$ encodes two contents. We shall distinguish between the kind of encoding involved by calling one, in the case of the proposition, *$\alpha$-encoding*, and the other, in the case of the implicature, *$\beta$-encoding*. We can then say:

> **Dual**:   $N[..S_j..]$ $\alpha$-encodes a proposition: $\varepsilon$.
> $N[..S_j..]$ $\beta$-encodes a property: $\iota$.

**Dual** records the fact that $N[..S_j..]$ is a dual content sentence. Moreover, **Dual** assumes, given the technical notion of encoding introduced above, that implicature is semantic content in this sense: it is content fixed by rule and content, which, is embeddable in logical compounds. I have not yet shown this, but will do so shortly. Given **Dual**, we can specify the following inter-subjective conditions for evaluation:

> **IF**: An utterance by U of $N[..S_j..]$, which $\alpha$-encodes $\varepsilon$ and $\beta$-encodes $\iota$, is judged assertable by audience H iff H believes that $\varepsilon$ obtains and H accepts $\iota$.

**IF** captures the idea that implicatures are not like propositions, which we can talk of in terms of either obtaining or not, depending on what the states of affairs in the world are, but mental properties, which speaker and audience can instantiate.

## 1.1 Implicatures and Embedding

That is the first major claim about the nature of implicature. The second concerns its embeddability. Sentences of the form $N[..S_j..]$ can embed and enter significantly within logical compounds and valid arguments. Thus conventional implicatures can enter into logical form. Here are some cases of such embedding:

(2) Either Misha went *but* left early, or *even* he didn't go.

(3) *Either Jane is deeply religious *but* pious *nevertheless* or she is not religious.

(4) It is not that she dislikes him *but* dates him *nevertheless*. She dates him because she dislikes him.

(5) Either she dislikes him *but nevertheless* dates him, or she dates him because she dislikes him.

(6) If there was a keg of beer, then *even* Granny would have got drunk.

(7) If he is wearing a Union Jack, Union Jack wearers are Englishmen and all Englishmen are brave, then he is English, and *therefore*, he is brave.

(8) If *even* John is given amnesty, there will be a peace deal.

There is a lot to discuss about what's going on here. First, there is the issue of *projection*. Sometimes implicatures project; they become implicatures of the whole utterance. (2) is a case of that. The implicature about contrast is an implicature of (2) as a whole. We see this in (3) which is infelicitous because the projected implicature is unacceptable, and so (3) as a whole must be rejected.

The other cases, (4) to (8) are cases in which the implicatures are not projected. Nevertheless, the implicatures are present and *active* in the sentence, and, furthermore, the logical operators concerned are sensitive to the implicatures. At least some of the implicature content of each embedded implicature-bearing sentence is semantically embedded. Thus the logical operators do not function purely truth-conditionally. (4) is a case in which negation takes an implicature in its scope. In (5) disjunction takes an implicature in its scope, and so on. The logical compounds here depend for their assertability on the presence of implicature. Remove the implicature, and the result alters entirely with respect to its assertoric content. Take (8). It simply may not be the case that if *John* is given amnesty there will be a peace deal.

What *even* in (8) adds to that is that the supposition encompasses everyone in a certain class being given amnesty with John as the extreme case. Under those circumstances there will be a peace deal. Implicature then is entering into the scope of the operators, and they in turn are sensitive to its presence – see Barker (2003) for some relatively detailed considerations about how this works and further arguments of support for this conclusion.

That means that implicatures are components of semantic content – implicature is associated in a rule governed way with a sentence, and can enter into the scope of logical operators – and so we can say, in my technical sense, that it is *encoded*, or, as I say, the implicature property $\iota$ is β-encoded.

If that is correct, then we can draw a significant conclusion about the nature of semantic content of sentences. Semantic content is content encoded by sentences that enters into the scope of logical operators. So some components of semantic content are non-truth-conditional and thus **Content Monism** is false.

> **Content Monism**: The semantic content of a sentence $S$ – the content $S$ possesses by virtue of linguistic rules and context, and upon which logical particles may potentially operate – is to be identified with $S$'s truth-conditional content.

According to **Content Monism**, a given sentence $S$ only has one type of content associated with it: its truth-conditional content. This is wrong. Rather words like *even, but, nevertheless* can contribute another content which is semantic, in that it embeds and enters into logical form.

The demise of **Content Monism** is serious for orthodox thinking. The main casualty is the T-schema. Most theorists take the T-schema, one version of which is given below, to be a truism or platitude, a philosophically neutral fact, one whose correctness needs to be recognised by any adequate account:

> **Disquotation**: Where a quotational expression of the form '$S$' denotes an interpreted sentence type, all instances of the following schema are assertable: '$S$' *is true iff S*.

But the T-schema is not valid – **Disquotation** is false if **Content Monism** is false. It is possible for sentences $N[..S_j..]$ to be true but infelicitous – its implicature condition fails. In which case it is possible for '$N[..S_j..]$' *is true* to be assertable for a speaker but not $N[..S_j..]$. To give an example: *Even Hitler was evil* is, technically true, but it is infelicitous, and thus unassertable, in the relevant sense of unassertable. Thus we must reject the disquotational principle **Transparency** below – which is a natural counterpart to **Disquotation**:

> **Transparency**: Where a quotational expression of the form '*S*' denotes an interpreted sentence type, the assertability conditions of *"'S' is true"* are identical to those of '*S*'.

The rule-based commitments of *S* and '*S*' *is true* can differ. Semantic ascent has the affect of altering content. Semantic ascent and descent are not contentfully innocent. Because that is so, there can be no equivalence between '*S*' *is true* and *S*. **Disquotation** is false.

Rejection of the T-schema has many consequences. First, minimalism about truth cannot be maintained. Our grasp of the truth-predicate cannot reside in asserting all instances of the T-schema.[2] Secondly, disquotational semantics of the Davidsonian kind cannot be right. According to disquotational semantics, theories of meaning are truth-theories of a Tarskian kind fitted to natural languages – constrained by principles of interpretation. However, no semantics can work this way, since not all instances of the T-schema for a given language are affirmed.[3]

A third consequence of rejection of **Disquotation** and **Content Monism** pertains to how we should conceive of truth-bearers: the objects to which truth-judgements are applied. As the consequences of this argument will concern us greatly, I will now focus on the argument, laid out below:

(i) The canonical form in which we denote truth-bearers in a language is through *that*-clauses, as in *that the sky is blue*.

(ii) Implicature-bearing sentences can be content sentences of *that*-clauses, as in *that **even** the best philosophers get confused.*

(iii) *That*-clauses featuring implicature operators can enter into truth-ascriptions, as in *It is true that even the best philosophers get confused*. But they can also equally have other kinds of evaluation. Consider *That even Elvis was famous is an odd thing to think.*

(iv) Given that truth-bearers are canonically picked out by *that*-clauses, the former are open not only to truth and falsity evaluation but also felicity and infelicity.

---

[2]It might be objected that one might re-express minimalism as the claim that a given sentence *S* is true iff $S^-$ is true, where $S^-$ is *S* minus its implicature operators. But this will not work, since some negations take implicature in their scope, and so their truth-value depends on the presence of implicature. Thus *S* is true, but $S^-$ may not be.

[3]Another consequence is that since logical connectives are not truth-conditional, validity cannot be defined in terms of truth – as for example necessary truth-preservation.

(v)   Propositions have only one evaluative pole – truth and falsity.
      There is no room for a second polarity – felicity and infelicity.

(vi)  The bearers of truth cannot be propositions. They must be
      entities that can incorporate both said-content and unsaid
      (implicature) elements. The one thing that can do that is
      something like sentences encoding a proposition and poten-
      tially an implicature.

The conclusion of this argument entails that **TB1** is false. To be capable
of both truth/falsity and felicity/infelicity polarities, truth-bearers
have to be things like sentences encoding both propositions and
potentially implicatures. Which is to say that they are meaningful
sentence types or kinds of speech-act types, and not propositions in any
extra-linguistic sense.

If this is right, then the right view about truth-bearers must be
closer to **TB2**: sentences encoding propositions. Though now we have to
complicate this a bit. We need to introduce a distinction between two
kinds of encoding. As proposed above, we used the terms $\alpha$-encoding
and $\beta$-encoding. Truth-bearers are sentences that $\alpha$-encode a proposition and potentially $\beta$-encode a mental property.

## 2   Truth, Truth-Bearers and Propositions

Based on that analysis, it seems that we should now investigate the $\alpha$-
encoding/$\beta$-encoding distinction. To be complete, a theory of truth-
bearer and semantic content needs to provide a theory of $\alpha$-encoding,
which is a theory of said-content, and a theory of $\beta$-encoding, which is a
theory of implicature, that is, of the rule-based but unsaid – non-truth-
conditional – components of sentences. However, I now want to show
that this task cannot be completed. The main problem here is that once
we have given up **Content Monism** and the T-schema, we lose any
ability to account for said-content in terms of the theoretical construct
of a proposition. This means that not only must **TB1** go, but also **TB2**.
We must completely re-conceptualise how we look at truth-bearers.

Let us assume **TB2** – now rewritten in terms of the concept of
$\alpha$-encoding, which is a refinement of encoding. That is, **TB2** reads: *a
truth-bearer is a sentence $\alpha$-encoding a proposition*. Propositions are
assertion-independent entities that through the relation of $\alpha$-encoding
are associated with sentences as their said-contents, enabling those
sentences to be truth-apt. What is $\alpha$-encoding? It seems reasonable to
suggest that facts of $\alpha$-encoding are underpinned by facts about the
norms speakers follow in using sentences. What is the norm that

speakers follow that determines that a particular proposition «P» is α-encoded by a sentence $S$? A natural suggestion is that a norm invoking truth underpins encoding, something like:

> **E1:** A sentence $S$ α-encodes «P» if and only if speakers conform to the norm that they utter $S$ with the intention that $S$ be true if and if «P» obtains.[4]

In order for speakers to be able to follow **E1**, they need to have access to some concept of truth. We need some independent specifications of what truth is. We cannot say that truth is just the property that a sentence $S$ has if and only if the proposition encoded by it obtains. That is too tight a circle to provide any illumination. We are looking for features of truth prior to the stipulation of **E1**. The property picked out by *true*, assuming it picks out one, cannot be the disquotational property, since the T-schema is not generally correct. Why not propose that truth is the goal of assertion, the property we want our assertions to have? This won't work. As well as being true, we also want our assertions to be felicitous, and generally conversationally correct. So the description, *aimed at in assertion*, does not isolate truth. What of the idea that truth is that feature of beliefs that makes them useful, such that no matter what our desires are, by having such beliefs we will be successful? Again, it is not evident that success distinguishes truth from other forms of correctness. Implicature-bearing sentences are such that believing them aids achievement, but not all their content is truth-apt. Thus being a truth-bearer cannot be constituted through conventions about success. The concepts of the goal of assertion and success are too coarse to distinguish truth from other kinds of evaluation.

The problem with invoking truth is that we have not yet a means of distinguishing it from felicity – the property that sentences have if their said-contents and implicatures are met. It might seem however that the concept of truth as correspondence provides the key to distinguishing said-content from implicature. Suppose that truth is the property a sentence has when it represents how things are. More precisely, let us propose that sentences can represent actual states of affairs, which we can treat as propositions that obtain. We might now

---

[4]See Lewis (1975) for a detailed theoretical framework in which a version of such a general approach would be couched. None of the arguments I give below depends upon the details of the account. Furthermore, none of the arguments below particularly depends on an entity-interpretation of propositions. The arguments also apply to views according to which a sentence's α-encoding a proposition means that it is has certain truth-conditions.

distinguish said-content from implicature by invoking two kinds of rules. First there is the rule for said-content:

> **Rep**: In using $S$ speakers conform to the norm that they utter $S$ if and only if they intend to represent by $S$ that «P» obtains.

So «P» is the said-content of a sentence just in case it is uttered according to such a norm of representation. That is, we accept:

> **E2**: A sentence $S$ α-encodes «P» if and only if speakers conform to a norm that they utter $S$ if and only if they intend to represent by $S$ that «P» obtains.

Implicatures work according to a different norm. One idea is that we invoke what we might call *when*-rules, rules that specify what speakers can utter when they have a certain state. Let '$N^\frown S$' by the act of attaching an implicature operator $N$ to a sentence $S$. Suppose that $S$ has the propositional content «P», and that $NS$ carries the implicature associated with the property $\Sigma$. We now invoke a *when*-rule to characterise the content of '$N^\frown S$':

> **W**: In using '$N^\frown S$' speakers conform to the norm that they utter '$N^\frown S$' when they have the state $\Sigma$.

Speakers following *when*-rules, we might claim, enable them to correlate properties such as possessing $\Sigma$ to be correlated with their utterances of sentences $NS$. The sentence $NS$ then has the truth-condition that «P» obtains – given by **Rep** – and an implicature condition introduced by '$N^\frown S$' with respect to the property of possessing $\Sigma$ – given by **W**. $NS$ does not have the truth-condition that «P» and «U has $\Sigma$» obtain. In short, we analyse the distinction between said-content and implicature by appeal to the distinction between rules of representation and *when*-rules.

The main objection to this approach is that the distinction between rules of representation as opposed to *when*-rules is not clear. Jackson and Pettit (2003) argue that if there is a regularity linking U's believing that she has $\Sigma$ and uttering $S$, then that constitutes that S represents that U has $\Sigma$. If so, where there is a *when*-rule, U's utterance of $S$ will represent that she has $\Sigma$. Consequently, U's utterance of '$N^\frown S$' will be true if and only if «P» and «U has $\Sigma$» obtain. But that, of course, is exactly what we do not want, since implicature is not truth-conditional. There is a more cogent way of arguing that '$N^\frown S$' functions as a representation of U's having $\Sigma$. In uttering '$N^\frown S$', U intends that H take away the information that U has $\Sigma$ by noticing that U has uttered '$N^\frown S$'. U's utterance of '$N^\frown S$' clearly functions as an

# 6    Monism About Reference: One Notion, Not Two?

If there is only one kind of reference, be it word reference or speaker reference, there can hardly be a tension between the contrasting characteristics of two notions of reference, let alone a proof along the lines of the previous section of an outright inconsistency. The quotations from Quine and Strawson in Section 1 represent opposite strands of this reaction to the puzzle. Quine's view is less widely supported today. Those who accept that a given word refers to something tend to require that its doing so depends in some way on people using it or having used it to refer to that thing, though perhaps not solely on this. Strawson's view is initially more plausible. According to him and Linsky (and see also Bach, 1987: 40), words don't refer at all, save in an entirely derivative sense, and the very question of which two-place reference relation is the fundamental one – i.e. the two-place relation between words and objects or the two-place relation between speakers and objects – is misconceived. Talk of words referring or of speakers referring, in each of which reference is superficially a two-place relation, distorts the nature of the three-place relation that reference really is, i.e. a matter of a speaker$_I$ using a word$_{II}$ to refer to an object$_{III}$.[8] The NRA slogan arguably exploits a parallel confusion: it is not that guns$_I$ kill people$_{II}$, or that people$_I$ kill people$_{II}$. Rather, people$_I$ use guns$_{II}$ to kill people$_{III}$. The use of distinct shorthands, in each of which the three-place relation appears to be two-place, creates the illusion of a substantial debate.[9]

In what follows I will, first, offer a reason for being suspicious of this form of monism. But for those who find this reason unpersuasive I will go on to present a monist-friendly version of the puzzle: an inconsistency similar to that of the previous section but reached without the assumption that words refer (or designate, etc.).

---

[8]Whether the relation is in fact four-place – a speaker$_I$ using a word$_{II}$ to refer some audience$_{III}$ to an object$_{IV}$ – is not a pressing issue here. My own view is that the actual existence of an audience is unnecessary. What matters is that the speaker thinks there is an audience, since only then can he or she form the intention to have that audience think of the act as a reference to the object. A similar line cannot be taken on the existence of the object. One cannot refer save to something that really exists. I touch on this in Section 9.

[9]There is a question over the nature of the shorthand. It is hardly synecdoche or metonymy. 'The (hired) gun killed the child' in a Raymond Chandler novel means that the person carrying the gun killed the child; but while the NRA slogan may be confused, it is not so confused as to be saying that people don't kill people, people kill people. The shorthand is more plausibly seen as a form of ellipsis. The criticism I offer of the 'shorthand' position is neutral on how it is developed.

indicator for H that U has $\Sigma$. Representations of states of affairs for intentional creatures are symbols intended to give information about states of affairs. How then can U not be intending that '$N^\frown$'$S$' function as a representation? It seems, '$N^\frown$'$S$' just is a representation. If so, '$N^\frown$'$S$' and *I have* $\Sigma$ both function as representations. Thus sentences carrying implicature end up being reports about the speakers' subjective states. But this they are not.

Another objection is that truth cannot be representational in this sense, as **Rep** requires. After all, are logically complex sentences representational? If they are that commits us to features in reality corresponding to negation, universal quantification, etc. It would seem we must accept logically complex constituents in reality. I think, however, that is highly objectionable.

Appeal to truth in analysing $\alpha$-encoding is not proceeding well. Why not suggest that truth is primitive and has no analysis, and simply affirm **E1**? Bringing in truth as a primitive concept is perhaps acceptable when we have the T-schema in place. Then at least we have some access to the truth-predicate. We can say it conforms to the T-schema, is a kind of success condition, and has such entities as its bearers. But the T-schema fails, and so this won't work. Using a primitive conception of truth, without the T-schema, to provide a theory of said-content, or $\alpha$-encoding, is not plausible.

There is another way of analysing $\alpha$-encoding that might seem to be available. That is to appeal to belief, namely, the idea that content is attached to sentences by virtue of the practice of correlating having a belief with content «P» with utterance of $S$. That is, we accept something like:

**E3**: A sentence $S$ $\alpha$-encodes «P» if and only if speakers conform to a norm that they utter $S$ if and only if they believe that «P» obtains.[5]

However, **E3** is falsified by all those sentences whose utterance are correlated with belief, but which possess content that is not truth-conditional, implicature-bearing sentences being in this case the prime example. In asserting (1) – *Even Granny got drunk* – a speaker manifests beliefs, conveyed by the sentences:

(i) Granny got drunk.
(ii) It is comparatively surprising that Granny got drunk.
(iii) Others got drunk.

---

[5]We can think of variations of this analysis such as: $S$ means that P in L iff speakers of L conform to a convention to utter $S$ with the intention of getting H to believe that P (see Schiffer, 1972).

Furthermore, one could argue that in using the sentence *Even Granny got drunk*, U conforms to a norm like that specified in the right hand side of **E3**. If so, given **E3**, all the commitments of *Even Granny got drunk* are truth-conditional. It might be objected that in the case of the subjective-probability component of (1) – corresponding to sentence (ii) above – that there is no proposition in the offing, since, as we argued in Section 1 above, it is better to look at implicatures in terms of properties rather than propositions. The problem for the orthodox view wielding **E3**, however, is that there must be a proposition corresponding to (ii) since it is a truth-apt sentence, and so, given **E3**, it follows that the probability component of (1) does correspond to a proposition. If so, our conclusion stands: (1) is entirely truth-conditional. But evidently it is not. And so, **E3** cannot be the correct explanation of propositional encoding.

**E3** is inadequate as it stands but can it be supplemented by some further condition enabling us to isolate truth-bearers? Some theorists – e.g., Wright (1992) – have been attracted to the idea that embeddability is a means of identifying discourse with *assertoric* content. Wright (1992) proposes that truth-apt sentences can enter into the scope of negation, the antecedents of *if*-sentences, and believe-that contexts. These thoughts inspire the following improvement on **E3** as an account of encoding:

> **E4**: A sentence $S$ encodes «P» if and only if speakers conform to the norm that they utter $S$ if and only if they believe that «P» obtains, (*ii*) $S$ embeds in the antecedents of conditionals, can enter into the scope of negation, and be an object of belief.

**E4** is just as bad as **E3**. Implicature is non-truth-conditional content that should, if **E4** is right, be truth-conditional content. First, there are rule-based regularities that link utterance of $N[..S_j..]$ with beliefs that certain conditions obtain. Secondly, sentences of the form $N[..S_j..]$ can embed along with their implicatures. Implicature can come within the scope of negation. In short, implicature meets all the embeddability criteria set out by Wright. If so, **E4** fails to isolate truth-bearers.[6]

---

[6]There are other problems for **E4**. Rhetorical questions are true but don't embed. Embeddability is not a defining feature of truth-aptness. A more general matter is whether facts of embedding constitute truth-aptness. It is hard to see how. Why is it that we accept this kind of embedding pattern rather than another? Is this an arbitrary, conventional fact about languages? If so, we might expect different languages from English to allow different kinds of embedding. But in fact, I expect, we do not find this. If so, we need to explain the actual pattern of embedding. But to do that we need an independent account of the nature of embedded contexts, and an independent account of the nature of potentially embeddable sentences, declaratives, imperatives and interrogatives, resulting in an account of the

Another idea is to bring in assertion to define encoding, but not to define assertion in terms of truth or belief. One suggestion is Brandom's (1983) analysis. Brandom contends that U asserts that $S$ iff ($i$) U undertakes to justify $S$, if asked to, and ($ii$) permits speakers to use $S$ as a premise in arguments. So we might propose:

**E5**: A sentence $S$ encodes «P» if and only if U can use $S$ to literally assert that P.

Again there are problems. The first is the appeal to literalness: to say that U is literally asserting that P with $S$, we mean that «P» is part of semantic content of $S$. But that means that $S$ encodes «P», which involve the very notion we are trying to explicate. The second is that implicature-bearing sentences can meet both ($i$) and ($ii$) of Brandom's conditions. ($i$) In uttering $N[..S_j..]$, U will undertake to justify acceptance of ι if asked to. ($ii$) In uttering $N[..S_j..]$, U permits speakers to use $N[..S_j..]$ as a premise in arguments. Take the case of *but*-sentences and the following inference:

Fred was poor but nice. Jane was poor but nice, etc. Therefore, everyone was poor but nice.

In this case, implicature-bearing sentences are premises in an argument. If so, implicatures pass both of Brandom's tests, and so must be asserted content. If that is so, by **E5**, then they must correspond to propositions encoded by sentences. But they do not.

Could it be that our problems so far in providing an adequate theory of said-content are the result of not having a specific theory of what propositions are? Let us assume a structured meaning approach to propositions. On this view, a proposition is a set-theoretic object made up of entities denoted by constituents of sentences. So the sentence, *T is F* encodes $\langle T, F \rangle$ because these constituents are denoted by *T is F*. *T is not F* encodes $\langle Neg \langle T, F \rangle \rangle$ because its constituents denote those in the n-tuple. What is Neg? We might propose that Neg is a function from a structured meaning onto a truth-value. But structured meanings cannot be truth-bearers for, as argued in Section 1, truth-bearers must be subject to two kinds of evaluation: truth and felicity. We may also ask what is truth such that ordered n-tuples can be true? It seems we should construe Neg as a function from the truth of one sentence to the falsity or another, etc. But this understanding invokes truth. Again, we need some independent handle on truth if the whole exercise is not merely an

---

pattern of embedding we do find. But that means we need an independent account of truth-aptness. But this is exactly what **E4** does not give us.

empty formal exercise. Unfortunately, for reasons already given, we have no such independent handle on truth.

These last remarks should put in doubt another option, which is that we can explain encoding in terms of some structural view of propositions, that is:

> **E6**: A sentence $S$ α-encodes «P» if and only if $S$ has a constituent isomorphic structural relation to «P», generated by the constituents of $S$ denoting constituents of «P».

This kind of approach fails for reasons that should be clear; we need a theory of propositional constituents, but as we saw, in the case of negation, we do not have one that does not already invoke truth.

## 2.1 Conclusion

Our goal in this section has been to find an analysis of said-content, understood as the proposition α-encoded by a sentence. The problem is that we have not been able to provide an analysis of α-encoding. The usual tools for explaining truth-aptness and said-content, the T-schema, embeddability, correlation with belief, disciplined use of language, syntax, etc. all fail to provide illumination. If this is right, the conception of truth-bearers captured in **TB2** is unworkable. Said-content cannot be a semantic notion, which is to say, one that is constituted by a proposition's being semantically connected to a sentence. What kind of a phenomenon is said-content? It has to be a pragmatic phenomenon, which is to say, one that is constituted by speech-act dimensions of language use. The next section attempts to provide just this sort of account.

## 3 A Pragmatic Treatment of Truth-Bearers

The theory I propose is that said-content is a pragmatic or speech-act based phenomenon, one whose explication is linked to the analysis of assertion. Thus I reject the idea that the nature of said-content is something prior to, independent of, assertion. To understand said-content, and truth-bearers, we must first analyse assertion. But, if the conclusions above are correct, we need to analyse assertion without appeal to propositions. That means we need to analyse assertion without appeal to the distinction between sense and force, since this distinction, applied to assertion, discerns in assertion a sense-component, a proposition and a force-component, some action-type that involves deployment of the proposition.

I now examine a line of enquiry that shall lead to the kind of theory of assertion we need: one without the force/sense distinction.

Let me first offer what I think is a neutral characterisation of the kind of act assertion is: Assertion is an act in which U utters a sentence and thereby *defends* a mental state Π. To *defend* a mental state Π is to manifest through a symbolic act, like uttering a sentence, epistemic authority for Π. Manifestation means that an audience can interpret the speaker as taking on epistemic authority. Epistemic authority is being disposed to offer (what U takes to be) sufficient reason for Π.

So much is relatively uncontroversial – see Alston (2001). What is controversial, as we shall see, is the character of the mental state Π defended in assertion. The orthodox view is that Π is a belief-state. Thus, in asserting that P, U utters a sentence S and defends a belief that P. But here is the problem. By treating Π as a belief-state, we are doomed to re-introduce propositions as bearers of truth. If Π is a belief-state, then as Π is prior to assertion, belief-states are prior to assertions. But then as beliefs are truth-apt states, there are truth-apt states prior to assertions. The idea will inevitably arise that belief-states are truth-apt because they are propositional attitudes. Their truth-aptness resides in the fact that they have propositions as objects, and those propositions are truth-apt. In which case, propositions will be the primary bearers of truth, as **TB1** proposes.

If we are going to escape propositions then we cannot identify the Π-property, the state defended in assertion, with a belief-state. Indeed we must adopt the view that Π, although a mental state, is not one capable of being judged true or false: it is pre-truth-apt or pre-doxastic. Instead, we only get to the level of truth-accessible content when we get to acts of assertion: the act of defending a mental-state property Π. The primary truth-bearers are assertions: acts of defending Π-properties, and not Π-properties themselves. This is the line taken by the pragmatic concept of truth-bearers. The difference between the orthodox view and the pragmatic view is summed up in the table below:

|  |  | Orthodox Semantics | Pragmatic Conception |
|---|---|---|---|
| ***Act*** | Assertion: Production of S defending Π. | Truth-apt (Secondary) | Truth-apt (Primary) |
| ***State*** | Π | Truth-apt (Primary). Belief-state ontologically prior to assertion. | Not a belief-state. Non-truth-apt. |

How could the mental property Π defended in assertion, the Π-property, not be itself a truth-apt state? I give some idea of how this might work by looking at the case of representational states. Suppose that some assertions involve defending states that are representational. Say that in uttering *Snow is white*, U defends a representational state: representing snow's being white. A representational state like this is not, as such, a belief-state. Consider the desire state of wanting snow to be white. This is not belief-state, but it is, apparently, a representational state. This fact suggests that a representational state, *in itself*, is not truth-apt or a belief-state. Of course, one might object that if we think of assertion of *Snow is white* as involving defence of a representational state, this will be a representational state with a certain *direction of fit* – in the sense of Searle (1983). The direction of fit will be the opposite of that possessed by the representational state that is connected with the desire that snow be white; the former will be state-world – the state must fit the world – the latter world-state – the world must fit the state. But what is direction of fit beyond the metaphor of fitting? There is no obviously adequate way of cashing out the idea – see Sobel and Copp (2001). It is here that the pragmatic view, according to which Π-properties are not truth-apt as such, can begin to look attractive.

The representational state defended in the assertion of *Snow is white* is not, *per se*, a belief-state or truth-apt. It is only when this representational Π-property becomes associated with *defence* that there is a truth-apt state. It is the relational property of being defended that renders representational states belief-states. Which is to say, what is truth-apt is the disposition to defend the representational state, not the representational state *in itself*. But this is synonymous with the view that it is acts of defending Π-properties – which may or may not be representational – that are the truth-apt states, and not the Π-properties themselves.

The basic bearers of truth are dispositions to defend Π-properties. But to really understand this claim we need to understand how the truth-predicate functions. The truth-predicate is that device we use to express our commitment to the Π-property defended in an assertion or belief. That means that in asserting *N is true*, where *N* denotes some truth-bearer, U defends commitment to the Π-property of *N*. Truth is not a property of correspondence or coherence, nor is it the metaphysically lightweight property of Horwich's (1998) minimalism. We might dispense with talk of properties altogether. That is because the present theory is a theory of the function of the truth-predicate, rather than a theory of what truth is.[7]

---

[7]One can still talk of the property of truth, if one wants. But that comes later, when we develop a theory of property talk that allows us to talk of properties even where, as is the case with the truth-predicate, there is no property in the metaphysical sense. See Barker (2007b).

It is not part of the pragmatic view that all Π-properties are representational. Far from it. There is a significant plurality of states. For example, in asserting value-sentences, such as *Haggis is tasty* or *Murder is wrong*, speakers defend Π-properties that are affective states, states of gustatory approval or moral disapproval. Logically complex statements involve the defence of various kinds of dispositional state, which are not representational in themselves. Negations, disjunctions, universal-statements and so on, are all characterised in terms of the kinds of functionally complex dispositional Π-property states that are defended in their assertion. The task of language activity is to characterise these functional states. I will not attempt to do that here – see Barker (2004, 2007b) for details.

To get this approach to work we must treat reason relations as capable of holding between mental states that are not truth-apt. But one might object that this cannot be because reason is analysed, in part, by appeal to truth. The pragmatic view rejects this idea. Reason relations can hold between states that in themselves are not truth-apt. For example, relations of reason, rational connection, can hold between desire states, which are not truth-apt states. Thus desiring something salty, oaty and with kidney-oniony flavour is a reason for desiring haggis. Of course, there is still the question of how to analyse the reason relation. I will not attempt that here. But I show in Barker (2004, 2007a, 2007b) that an analysis is possible that makes no reference to truth.

If this treatment of assertion can be made to work, it would constitute an analysis of assertion without appeal to propositional content. We have made the first step towards an analysis of truth-bearers without appeal to propositions. But, it might now be objected that we still need propositions. That is because we need propositions to explain the embedding of declarative sentences in the scope of logical operators, where they are contentful but unasserted.

There is no major problem here. We solve the problem of embedding by invoking the concept of a *proto-assertion*. To proto-assert is to *present oneself as having*, or *advertise*, defence of a Π-property. To advertise is to intentionally engage in a behaviour characteristic of a speaker who, given she wants to defend a certain Π-property, utters a sentence S. It does not follow from the fact that she so utters S, advertising the defensive stance, that she actually has it, or that she intends her audience to believe that she has it. She may in fact intend that her audience believe she lacks it. For example, in asserting ironically that Bush is a genius, the speaker utters a sentence *Bush is a genius* and advertises a defensive state. But she lacks that stance, and intends that her audience recognise this fact, meaning to communicate that she has the opposite stance.

Think now of logical embeddings as being like irony. In asserting *either P or R*, the sentences *P* and *R* are embedded and unasserted. But that does not prevent them from being performed in proto-assertions: the speaker advertises defensive purposes, which she lacks. The particular tokened sentences *P* and *R* within *either P or R* are not uttered with the purpose of defending a Π-property. (Of course, U may in fact have a disposition to defend the Π-properties concerned, that is, she may believe *P* and *Q*. It is just that in the embedded instances, U is not in fact undertaking to defend the states there and then.)[8]

## 4    Said and the Unsaid: Conventional Implicature

I have argued for the view that said-content is a pragmatic notion that can be articulated through the idea of defence of a Π-property. This theory will be open to dispute if we fail to provide a theory of implicature, which entails that implicatures are not said-content. Let us then turn to the theory of implicature. Instead of the picture we developed in Section 1 above, according to which an implicature-bearing sentence $N[..S_j..]$ encodes in one way a proposition, ε, and in another way a mental state property, ι, the view sketched in the last section is that $N[..S_j..]$ is associated with two properties. One of these properties Π is that which is defended in uttering $N[..S_j..]$. That act of utterance with the purpose of defence is the assertion. But the other property ι cannot be defended in this way for then implicature would just be part of the assertion and hence contributory to truth-conditions. The problem of conventional implicature boils down to specifying U's dialectical relation to ι, if it is not defending.

In asserting (1), U produces an utterance with two implicatures, whose mental properties are Ψ1 and Ψ2 below:

(1)   Even Granny got drunk

Ψ1:   having a high relative subjective-probability that Granny did not get drunk.

Ψ2:   believing that others (in some class) got drunk.[9]

---

[8]See Barker (2004, 2007b) for extensive discussion of proto-assertion. I provide there a causal reduction of proto-assertion.

[9]I say *belief-state*. But really the state here is the Π-property corresponding to the sentence *Others in class F got drunk*. I shall retain the reference to belief-state to make things a little expositionally easier.

As I have argued, in making an assertion, U utters a sentence $S$ with the purpose of defending a mental state $\Pi$. In contrast, U does not concatenate *even* to *Granny got drunk* with the purpose of defending the states $\Psi$1-2. If U is sincere and clear-minded in uttering (1), she will, in fact, take epistemic authority for $\Psi$1-2; U will have reasons for those states. But the purpose behind concatenation of *even* with *Granny got drunk* is not to defend $\Psi$1-2. That is, the purpose of her act is not to manifest her epistemic authority – to display reasons – and thus her openness to dialectical dispute about instantiating $\Psi$1-2. In uttering (1), U may manifest the fact that she has reasons for acceptance of $\Psi$1-2. But that is a bi-product of her act. Compare using a name. In asserting 'Bush is president', U manifests that she believes Bush exists, but she is not asserting *Bush exists* despite manifesting her belief that he does.

If U's purpose in implicating is not to defend the properties $\Psi$1-2, what is it? Implicature is tied up with what is taken for granted, that is, with presupposition. On the standard conception of pragmatic presuppositions – given by Stalnaker (1974) – presuppositions are parts of background beliefs that speakers bring to conversations. Pragmatic presuppositions trigger use of such background beliefs. But there is a major problem with this idea. We can assert implicative statements and inform people. For example, I inform you that she is poor but nice, indicating that there is a contrast between poverty and niceness. You may not have believed in this contrast before my utterance, but then go on to accept the utterance. But if presupposition accesses background beliefs brought to conversations this must be infelicitous. A possible solution to this difficulty is the idea of *accommodation* – Lewis (1979). Hearers update their beliefs. But this solution creates its own problem: what is the contrast between assertion and presupposition if updating is possible? Lewis does not really say.[10]

There is another view about implicature offered by Blakemore (1987). This is that the function of implicature is securing the relevance of illocutionary acts. Implicatures help us process the utterance in relation to its purpose. We might then accept something like:

**Implicature**: In performing an act of implicating in attaching $N$ to *[..$S_j$..]*, U intends that H appeal to her acceptance of $\iota$ in determining *[..$S_j$..]*'s relevance.

---

[10]See Gauker (2002), who provides an interesting critique of the Stalnaker/Lewis analysis of presupposition along these lines.

To illustrate this idea, in uttering (1), U intends that H use her acceptance of Ψ1-2 in determining the relevance of her assertion of *Granny got drunk*. That is, given that Ψ1 is the state of finding Granny's drunkenness comparatively surprising, and Ψ2 is believing others got drunk, U is offering in asserting *Granny got drunk* a surprising instance of a generality. Of course, U is presupposing that H has these states to draw upon. H may not instantiate Ψ1-2. If so, H will either accommodate or dispute acceptance of such states. In the latter case, H will judge U's utterance of (1) to be infelicitous, and not false. It is not judged false because U is not defending Ψ1-2. Rather, U is taking acceptance of Ψ1-2 for granted. **Implicature** then explains why implicatures are not truth-conditional. The dialectical stance towards the mental properties concerned is not that of defence but of taking for granted.

An objection to this theory is that it is overly intellectual: it requires U to have a conception of implicature properties, like Ψ1-2, having a role in determining a speech-act's relevance in a conversation. However, it is not clear that U has to explicitly grasp the character of the intended state in order for it to be said that U intends this state. U's explicit grasp may simply be to induce in H a state, that which is associated with utterance of application of $N$ to $[..S_j..]$. If so, given that speakers do in fact act as **Implicature** specifies – they appeal to acceptance of ι in determining the relevance of assertion of $[..S_j..]$ – U will in fact, achieve the goal laid out in **Implicature**.

Again, as in the speech-act analysis of said-content in terms of defended states, this treatment of implicature has no difficulty in explaining the embedding of implicature. The content of implicature-bearing sentences is given by proto-act types – in the sense specified in Section 3 above – and implicative proto-acts can be components of such types. Utterances of logical compounds are expressions of commitment to the performance of proto-illocutionary acts within their scope.

## 5 Conclusions

What does the present analysis offer that is not provided by orthodox semantics? It provides an analysis of the said-content, unsaid-content (conventional implicature) distinction, which is a distinction falling within semantic content, which is to say, content that is rule-based and embeddable in logical compounds. The proposed analysis drops reference to propositions, encoded by sentences, as an explanatory tool, and replaces it with mental properties, Π-properties, that have a distinct functional role in production of speech-acts depending on whether they underpin said-content or unsaid-content. In the case of said-content the properties are defended, in the case of implicature they are taken for granted, which is to say, their defence by audiences is assumed.[11]

# References

Alston, W. 2001. *Illocutionary Acts and Sentence Meaning.* Ithaca, NY: Cornell.

Barker, S. J. 2003. Truth and conventional implicature. *Mind* 112:1–33.

Barker, S. J. 2004. *Renewing Meaning.* Oxford, UK: Oxford University Press.

Barker, S. J. 2007a. Semantics without the distinction between sense and force. In S. L. Tsohatzidis, ed., *John Searle's Philosophy of Language: Force, Meaning and Mind*, pp. 190–210. Cambridge: Cambridge University Press.

Barker, S. J. 2007b. *Global Expressivism: Language Agency Without Semantics, Reality Without Metaphysics* [online], University of Nottingham ePrints. Available at: http://eprints.nottingham.ac.uk/696/ [30 Oct 2007].

Blakemore, D. 1987. *Semantic Constraints on Relevance.* Cambridge: Cambridge University Press.

Brandom, R. 1983. Asserting. *Noûs* 17(4):637–650.

Gauker, C. 2002. *Words Without Meaning.* Cambridge, MA: MIT Press.

Horwich, P. 1998. *Truth.* Oxford: Oxford University Press.

Jackson, F. 1987. *Conditionals.* Oxford: Basil Blackwell.

Jackson, F. and P. Pettit. 2003. Locke, expressivism, conditionals. *Analysis* 63:86–92.

Lewis, D. K. 1975. Languages and language. In K. Gunderson, ed., *Minnesota Studies in the Philosophy of Science.* vol VII. Minneapolis, MN: University of Minnesota Press.

Lewis, D. K. 1979. Score keeping in a language game. *Journal of Philosophical Logic* 8:339–359.

MacFarlane, J. 2005. Making sense of relative truth. *Proceedings of the Aristotelian Society* 105:321–339.

---

[11]This chapter argues that truth-bearers are pragmatic, in the sense that their characters cannot be understood independently of assertion. The simplest view is that this means that truth-bearers are assertions, or assertion-types, or even proto-assertions, or types. There are various reasons to be unhappy with the idea that truth-bearers are acts in this sense. See MacFarlane (2005). In Barker (2007b) I propose an alternative in which, although truth-bearers can only be understood by appeal to a prior notion of assertion, we do not identity truth-bearers with acts. They are neither propositions, in the orthodox semantic sense, nor acts. This alternative view requires the development of apparatus that cannot be discussed here, for reasons of space.

Richard, M. 1990. *Propositional Attitudes: An Essay on Thoughts and How We Ascribe Them*. Cambridge: Cambridge University Press.

Schiffer, S. 1972. *Meaning*. Oxford: Oxford University Press.

Searle, J. 1983. *Intentionality*. Cambridge: Cambridge University Press.

Sobel, D. and D. Copp. 2001. Against direction of fit accounts of belief and desire. *Analysis* 61:44–51.

Stalnaker, J. 1972. Pragmatics. In D. Davidson and G. Harman, eds., *Semantics of Natural Language*, pp. 380–397. Dordrecht: Reidel.

Stalnaker, J. 1974. Pragmatic presupposition. *Journal of Philosophical Logic* 2:447–457.

Wright, C. 1992. *Truth and Objectivity*. Cambridge, MA: Harvard University Press.

# 5

# Towards a Radically Pragmatic Theory of If-Conditionals

GUNNAR BJÖRNSSON

## 1   Overview

It is generally agreed that constructions of the form "if P, Q" are capable of conveying a number of different relations between antecedent and consequent, with pragmatics playing a central role in determining these relations. Controversy concerns what the conventional contribution of the if-clause is, how it constrains the pragmatic processes, and what those processes are. In this chapter, I begin to argue that the conventional contribution of if-clauses to semantics is exhausted by the fact that these clauses introduce a proposition without presenting it as true so that the consequent can be understood in relation to it. Given our cognitive interests in such non-truth-presentational introductions, conditionals will make salient the wide but nevertheless disciplined variety of contents that we naturally attribute to them; no further substantial constraints of the sorts proposed by standard theories of conditionals are needed to explain the phenomena. If this is correct, it provides prima facie evidence for a radically contextualist account of conditionals according to which conditionals have no truth-evaluable or intuitively complete content absent some contextually provided, sufficiently salient relation between antecedent and consequent.

*Making Semantics Pragmatic*
Ken Turner (ed.).
Current Research in the Semantics/Pragmatics Interface, Vol. 24.

## 2    The Challenge: Making Sense of Great but Restricted Variation

As illustrated by the following list, if-conditionals are capable of conveying a wide variety of relations between the antecedent (the content represented by the if-clause) and the consequent (the content represented by the main clause):

  (1) If you are really hungry, you will have a hard time concentrating.
  (2) If you are really hungry, you didn't eat enough.
  (3) If you are really hungry, you should order something else.
  (4) If you are really hungry, Bill still won't offer you any of his food.
  (5) If you are really hungry, there are some old sandwiches in the kitchen.
  (6) If you are really hungry, please do have a sandwich before we leave!
  (7) Did he break anything? And if he did, does he have insurance?
  (8) I don't know whether my friend has a student ID, but if she does, is she entitled to a rebate?
  (9) If we are only talking about taste, you should order the fried mozzarella sticks.[1]
 (10) If you believe Gottfried, everything is fine and dandy.
 (11) If you look to your right, the book is on the top shelf.
 (12) If you are Lance Armstrong, what do you do next to improve?
 (13) If you know what a *dundertabbe* is, that is exactly what she did.
 (14) If I may toot my own horn, our group made the transition *months* ago.

Sentence (1) through (3) would be used to communicate that the case at hand is such that being really hungry *causes* having a hard time concentrating, *indicates* that one did not eat enough, and *provides a sufficient normative reason* to order something else, respectively, whereas (4) would be used to communicate that the case in question *isn't* such that being really hungry *undermines* the other person's disposition not to offer food. Sentence (5) states that there are some old sandwiches in the kitchen, and indicates a condition – that the addressee is really hungry – under which that stated fact would be *relevant.* Sentences (6) and (7) would be used to make a *conditional command* and a *conditional question*, respectively, where the if-clause states a condition

---

[1]From Jamie Dreier, in conversation.

under which the main clause commands action or requests an answer. while (8) would be used to categorically ask a question about a conditional content. The antecedent of (9) would be used to *restrict the practical modal* expressed by the consequent, whereas the antecedents of (10), (11), and (12) would be used to *indicate the perspective* from which the consequent should be understood, and those of (13) and (14) to express that the speaker is not taking for granted that the hearer understands the expression (anaphorically) employed in the assertion made by the main clause, or that it is appropriate to bring up one's own achievements as done by uttering the main clause.

Consider three interesting features of this variety of relations. The first is that it seems *radically* diverse. Some of these relations are, intuitively, relations of conditionality: the main clause is conditional on the if-clause in some way: witness (1), (2), (3), (6) and (7), and (8). Others are not: the truth of the main clause is independent of the if-clause, and the speech act performed is performed regardless: witness (5) and (11) through (14).[2] Likewise, whereas some relations seem to be between the antecedent and a speech act made by the main clause – most clearly (6), (7), (13), and (14) – others seem to create complex contents that are themselves objects of speech acts – most clearly (1), (2), (4), and (8), and perhaps also (9) and (10).[3]

The second interesting feature is that, although radical, this diversity is also strongly *restricted*. Though interpretation of the relation between clauses is flexible, it seems considerably less flexible than that of demonstratives like "this" or "that." We clearly do not ascribe whatever relation would make the conditional true, or whatever relation happens to be most salient in the context where the conditional is uttered: "If P, Q" never expresses that P would make Q less probable, or that P is more desirable than Q. One way in which such restrictions on contents are revealed is in restrictions on acceptability or truth of conditionals, and philosophers have attempted to characterize such restrictions in general terms. Among constraints that concern the truth-conditions of conditionals, the best known and most widely accepted is that the truth-conditions of the corresponding material implication should obtain: "If P, Q" is only true if $\neg(P \wedge \neg Q)$.[4]

---

[2](9) and (10) might also belong to this category (see Section 11.)

[3]Some think that (5) is a speech act conditional; I suspect that such conditionals are primarily understood as conveying a relevance relation between a possibility expressed by the antecedent and the (putative) fact expressed by the consequent (see Section 8.)

[4]Among constraints concerned with epistemology or psychology, the best known is probably Ernest Adams' (1975) proposal that the degree of credence that a person gives to

The third striking feature is that, for "If P, Q" to seem felicitous, it is typically not enough that some such general constraint is satisfied: some relation *of the right sort* between P and Q needs to be made salient enough, as it is in examples (1) through (14). For example, even if I find it highly likely both that Berne is the capital of Switzerland and that John Lennon was killed in 1980, I am not thereby ready to accept (or reject) the truth of:

(15)  If Berne is the capital of Switzerland, John Lennon was killed in 1980.

Apparently, to agree with (15), it is not enough that one should find it likely that the material implication holds.[5] Moreover, the reason that (15) fails to be clearly truth-evaluable is not (or not just) that it violates conversational maxims by stating something weaker than could be stated given that both antecedent and consequent are highly likely, namely, the conjunction of antecedent and consequent. Trivialities do not in general seem nonsensical: although people seem to think that the utterance of "I weigh more than 3 pounds and more than 2 pounds" is puzzling, they also think that what is said is obviously true in a way that (15) is not. At the same time, it is clear that pragmatics plays a crucial role in explaining why conditionals like (15) resist truth-evaluation. Suppose that we are playing a game where we are handed two cards, one of which contains falsehoods and the other truths, and that our objective is to decide which card is which. In a context where we have found both antecedent and consequent on the same card, (15) would seem to express

---

an indicative conditional, "if P, Q" is the person's subjective probability of Q on the supposition of P. I do think that the explanatory model developed here can explain the intuitions that do conform to Adams' proposal, but since I think that the proposal is problematic for a wide range of cases and since a proper discussion of these cases and of subjective conditional probabilities would require too much space, I will focus on the requirement that the material implication holds. (We will note some exceptions to that requirement too, but they are considerably easier to deal with.) Problems for Adams' proposal include: (I) Conditionals that do not seem truth-evaluable, such as (15) and (33). (II) Conditionals that intuitively convey that the consequent follows from the antecedent but have consequents that have a fairly high probability independently of the antecedent (Lycan, 2001: 70). For example, I find it 50% likely that I will have a cup of tea before going to bed and 90% likely that it will rain tomorrow, independently of whether I go to bed or not, but the following seems false:
(i)    If I have a cup of tea before going to bed, it will rain tomorrow.
For some further difficulties for Adams' proposal, see Morton (2004).

[5]Nor is it enough that one's subjective probability that John Lennon was killed in 1980 is high on the supposition that Berne is the capital of Switzerland.

an epistemic consequence relation and would seem unproblematically true.

The challenge then is to characterize both the conventional contribution of the "if P, Q" form and the pragmatic processes through which the constrained diversity of contents is derived. A full characterization would demand answering a number of difficult questions: To what extent, if any, is the lexical item *if* ambiguous? Is the conventional contribution of if-clauses to consequence conditionals like (1), (2), and (3) different from the contribution of such clauses to other conditionals: independence conditionals like (4), relevance conditionals like (5), conditional speech act constructions like (6) and (7), modal conditionals like (9), perspective shifters like (10), (11), and (12), "cautious" speech act conditionals like (13) and (14)? Can some of these, or all, be understood as pragmatic enrichments of a weaker, more abstract conventional content? If they can, is that conventional content truth-evaluable, or is pragmatic enrichment needed to reach a minimal truth-evaluable content, as examples like (15) suggest?

In what follows, I will begin to argue for a contextualist account of conditionals according to which the conventional contribution of the if-clause *radically* underspecifies the relation between antecedent and consequent intuitively expressed by the containing sentence. The argument takes the form of an inference to the best explanation, building on an uncontroversial assumption about the conventional contribution of if-clauses. This assumption, *non-truth-presentational introduction*, is that an if-clause introduces a proposition without presenting it as true so that the main clause can be understood in relation to it. I will suggest that the constrained variability of intuitive relations expressed by conditionals can be explained given *non-truth-presentational introduction* and the assumption that the content intuitively assigned to a given conditional involves the relation that is made most immediately salient by antecedent and consequent given that contribution. Since no further assumptions need to be made about the conventional contribution of if-clauses, there is no need to postulate any such further contribution. The upshot is that conditionals have no truth-evaluable or intuitively complete content absent some contextually provided salient enough relation between antecedent and consequent. I call this view *relational contextualism*.

A full argument would obviously have to look at competing explanations of the phenomena and show in some detail how these explanations are less satisfying. I have taken steps in that direction elsewhere (Björnsson, 2007, 2008, ms1, ms2); here, my main concern is to present the central pieces of my own positive explanation. Even if the comparative part of the argument should fail, however, I think that the explanations provided here will prove fruitful for those trying to understand conditionals and their role in reasoning and discourse. Since the pragmatic explanations build on a minimal, uncontroversial assumption about the conventional contribution of the if-clause, they are also likely to be available to theories that make more substantive assumptions.

The organization of the chapter is straightforward. In the next section, I make some preliminary remarks about factors that might affect the salience of relations between antecedent and consequent, and present non-truth-presentational introduction. In later sections, I look at different sorts of relations that conditionals are likely to make salient given this minimal conventional contribution, and explain how conditionals expressing these relations display just the behavior we expect. Before closing, I summarize the findings and discuss, very briefly, to what extent the argument supports relational contextualism.

Two major restrictions of the discussion should be noted. First, to limit the discussion, the examples discussed will all be of what is commonly classified as indicative conditionals. I have nothing to say here about the contribution of subjunctive or counterfactual forms, though I argue elsewhere that relational contextualism is well placed to accommodate such contributions and explain the peculiarities of counterfactual thinking. Second, I will say nothing here about the syntax of conditionals, or conventional restrictions on the syntactic role played by if-clauses; the concern here is with the contents conveyed by if-conditionals (Björnsson and Gregoromichelaki, forthcoming).

# 3   Preliminary Remarks About the Pragmatics of If-Conditionals

It is uncontroversial that pragmatic considerations play a crucial role in the interpretation of conditionals. The case of (15) illustrates how context might be needed to make conditionals intelligible, but it is clear that pragmatic considerations guide our understanding of relations between antecedent and consequent of the kinds exemplified by (1) through (14). For example, just about any declarative conditional can be understood as expressing either an epistemic or a causal consequence relation, given the right context. Consider (5) set in a context where it is believed that the addressee's hunger is a sure sign that there is a certain kind of food in the kitchen, or (11) set in a context where a magical book follows one's gaze around; or consider (9) set in a context where the rules of etiquette are such that a certain conversational topic calls for certain menu choices. Whatever the correct account is of the conventional contribution of the if-clause, there is no doubt that contextual factors affect the interpretation.

It is equally uncontroversial, and well illustrated by (1) through (14), that *the contents* of the if-clause and the main clause play an important role in determining what relation between the two we take the conditional to convey. Apparently, we attribute a relation of causal consequence when the two contents are of a sort that are likely to stand in that causal relation; we attribute a relation of relevance when it seems likely that the content of the main clause would be relevant to a need or goal indicated by the if-clause, and so forth. This illustrates that an important role is played by *general expectations* about what sort of relations hold between different conditions, or between conditions and speech acts. Moreover, we have already noted that expectations about relations holding in a *particular* context can affect interpretations, thus, for example, changing (5) from a relevance conditional to a consequence conditional.

The question, though, is why and how these factors play a role, and in particular what the conventional contributions of if-clauses are that mandate that role. I have already introduced the main thesis of this chapter: Our intuitive grasp of the following fact about conditionals both allows for the role of the various pragmatic factors and accounts for the strong restrictions on interpretations of conditionals:

> *Non-Truth-Presentational Introduction*: If-clauses introduce a proposition without presenting it as true so that the main clause can be understood in relation to it.[6]

Given the intended weak reading of "in relation to," *non-truth-presentational introduction* is true on any plausible account of the conventional contribution of if-clauses. In fact, it states what might be the most obvious facts about if-clauses: that they introduce a proposition, that they can be used in contexts where that proposition is not known to be true, and that they relate to their main clauses.

Controversy ensues when the relation in question is specified by different theories. According to the material implication analysis of conditionals, the conventional meaning of "if P, Q" is the truth-condition $\neg(P \wedge \neg Q)$ (Grice, 1975; Smith and Smith, 1988; Noh, 1998;

---

[6]Depending on how propositions are understood, this might need qualification to cover habitual or generalized conditionals, such as "if it rained, we stayed indoors playing cards" or "if a dog barks, it feels threatened," meaning roughly "whenever it rained, we stayed indoors playing cards" and "whenever a dog barks, it feels threatened." In such conditionals, the if-clause introduces a "gappy" proposition that is true or false only relative to a certain time or a certain individual. (If one wants to think of propositions as bearers of non-relative truth, *non-truth-presentational introduction* needs to be reformulated in terms of their gappy not-quite-propositional relatives.) However, the discussion here will be almost exclusively concerned with particularized conditionals.

Allott and Uchida, 2009).[7] According to possible worlds analyses, the conventional meaning is that Q holds in all relevant, or the closest, possible world(s) in which P holds (Stalnaker, 1981; Nolan, 2003). According to illocutionary theories, it is that Q is asserted under the supposition that P (Edgington, 1995: 287–291; Barker, 1995; Bennett, 2003: 124–126; Barnett, 2006). Finally, according to expressivist theories, the conventional meaning is given by the epistemic condition that the credence assigned to "if P, Q" is the probability of Q conditional upon P (Edgington, 1995; Bennett, 2003: Chapters 4–11).

What I will argue, in effect, is that none of these further characterizations of the conventional contribution of if-clauses are needed to explain constraints on the contents of conditionals. The reason is that introducing a proposition without presenting it as true activates a restricted range of cognitive or conversational purposes that provide an immediate cognitive context for the interpretation of the relation between antecedent and consequent. Only relations that are relevant to those purposes will seem to be part of the content of the conditional. Furthermore, only some relations relevant to these purposes are *straightforwardly* activated without added qualifications. In particular, relations that are straightforwardly activated by declarative conditionals either support modus ponens or imply that the consequent is categorically presented as true, thus implying the material implication (with some interesting exceptions).

The cognitive context into which we most often introduce propositions without presenting them as true is that of contingency planning. In Sections 4 through 8, we will look at a number of relations that are especially salient in that context, in particular relations of consequence, independence, and practical relevance. The vast majority of conditionals express one of these relations, and in particular the relation of consequence.

## 4　Consequence

Contingency planning largely consists of thinking about what might be the case or might be done, and what *follows* from that. To understand contingency planning, then, we need to understand our thinking about one thing following from another, or thoughts involving the consequence relation. One might suspect that the consequence relation is in

---

[7]Jackson (1987) defends the idea that material implication exhausts the truth-conditional conventional meaning of indicative conditionals, but thinks that there is a further constraint on acceptability.

turn best understood in terms of conditionals: to think that Q follows from P is to think that if P is the case, Q is the case. However, given that conditionals often do not express a consequence relation between antecedent and consequent, we still need an analysis of the thoughts involved in the *relevant* conditionals, that is, those that concern a consequence relation. In what follows I will suggest a way to understand such thoughts that fits with a plausible view of human cognition and is detailed enough to make intelligible the relation between such thoughts and conditionals.

To ease the exposition, I will use "A" and "B" as dummy predicates, and use "A*" and "B*" as names for propositions to the effect that some particular individual or ordered n-tuple is A, or that it is B, respectively.

To understand consequence relations and thoughts concerning such relations, start with the notion of a *regularity fact* – a fact to the effect that, within a certain domain, everything that is A is B – and the notion of the *supporting conditions* of such a fact – the conditions that define its domain. A regularity fact is especially interesting when (i) B is true about some but not all elements in its domain, and (ii) we can learn that it obtains and reliably identify elements of its domain as falling within that domain prior to establishing for each instance whether it is A or B. Call such regularity facts "lawlike."

Lawlike regularities might involve causes and effects (measles and fever), or two effects of the same cause (barometer falls and precipitation), or events in separate but regular processes (the departures of the Red Line and the arrivals within 5 minutes of Bus 5), but also facts standing in mathematical or logical relationships (the dividend's being a prime and the quotient's not being an integer; a conjunct's being false and the conjunction's being false). Some lawlike regularities are non-probabilistic laws without domain restrictions – mathematical and logical regularities, most clearly. Others hold for macroscopic objects within restricted spatiotemporal domains, say, or have supporting conditions with an irreducible *ceteris paribus* character that exclude "freak occurrences," or range over domains that are in some sense fundamentally indeterminate.[8] Moreover, many

---

[8] For this reason, one might think that physics is fundamentally indeterministic but still think that the fact that the ball fell to the floor *followed* from the fact that it was dropped: there is a universal correlation between these two kinds of events when things are arranged thus and so and *no freak event occurs*. Should the ball remain midair or fly sideways and land on the sofa, that is a freak event, meaning that the case is outside of the domain of the regularity.

lawful regularities are regularities of statistical events to the effect that whenever something is the case, the probability for (relative frequency of) something else is such and such.

Keeping track of and relying on various kinds of lawlike regularity facts and their domains is a fundamental cognitive task for any creature capable of adjusting its behavior to the circumstances and of learning new ways of doing so. This task relies on two capacities. It requires, first, a reliable mechanism that produces inferences from A* to B* and from ¬B* to ¬A*, and, second, a reliable capacity to identify elements of the relevant domain. We can call this recognitional and inferential ability a *concept* of the regularity fact in question, and we can say that the elements of its domain *fall under* or *satisfy* this concept.

Possessors of a regularity concept need not have correct or even explicit representations of the relevant A and B or the supporting conditions of the regularity. We often begin forming a regularity concept after encountering a few instances, only later learning exactly what conditions it relies on and the nature of the related properties. In many ways, learning about a regularity is like learning about a natural kind. Our primary way of learning about regularities is presumably through exposition to a wealth of its instances and induction-like processes. But a number of other ways are available: we can encounter a single instance of the regularity and recognize it as a case of a more general *kind* of regularity, thereby forming a concept of the specific lawlike regularity (learning that command+w closes the active window by seeing it happen once and taking it to depend on the normal designed functioning of the operating system, whatever that might be); we can similarly use knowledge of general regularities to deduce local regularities; we can quite simply be told that a certain kind of event is universally or most often accompanied by another kind of event, thus inheriting the concept from someone else who has actually encountered the regularity or done the deduction; or we can form such a concept in response to hearing a conditional ("if you press command+w, the active window is closed"). The last case is a bit like seeing a particular instance of a regularity as an instance of a more general kind of regularity, and a bit like being told explicitly that there is a certain kind of regularity that ranges over the present case.

Suppose that this story is roughly correct. Then it seems plausible that when we pre-theoretically think that a certain case is such that A *implies* B, or that B *follows from*, or *is a consequence of* A, we are taking that case to fall under the concept of some lawlike regularity. Moreover, it would be no wonder that consequence relations are highly relevant to the central cognitive interests we have in non-truth-presentational introductions of propositions, and so no wonder that this is what we intuitively take most conditionals to convey.

Taking a certain regularity concept to apply in a particular case disposes us to employ the concept's capacities in relation to that case. Most obviously it disposes us to infer $B^*$ from $A^*$ and $\neg A^*$ from $\neg B^*$, but it also disposes us to learn from the case at hand about the domain of the regularity, extending these dispositions to cases that strike us as relevantly alike. In order for these dispositions to reliably lead to true conclusions and further correct applications of the concept, the case at hand needs to actually fall within the domain of the regularity. In taking a regularity concept to apply in a particular case, then, we are in effect assuming, first, that within the domain of the regularity everything that is A is B and, second, that the case at hand falls within that domain. If we let $C$ be the supporting conditions for the regularity and $s$ the case at hand, what we are assuming can thus be said to have the following form:

$$\text{REG: } (x)((Ax \wedge Cx) \supset Bx) \wedge Cs$$

What I suggest, then, is that when we think that one condition follows from another in a certain way, these are the correctness or truth-conditions of that thought.[9]

Given this suggestion, it is clear why ordinary consequence conditionals support modus ponens and imply material implication. But other relations between propositions that do not support modus ponens are nevertheless highly relevant to contingency planning in much the same way. I have already indicated that regularity facts can relate probabilistic propositions and they can equally relate possibilistic propositions; such relations are naturally conveyed using conditionals with appropriately qualified clauses:

(16) If Sarah is not in her office, she has *probably* talked to Jane.

(17) If Sarah is not in her office, she *might* have talked to Jane.

---

[9]Notice that such a thought involves no *individual concepts* of other elements in the regularity's domain than $s$. This is why, on this account, thoughts about what follows from what are unlikely to seem to be about actual regularities, but rather about abstract relations between universals.

Talk about what needs to be the case for applications of a regularity concept to "reliably" lead to true conclusions and further correct applications of the concept can perhaps best be spelled out in historical, etiological terms: our continued employment of regularity concepts is explained by the fact that they tend to successfully guide actions in ways that rely on the successful tracking of regularities and location of cases within their domains (see, e.g., Millikan, 1984, 2000, 2005).

However, *makes it probable* or *makes it epistemically possible* are not salient candidate interpretations of the relation expressed by (18):

(18) If Sarah is not in her office, she has talked to Jane.

If they were, modus ponens would not be supported.[10] The question, though, is why they are not, given our guiding assumption that conditionals express relations that are particularly relevant to contingency planning. After all, relations of making probable or making possible are both highly relevant for such planning. And once the question is raised, it should be raised about relations of *exclusion*, naturally expressed using negated consequents:

(19) If Sarah is not in her office, she has *not* talked to Jane.

Again, we might ask why, if a relation's pragmatic relevance to contingency planning is what leads us to interpret a conditional as expressing it, we cannot see (18) as expressing what is expressed by (19), and thus as certainly not supporting modus ponens. Absent such an answer, the general pragmatic story looks implausible, in need of further conventionally given constraints.

　　There is a plausible answer, however, and one that covers all three alternative relations: *making probable, making possible*, and *excluding*. Contingency planning and hypothetical thinking involve constructing representations of alternative scenarios. When we construct a scenario where Sarah is not in her office and take her having talked to Jane to be a consequence of that, our scenario now contains the *conjunction* of antecedent and consequent, unqualified. However, if we take Sarah's having talked to Jane to merely be made probable or possible, or as being excluded by Sarah's not being in her office, something more complex is needed. In the last case we need to negate the consequent before forming the conjunction; in the former cases we might need to handle two scenarios in our planning, one involving the antecedent and the consequent and the other the antecedent and the negation of the consequent, or perhaps something like a decision theoretic action tree with the consequent on one branch and its negation on a sister branch.

---

[10]Probabilistic cases raise a host of difficult problems that I cannot deal with here. Edgington (1995, 2008) has argued that various truth-conditional theories are unable to account for probabilistic judgments about conditionals. I try to argue elsewhere that the full set of phenomena, including cases that pose troubles for Edgington's view (see Morton, 2004), is adequately dealt with using a contextualist account of the sort defended here.

In either case, the qualifications involved in (16), (17), and (19) correspond to qualifications that we need to make when we represent alternative scenarios in our contingency planning. Since the qualifications are highly relevant to contingency planning and since they are not marked in (18), the unqualified consequent prevents the alternative interpretations. (Compare charade communication: having symbolized, in turn, a crocodile and hunger, the audience might take the message to be that the crocodile is hungry, but not that the crocodile *might* be or *probably* is hungry, or that it is *not* hungry.)

Although REG supports modus ponens, and although I have argued that consequence conditionals express content of that form, we should note that the story here *allows* for conditionals that do not: depending on context, it might be clear that the supporting conditions are not unqualifiedly presented as true. Here is one telling example, adapted from Allan Gibbard, via Bill Lycan (2001: 63):

(20) I'll respond politely if you insult me, but I won't if you insult my wife.

Suppose that the addressee proceeds to insult both the speaker and his wife, and that the speaker's response is very impolite. Intuitively, this is perfectly consonant with what has been said, but then the first conjunct cannot support modus ponens: it has a true antecedent but a false consequent. What goes on here, it seems, is that the speaker does not assert that *all* the supporting conditions hold for the relevant consequence relation, only some relevant subset.[11]

Once we begin thinking about such cases, it seems possible that many consequence conditionals only present part of their supporting conditions as true. Suppose that I tell a friend who needs to go to the airport that he will be there with plenty of time to spare if he leaves three hours before departure, but that a major earthquake blocks both railway and roads leading to the airport for several days. At the very least, it is not completely clear that my utterance implied that there would be no earthquake (or that my friend wouldn't be hit by a car when crossing the street to fetch a taxi, or that he wouldn't die of a heart attack just after leaving). Obviously, this point generalizes to other consequence conditionals with supporting conditions that might

---

[11]The conditional promise aspect of (20) is inessential to the phenomenon:

(i)   I know these gals: they are tough but not irresponsible. They'll play an even tougher game if it is raining or sleeting, but they'll stop immediately if there is lightning.

be undermined by freak events that both speakers and hearers can justifiably ignore.[12]

If this is correct, one sort of qualified consequence relation might be communicated without *explicit* qualifications of the conditionals, and that might seem to contradict our previous explanation of why *makes probable* and *excludes* typically require such qualifications. But this sort is different: in constructing representations of scenarios for contingency planning we regularly do disregard freak occurrences unless their possibility has been explicitly raised. They are not part of our representations of possibilities, but rather of a general understanding that such representations are simplifications.

## 5   Independence

We now have a pragmatic explanation of why, given *non-truth-presentational introduction*, conditionals will be taken to express consequence relations that support modus ponens (at least under normal circumstances), but not similar but weaker relations. However, there is another class of relations that are highly relevant to contingency planning but resist this explanation. These are *independence* relations, expressed in conditionals like (4) above and in (21) and (22) below:

(21)  If you ignore him, he'll still adore your.
(22)  Even if we downsize, we still have to pay the computer licenses.

Intuitively, such conditionals convey that the consequent holds independently of the antecedent. In most cases, such interpretations depend on semantic markers like "even" or "still." Contrast (21) and (22) with (23) and (24), which seem to force consequence readings:

(23)  If you ignore him, he'll adore you.
(24)  If we downsize, we have to pay the computer licenses.

However, the requirement of semantic markers cannot be explained with reference to a need for corresponding explicit markers in our representations of hypothetical scenarios, as in the case of probabilistic, possibilistic, or exclusionary relations: the hypothetical scenarios

---

[12]For further discussion of counterexamples to modus ponens from a contextualist point of view, see Lycan (2001: 57–69). Although Lycan's event theory provides a very different semantic framework for consequence conditionals than that offered here, most of his points translate with only minor adjustments.

reflecting independence conditionals will contain the conjunction of antecedent and consequent, unqualified, just as for consequence conditionals. If our explanation of why consequence conditionals need no marker is correct, there must be some other explanation of the requirement in the case of independence conditionals.

A first suggestion invokes the ubiquity of independence relations: any arbitrary fact is causally and epistemically independent from just about every other fact. Perhaps, then, independence interpretations are not naturally available for (23) and (24) because they do not stand out. Compare pointing: if I point and say "look at that" but there is nothing particularly remarkable in the direction of my finger, my interlocutors might not get what I am referring to. In comparison, consequence relations are much more telling. But this cannot be the whole story; if it were, independence interpretations should be easily available when the independence relation does stand out, and cases suggest that is not enough. The independence relation expressed by (21) is out of the ordinary, but still not available for the interpretation of (23).

Something more is apparently needed to explain the requirement of markers, and I suspect that the complete explanation involves the fact that *explicitly* or *consciously* thinking that B holds independently of A is a much more complex state of mind than thinking that B is a consequence of A. For that reason, it needs more specific prompting to be activated by an utterance and for the independence relation to be made salient.

Because of the ubiquity of independence relations, we most likely operate with a general presumption of independence. If we think that B* and do not take some A* to affect the probability of B*, we reason and act *as if* B* holds independently of A*, even if we have no explicit representation of this particular independence, or perhaps not even an explicit representation of A*. This morning, for example, I thought that I would be working on this chapter, and I presumably acted as if this was independent of whether my left and right hands would touch during breakfast. But I had no explicit or conscious thought that working on the chapter was independent of hand touching.

Given that independence is a default assumption, conscious or explicit thoughts to the effect that B* is independent of A* would consist in the conscious or explicit representation of a negative outcome of an explicit *test* for dependence, or the negation of claims of dependence. Contrast this with the thought that A* implies B*, which, I have suggested, consists in the simple activation of a basic inferential mechanism. Because of this contrast between our explicit thoughts about independence relations on the one hand, and about consequence relations on the other, we can expect the activation of the former to need much more specific prompting. It thus makes sense that conditionals are not easily understood as conveying independence relations in the absence of markers like "even" or "still."[13]

One would of course want to know just *how* such markers point us toward an independence relation. This is not the place to fully analyze these markers – there is considerable literature on the topic – but it is *intuitively* clear how they do their job.[14] "Even" seems to indicate that its target was less likely to figure in the relevant context than some relevant alternative(s): "Even Granny had some of the wine" indicates that Granny was less likely than some relevant others to have some of the wine; "Granny even had some wine" indicates that having some wine was less likely than some relevant alternative activities of hers. When "even" modifies conditionals, it seems to indicate that the consequent is less likely given the if-clause than given some relevant alternative condition: "The light is on even if you flip the switch

---

[13]By contrast, it is unclear whether explicit representations of possibilistic and probabilistic relations must be more complex than representations of consequence relations; what seems clear, and what I appealed to in the previous explanation, is that the *hypothetical scenarios* built from such relations must be more complex than those built from consequence relations.

Notice that the claim here is that the comparative inaccessibility of independence relations as contents of conditionals is not *merely* due to their ubiquity. I am not saying that there cannot be unmarked independence conditionals; there are: "Don't worry, they're a tough bunch. They'll play Saturday if it is raining, for sure." However, those that seem most natural typically involve appended rather than prepended if-clauses, again showing that independence relations are less accessible than consequence relations, which are naturally expressed in both orders. (One might wonder why the consequence relation becomes more prominent with prepended than with appended if-clauses. I see two possible reasons. One is that an appended if-clause allows us to start processing the consequent, possibly priming a non-conditional reading, before relating it to the antecedent, thus favoring an interpretation on which the consequent is presented as true. Another is a difference in phenomenology and processing between the two kinds of relations. Based on my own phenomenology, consequence relations seem to be most naturally experienced and processed starting with the ground and proceeding to the consequence – hence talk about what "follows" from what – whereas the experience of independence relations naturally begins with the independent condition before proceeding to that from which it is independent. This should make relations more accessible from conditionals that present clauses in the same order: consequence conditionals with prepended if-clauses and independence relations with appended ones.)

[14]For analyses of "even" with attempts to explain the character of "even if" conditionals, see Lycan (2001: Chapters 5–6) and Bennett (2003: Chapter 17).

down."[15] Similarly, "still" indicates constancy in one dimension across change in another (time, space, events, conditions), conversationally implying that such constancy might not have been the case: "Farther east, the forest is still dense"; "Granny is still singing"; "It was better than the last one, but still not good enough." In conditionals indicating independence, the implied constancy is across relevant possible conditions, one among which is indicated by the antecedent: "If you take the scenic road, you will still be there on time." Other locutions indicating constancy can serve the same function, at least in the right context: "stay," "continue," "go on," "remain": "If I flip the switch down, the light stays on," "The game will continue if it starts to rain," "Life will go on if she leaves you, you know," "If the battle is won, the war remains."[16]

If this is right, then independence conditionals would seem to represent contents of the following shape:

$$\text{IND: } (x)(((A_1x \lor A_2x \lor \dots A_nx) \land Cx) \supset Bx) \land Cs$$

Intuitively: the case is such that B holds in all such cases in which some from a range of alternative conditions, $A_1$ through $A_n$, hold. When the alternative conditions are exhaustive, the independence relation

---

[15]We often use "even if" in contexts where it is taken for granted that the antecedent holds. For example:

(i)   Even if we know that there are some people who are happier, ... we also know that they rarely become so by being educated as outlaws (Williams, 2006: 48).

(ii)  Even if liberty or freedom of this kind is something to write home about, it is so only when one feels obliged to write and has nothing momentous to report (Mele, 2009: 84).

It is noteworthy that "If P, still Q" conditionals do less well in communicating the truth-presenting nature of the if-clause in such contexts. The explanation, I suggest, is that our *primary* interpretive task with "even if" conditionals is to find the relevant comparison between the targets for "even" and some relevant class of comparison objects, providing a context where the introduction of a proposition not presented as true indicates that the relevant comparison is between *possibilities*. This removes the pressure to identify some other purpose for the non-truth-presentational introduction, including the purposes of contingency planning, expression of uncertainty and perspective taking.

[16]Relatedly, independence relations can be expressed using pairs of conditionals, as in "You are damned if you do, and damned if you don't." In such cases, though, neither consequence nor independence relations are expressed by the individual conditionals. Rather, they express a relation that seems to be neutral with regard to consequence and independence: a relation of "accompaniment," we might say.

implies that B holds in the case and that the conditional is a "semifactual," implying the truth of its consequent.[17]

I will mention one more semantic marker that seems capable of suggesting an independence relation: negation. Here are three typical examples:

(25) If you don't invite him to the party, he won't blame you.
(26) The substance won't ignite if you touch it.
(27) If you ask him, he won't bite your head off (Lycan, 2001: 21).[18]

Given the right context, these conditionals could be understood as consequence conditionals, but the contents of the two clauses strongly invite an independence reading. Even without recourse to "even," "still" or relatives, such readings seems comparatively accessible when consequents are put in negative terms. The question is why.

One possible explanation of why negative consequents make independence relations more easily accessible is that, unlike their positive counterparts, they contain the explicit representational elements of their contradictions: representing that *the substance will not ignite* already involves representing that *the substance will ignite*, since this is the representation that the negation operates on. (The kindergarten illustration of this phenomenon is the exhortation *not to think of a pink elephant*, the uptake of which already involves a violation.) This is turn suggests that the conditional will prime representations of possible relations not only between antecedent and consequent but also between antecedent and the positive counterpart of the negative consequent. If it is more plausible that a consequence relation would hold between the latter, the relation between antecedent and consequent will in turn be seen as an independence relation that rules out that consequence relation. However, if it is more plausible that a consequent relation would

---

[17]The expression "semifactual" comes from Goodman (1947: 114–115) (see also Lycan, 2001: 20–21, 31–36).

The following might be an example where the alternative conditions are non-exhaustive: "Even if we beg with a pretty 'please,' he still won't help. We need to pay him."

Like consequence conditionals, independence conditionals need not express that all supporting conditions of the consequence relation hold. Here is the example from which (20) was derived: "I'll be polite even if you insult me, but I won't be polite if you insult my wife" (Lycan, 2001: 63).

[18]For an early treatment, see Davis (1983), who calls conditionals without a-temporal "then" at the beginning of the main clause "weak."

hold between antecedent and consequent, that is still how the conditional is read:

(28) If you ignore him, he won't adore you.

(29) If we downsize, we will not have to pay computer licenses.


# 6   Embedding and Its Limits

Examples like (15) ("If Berne is the capital of Switzerland, John Lennon was killed in 1980") show that "if P, Q" constructions are likely to strike us as unintelligible unless they make immediately salient some relevant relation between P and Q. On the other hand, it is clear that we can understand conditionals while having a very thin grasp of the sort of relation expressed. Consider:

(30) Kripke was there if Strawson was.

Apart from our lack of knowledge about the referent of "there" and the relevant time, this conditional seems intelligible enough even though we have no definite idea about how Kripke's presence was tied to Strawson's and no idea of whether Kripke's presence at the event is supposed to be causally or merely epistemically related to Strawson's. Perhaps Kripke was eager to talk to Strawson, or perhaps Strawson only went to one event of the relevant kind during the relevant period, and met Kripke there?

The reason why (30) strikes us as intelligible and truth-evaluable (but not by us), whereas (15) does not in the absence of a special context, seems to be that the former triggers representations of ways in which the consequent follows from the antecedent. No definite consequence relation comes to mind, but rather a somewhat vague disjunction of such relations. If we can rely on the obtaining of those vague and disjunctive consequence relations, we know enough to run modus ponens and modus tollens on (30). For that restricted purpose, even a vague and disjunctive idea of values for the contextual variable might be salient enough.[19]

The possibility of understanding a paradigmatic conditional with only a vague or disjunctive content in mind solves a well-known puzzle concerning conditionals embedded in various contexts, such as in antecedents of other conditionals. On the one hand, many such

---

[19]That doesn't mean, though, that we understand conditionals as having more specific contents *by* first grasping these non-specific relations and then pragmatically enrich them. In most contexts, more specific relations will tend to be more salient, and thus more likely to attract our interpretation mechanisms.

constructions involving consequence or independence conditionals seem perfectly intelligible:

> (31) If Jack will be happy if you hold his hand, he will be ecstatic if you give him a kiss.
> (32) If they will play even if it snows, they are tougher than I thought.

On the other hand, some are very hard to grasp, even though the embedded conditional is not. Take the standard illustration, from Allan Gibbard (1981: 235):

> (33) If Kripke was there if Strawson was, then Anscombe was there.

The antecedent here contains (30), and both it and the consequent seem to make sense independently. (33) as a whole does not, however. This contrast has been taken to suggest that there is no general way of decoding embedded conditionals, and thus to provide prima facie evidence that conditionals lack truth-conditions (Edgington, 1995: 280–284; Bennett, 2003: 95–102; Barnett, 2006: 548). But occasional failures to embed is just what we should expect given relational contextualism, that is, given that truth-evaluable contents are assigned pragmatically. The reason that (33) seems unintelligible is simply that our vague and disjunctive understanding of (30) makes the antecedent of (33) correspondingly indeterminate. Because of this, it is *very* hard to see how it might relate to the consequent, for it is hard to see how the consequent could follow from such an indeterminate affair. (33) appears to be almost completely unintelligible for the very same reason that (15) does: it does not make immediately salient any relevant enough relation. Given this account, the seeming unintelligibility of certain embedding constructions only provides another illustration of the fact that *some* conditionals lack definite enough contents to be truth-evaluable.

## 7  Epistemic Context Dependence

According to the guiding hypothesis of the last sections, the interpretation of conditionals is constrained by the assumption that the relation between antecedent and consequent is relevant to the purpose of non-truth-presentational introduction of the if-clause. Given this constraint, I have argued, we should expect most conditionals to be consequence conditionals, and to support modus ponens. This provides the beginning of an explanation of the central *logical* properties of conditionals. In this section, I will argue that the same assumption lets us understand the way in which indicative conditionals are sensitive to epistemic perspectives.

Consider the following so-called *stand-off* case: a case where two conditionals with identical antecedents and incompatible consequents might be perfectly appropriate in their respective contexts (Gibbard, 1981: 231–232). Ann and Beth both know that the treasure is hidden in one of three chests, C1, C2, and C3. Each has a quick peek inside one of the chests, but cannot communicate her finding to the other. Ann peeks inside C3 and sees that it is empty. Consequently, she accepts (34) below, while rejecting (35):

(34) If the treasure is not in C1, it is in C2.
(35) If the treasure is not in C1, it is in C3.

Beth, on the other hand, peeks inside C2 and sees that it is empty. *She* confidently accepts (35) while rejecting (34). They seem to make opposite judgments, but given Ann's and Beth's epistemic circumstances, each seems correct in her judgment, basing it on true premises and sound reasoning (Edgington, 1995: 293–296; Bennett, 2003: 83–88). Obviously, they make their judgments in circumstances of partial ignorance, and the fact that they are ignorant about different facts explains their different judgments. But each is aware of this ignorance and correctly thinks that it should not undermine confidence in her judgment. In assessing the two conditionals, then, Ann and Beth are clearly not concerned with assessing the same *objective* state-of-affairs, but rather with states-of-affairs that relate, somehow, to their epistemic circumstances.[20]

The literature contains various attempts to understand just what that relation is. One is to say that indicative conditionals express subjective conditional probabilities, rather than representing reality as being a certain way and thus being capable of corresponding or failing to correspond to actual states-of-affairs ([Adams, 1975; Edgington, 1995; Bennett, 2003). Another preserves the assumption that conditionals have truth-conditions or represent states-of-affairs, but takes the content or truth-conditions of conditionals to involve a relation to the epistemic context in which the conditional judgments are made, or perhaps the epistemic context in which it is assessed (Stalnaker, 1981;

---

[20]For example, if Ann had merely been judging whether the corresponding material implication holds, she would not have had grounds for rejecting (35), rather than assigning it, say, a .5 probability.

Nolan, 2003; Weatherson, 2009)[21]. The explanation that falls out of the current approach is, not surprisingly, that epistemic context can make salient certain relations rather than others but also that it can – sometimes – become part of the very content of the conditional.[22]

The first part of the explanation is that, generally speaking, subjective factors are likely to affect the content we intuitively ascribe to conditionals. For example, different concepts of regularities ranging over antecedent and consequent will be differently accessible depending on whether we think that they apply in the case at hand, since such concepts will be especially relevant to both contingency planning and for inferences about the actual case, other things being equal. If we had believed that barometers magically influence the weather, (36) below would naturally have been understood as expressing a direct causal consequence relation.

(36) If the barometer falls, it will rain.

This provides a plausible explanation of why Ann accepts (34) and Beth (35). Both know that the treasure is in one of two places – Ann that it is in either C1 or C2 and Beth that it is in either C1 or C3 – and both know that when something is in exactly one of two places and isn't in the first, it is in the second.

The same explanation does not, however, tell us what content Ann assigns to (35) (or Beth to (34)) before rejecting it. Intuitively, they do not have any definite consequence relation in mind; rather, what they reject is that there is any consequence relation of the relevant sort. As noted in the previous section, we can attribute vague or disjunctive contents to conditionals as long as the cognitive upshots in the relevant cognitive context are clear enough. Since Ann finds herself in a cognitive context where relations allowing her to infer things about the whereabouts of the treasure are highly relevant, she would thus understand (35) to convey that the consequent follows from the antecedent in some way relevant to such reasoning. When she rejects (35), she is rejecting the idea that any such consequence relation holds.[23]

---

[21]On Weatherson's view, the proposition expressed by a conditional is a function of the context of assessment, not just the context of utterance.

[22]It thus avoids some of the criticism that Bennett (2003: Chapter 6) directs at "subjective" theories of the content of conditionals.

[23]The pragmatic "definition" should be understood as fixing the reference of the regularity concept rather than as providing essential properties of the regularity. (Compare: In interpreting the sentence "Just as a man entered the room, John fell asleep," we token a concept of an *individual* man. If the concept has a reference, it must be a man who entered the room, but if there is such an individual, that individual could have been elsewhere, and could have been a woman.)

Her reason for rejecting this is twofold. First, she knows that the treasure isn't in C3. This fact rules out that Ann could infer the consequent from the antecedent if she should learn that the treasure isn't in C1, thus blocking the most obvious use of the conditional.[24] Second, Ann knows of nothing that would allow her to infer that the treasure is in C1 from the fact that it isn't in C3. Thus, no consequence relation between the two conditions could be relevant in the normal way to her contingency planning: productive use of both modus ponens and modus tollens is ruled out. (Obviously, the same holds, mutatis mutandis, for Beth and (34).)

We have seen, then, how epistemic circumstances affect the content assigned to a conditional in those circumstances, and so affect whether an "if P, Q" construction will seem acceptable or not. In the case where no definite consequence relation could be assigned, the epistemic circumstances could still make it clear enough what sort of consequence relation would be relevant, or that none would, thus providing sufficient ground for rejecting the conditional.

In other cases, the relevance of consequence relations is undermined in more subtle ways. Suppose that Clara is reasonably confident that the treasure is in C1, and so reasonably confident that it is in either C1 or C2. For Ann, confidence in that disjunction inclined her to accept (34), but Clara is unmoved. The reason is not that she knows that the antecedent is false, thus ruling out inferences from antecedent to consequent and making modus tollens redundant, analogously to how Ann's knowledge that the treasure was not in C3 ruled out the employment of any consequence relation expressed by (35). For although Clara is reasonably confident that the antecedent of (34) is false, she is not certain. Rather, she lacks inclination to accept (34) because her ground for accepting the disjunction is itself equally strong ground to think that the antecedent is false. Insofar as she relies on this ground, it rules out rationally inferring the consequent from the antecedent; conversely, if she considers the possibility that the antecedent is true, she is simultaneously suspending belief in the grounds for accepting the disjunction. For the same reason, her ground rules out productively or non-redundantly inferring the negation of the antecedent from the negation of the consequent: it supports that conclusion directly, without recourse to modus tollens. Because of this, the consequence relation supported by the disjunction that grounded Ann's acceptance of (34) would be groundless relative to the purpose of contingency planning in

---

[24]This is the ground to which people I have presented analogous cases immediately appeal when motivating their rejection of (35) when in Ann's circumstances.

Clara's epistemic circumstances, and thus not a candidate for the content of (34).[25]

If I have been correct about the explanation of how Ann's, Beth's, and Clara's epistemic circumstances determine what conditionals they accept, it leaves the question of why they would still assign a consequence content to the conditionals and judge that they cannot accept it, rather than think that there is no determinate enough content to accept or reject. The simple answer, it seems, is that the consequence reading is the most accessible, and is accessible enough. In cases where no consequence relation is particularly accessible and where one's epistemic context does not provide definite enough criteria for what a relevant consequence relation would be, acceptance or rejection becomes much less straightforward: this explains reactions to (15) ("If Berne is the capital of Switzerland, John Lennon was killed in 1980"). Similarly where other types of relations than consequence are made somewhat salient:

(37) If you need something to drink later on, the treasure is not in C2.
(38) If we are only talking about taste, the treasure is in C3.

Neither (37) and (38) have a clear sense, because the content of their antecedents make salient relations of relevance and perspective, respectively, for which their consequents fail to provide sensible relata. In the case of Ann's interpretation of (35) and Clara's of (34), neither of these problems arise: antecedents invite no non-consequential relation and both Ann and Clara find themselves in salient epistemic circumstances in relation to the treasure and its whereabouts.

Importantly, the explanation of epistemic context dependence offered here does not imply that *every* difference in epistemic context

---

[25]Instead of straightforwardly rejecting (34), people in Clara's position might well be inclined to rephrase the conditional in probabilistic or possibilistic terms: "If the treasure is not in C1, it *might* be in C2." The reason, I propose, is that probabilistic or negative judgments about conditionals are easily understood as pertaining to the consequent. Since there is no relevant consequence relation supporting "if the treasure is not in C1, it is *not* in C2," Clara would be unwilling to reject (34) without qualification.

Notice that Clara's refusal to accept (34) is based on the fact that her reasons for accepting the disjunction are reasons to reject the antecedent, not on her prediction that she would reject the disjunction if she came to believe the consequent. Conditionals like "If he embezzled, we will never know" can be perfectly acceptable and knowable even though we would predictably reject them if we learned that the antecedent was true or the consequent false. The reason is that our grounds for accepting them might do nothing to suggest that the antecedent is false.

implies a difference in the intuitive content of the conditional.[26] People who know that the treasure is in either C1 or C2 but not in which of the two can all have the same consequence relation in mind as Ann when tokening (34), independently of various and great differences in epistemic circumstances. Moreover, since we know that Ann's thought is based on this mix of knowledge and ignorance, we can understand the particular consequence relation she has in mind without sharing her particular epistemic context. It is true that epistemic contexts do play a role in fixing the relevant sort of consequence relation, and they seem to play an ineliminable role when conditionals are rejected without being given a definite content, as when Ann rejects (35). However, understanding just what content Ann rejects when rejecting (35) still does not involve grasping Ann's epistemic perspective in its entirety. It is enough to grasp the few aspects of it that I have spelled out here: that she knows that the treasure is not in C3 and lacks reasons to think that it must be in either C1 or C3.

Epistemic context dependence also explains one notable sort of apparent counterexample to modus ponens, due to Vann McGee (1985), and a peculiarity of embedded conditionals. Here is a standard version of the counterexample, concerning the 1980 US Presidential election, where Jimmy Carter was trailing Ronald Reagan with Republican John Anderson a distant third. The speaker has not yet heard the results and thinks:

(39) If a Republican won the election, then if it wasn't Reagan who won, it was Anderson.

This seems to be a perfectly intelligible consequence conditional, and a true one at that. Of course, Reagan did win the election, as the speaker was reasonably confident that he would, and he was a Republican. Still, this and (39) do not seem to provide grounds for thinking that:

(40) If it wasn't Reagan who won, it was Anderson.

This seeming violation of modus ponens is well explained by the pragmatic account on offer here. The embedding conditional is understood as a consequence conditional, and the most straightforward consequence relation takes the antecedent to indicate some of the supporting conditions for the embedded conditional, the remaining supporting condition being that Reagan and Anderson were the only

---

[26]Compare the views of Stalnaker (1981), Nolan (2003), and Weatherson (2009). Also see Bennett's (2003: Chapter 6) criticism of subjective theories of conditionals.

Republicans running; the regularity in question being that whenever there are only two relevant candidates for a certain status and the first candidate does not have that status, the other candidate does. When the embedded conditional is detached, however, that consequence relation is no longer available as a possible interpretation: the speaker's reason to accept the supporting conditions of that consequence relation – his reason to think that a republican won – would be his reason to think that Reagan won, and that reason would undermine both the application of modus ponens and the productive application of modus tollens. (The explanation exactly parallels the explanation of why Clare does not accept (34).) Instead, the most salient ground for ruling out candidates would be reference to polls, where Carter had been doing much better than Anderson.

What this means is that, strictly speaking, there is no violation of modus ponens, since the content of (40) is different from the content of the embedded conditional.[27] But the example neatly exemplifies how antecedents of conditionals can affect our understanding of the content of consequents; this will be important when we look in Section 11 at conditionals the antecedents of which invite perspective taking.

## 8  More Contingency Planning: Relevance, Conditional Intentions, and Speech Acts

Thus far, we have seen how the cognitive context of contingency planning creates a strong preference for readings of unqualified conditionals that support modus ponens and modus tollens. We have also looked at some ways in which semantic markers make independence readings of conditionals accessible, and seen how the pragmatic account of conditional interpretation offered here explains how attributions of specific consequence contents to conditionals depend on particular epistemic contexts without therefore becoming fully subjective. But the context of contingency planning makes relevant a host of other relations that should be mentioned briefly as they are responsible for some common uses of conditionals.

One relation that is absolutely central to contingency planning is that involved in conditional intentions, naturally expressed by conditionals with first-person action consequents like:

---

[27]This account of what goes on in the McGee case is similar to that provided in Lycan (2001: 66–68), though Lycan understands the scope for context dependence quite differently.

(41) If it snows tonight, we'll go to the mountains tomorrow.

Analogous relations are expressed as conditional commands, as in (42) below, or in the third person form by decision-making authorities, as exemplified by (43):

(42) If it snows tonight, wear your coat!
(43) If it snows tonight, Lindbergh and Scheffler report to headquarters at 2300 hours.

To respond cooperatively to a conditional command involves forming the corresponding conditional intention.

Conditional commands are a species of conditional speech acts, the cooperative use of which involves the formation of conditional commitments or intentions on the part of speakers or hearers. Other examples are conditional questions (expressed by (7): "Did he break anything? And if he did, does he have insurance?"), prompting addressees to form conditional commitments to produce an answer to the question provided by the consequent; and conditional bets, such as

(44) I bet that she won't wear her coat if it is snowing.

which require a commitment to honor the bet should the antecedent be true.[28]

Another relation of central importance to contingency planning is that of *being a fact relevant to the achievement of some possible goal.* Before deciding what to do under different contingencies, we need to know what can and cannot be done and what the potential costs involved are, and so keep track of facts that are potential means or obstacles to various actions and goals, or that affect the consequences of our actions. Such practical relevance relations are famously expressed by conditionals where the main clause indicates a means to an end made salient by the if-clause, as in (5) above ("If you are really hungry, there are some old sandwiches in the kitchen"). But they are also expressed by a host of other conditionals the consequents of which indicate something of practical relevance to a concern actualized by the antecedent possibility:

---

[28]For discussion of conditional speech acts, see Edgington (1995: 287–291), Barker (1995), Bennett (2003: 124–126), and Barnett (2006). For criticism of the idea that conditionals express conditional assertions and conditional commands, see Lycan (2006). Björnsson (2007) defends the idea of conditional commands, but argues against the idea that ordinary consequence conditionals express conditional assertions.

(45) If you decide to go downtown later, the bridge is closed from 9 p.m.

(46) If you decide to go downtown, there is a sale at SAKS.

(47) If you are thinking about skipping the afternoon session, John has sacked people for less.

(48) If he dies without a will, I am his son, though not from his first marriage.[29]

Since these conditionals convey that the consequent holds, they too imply that material implication holds. As with consequence relations, there are neighboring relations to this relevance relation that do not have that implication, such as that of *being a possibility relevant to the achievement of some possible goal*. However, just as with relations that neighbour consequence relations, the expression of these relations require explicit qualifications:

(49) If you decide to go downtown later, the bridge is [probably/ possibly/not] closed after 9 p.m.

The reason for this, again, is that such relations cannot be fitted into our cognitive map of reality without added probabilistic or modal qualifications, and so will be less easily activated than a consequent-implying relevance relation.[30]

Thus far, we have covered the most prominent relations of relevance for contingency planning involving thoughts about merely possible conditions: relations involved in contingency plans or conditional intentions; relations of consequences of contingencies, or independence of contingencies; and relations of relevance to various consequences or dependence relations relative to possible goals. The guiding assumption has been that conditionals are assigned contents that they make immediately salient and that such salience is primarily determined by the content's relevance to purposes for which it makes sense to introduce a proposition without presenting it as true. Applying the assumption to the most prominent purpose of non-truth-presentational introduction, that of contingency planning, I have argued that we could expect if-conditionals to express just the relations that they most commonly

---

[29]Example (48) is from Noh (1998: 294).

[30]Relevance conditionals are often described as speech act or discourse conditionals, with antecedents specifying the circumstances under which the consequent is discourse relevant. In Björnsson (ms1), I argue that this is wrong: relevance conditionals primarily convey contents relating facts to possible concerns, contents that often embed in unasserted contexts and as objects of propositional attitudes.

express: relations of consequence, independence, relevance, and conditional commitment. I have also explained why, given that assumption, we should not expect if-conditionals to express any of a number of neighboring relations. Furthermore, I have argued that the contents that we can expect to be expressed are contents that satisfy material implication: they either present the consequent as true or support modus ponens (at least under "normal" circumstances). I have also argued that we should expect some conditionals to resist intelligible embedding, and expect stand-off cases that illustrate epistemic context dependence. This goes a long way toward making sense of the restrictions that we see on the contents that are expressed by indicative conditionals.

To further indicate how this pragmatic approach can account for the variety of contents that are nevertheless possible, I will briefly mention three other kinds of purpose for which non-truth-presentational introduction makes sense – the expression of speaker uncertainty about speech act prerequisites, hypothetical reasoning from someone else's premises, and perspective taking.

## 9    Speaker Uncertainty About Speech Act Prerequisites

The most obvious reason to introduce a proposition without presenting it as true is probably that it is epistemically open and thus an interesting topic for contingency planning. At other times, however, uncertainty might concern prerequisites for the success or appropriateness of the speech act one wants to perform. Both speakers and hearers are highly sensitive to whether such prerequisites are satisfied. When the antecedent of a conditional expresses what could be a prerequisite for a speech act performed by the main clause, the conditional will therefore naturally be taken to express exactly this: uncertainty about whether this prerequisite for the speech act is satisfied. Such interpretations are triggered by (13) and (14), reproduced below as (50) and (51), as well as by (52):

(50) If you know what a *dundertabbe* is, that is exactly what she did.
(51) If I may toot my own horn, our group made the transition *months* ago.
(52) If I don't see you again before then, I hope you have a happy birthday.[31]

---

[31]Example (52) is from Siegel (2006: 180).

It is clear enough how the if-clauses of (50), (51), and (52) would express speaker uncertainty about prerequisites for, respectively, the intelligibility, social appropriateness, and appropriate timing of speech acts made by uttering the main clause. To give a general characterization of the content of prerequisite conditionals, let $R$ signify categories of speech act perfection, such as intelligibility and social appropriateness. Given this, prerequisite conditionals of the form "If P, Q" seem to express contents of the form: *The speaker is unsure whether P, which is an R-prerequisite for: Q.*

What we should note is that prerequisite conditionals do not, typically, express conditional speech acts. Whether or not the antecedent is true, the speaker of (50), (51), and (52) would have made her assertion, or expressed her birthday wishes. While prerequisite conditionals express relations to speech acts, they are thus importantly unlike conditionals with main clauses whose illocutionary force is conditional upon the antecedent.[32]

## 10   Non-Truth-Presentational Introduction Without Uncertainty

Thus far, we have looked at two cognitive contexts triggered by non-truth-presentational introduction: contexts of contingency planning, concerned with epistemically open possibilities, and contexts of uncertainty about prerequisites for the ongoing speech act. The former is easily made salient because contingency planning is such a central cognitive task; the latter because of our sensitivity to such prerequisites in communication. Given that these prominent contexts involve uncertainty about the truth of the antecedent, it is no wonder that in many contexts where P is taken for granted, "if P" will seem infelicitous:

---

[32]It might be worth noting that some conditionals seem to express both a conditional speech act and uncertainty about prerequisites for appropriateness of the speech act (conditionally) expressed by the main clause:

(i)    If you don't mind me asking, why didn't you respond to the allegations?

It might also be worth noting that prerequisite conditionals are unlike relevance conditionals, which do not concern speech acts at all. In many ways, then, the common practice of treating these three kinds of conditionals on a par as "speech act conditionals," "biscuit conditionals," or "relevance conditionals" glosses over fundamental semantic differences.

(53) John is heading out soon to buy some groceries. If he is, let him know if you need something from the store.

By adding "if he is," the speaker seems to introduce an element of significant uncertainty that jars with the prior assertion. Similarly, the following would sound odd to people with a modicum of knowledge about recent history:

(54) If Bill Clinton was President in the 90s, he didn't do enough to repeal "Don't ask, don't tell!"

On the other hand, "if P" can often be used without seemingly implying doubt concerning the antecedent:

(55) If he treats you like a slave, why don't you leave him?
(56) If I'm no longer going to be arrested for possessing cannabis for my own consumption, shouldn't I be able to grow my own?[33]
(57) A: John called; he is leaving now.
B: Excellent! If he is leaving now, he'll be here in 45 minutes. Let's prepare the food!

Conditional (55) might naturally be uttered in a context where the addressee has just complained about her boyfriend's behavior. Had "if" indicated uncertainty, however, the utterance would have put into question what the addressee had just said, rather than raised the question of what to do about it. Similarly, (56) fits naturally in a context where the truth of the antecedent is taken for granted, being implied by a recent government announcement. Finally, the person uttering the conditional in (57) would seem to be sure enough about the truth of the antecedent to act on it without hesitation.[34]

The contrast between the oddness of (53) and (54) and the naturalness of (55), (56), and (57) calls for an explanation. The first part of that explanation must be an account of a cognitive context where non-truth-presentational introduction makes sense even though the antecedent is already taken for granted; the second part must be an account of why that context is unavailable when we interpret (53) and (54).

Generally speaking, non-truth-presentational introduction makes sense when a proposition is meant to be the starting point or premise for further reasoning, but where there is no interest in presenting it as true. In contexts of contingency planning, the reason not to present a

---

[33]Example (56) is from Haegeman (2003: 321).
[34]These are what Iatridou (1991: 58–59) calls "factual" conditionals.

proposition as true is that its truth is not taken for granted. But there might be other reasons. One reason would be that one takes the antecedent to be false and hopes to show that it is by adducing evidence against it; another is to engage in reasoning on behalf of someone else with an eye to increasing consistency:

(58)  A:      My friend Joe, whom you haven't met, is very smart.
         B:      Oh yeah? If he's so smart why isn't he rich?

(59)  A:      This book that I'm reading is really stupid.
         B:      I haven't read it, but if it's so stupid you shouldn't bother with it (Iatridou, 1991: 59).

(60)  Mother:      Oh, you're cold. Your lips look blue with cold.
         Son:      If I'm cold, please let me use your shawl (Noh, 1998: 278).

The reason at play in (55), (56), and (57), however, seems to be a *lack of independent authority* concerning the truth of the antecedent: the speaker is merely repeating a proposition introduced by someone else or in a different context, taking it on their authority. This is confirmed by the fact that their antecedents are naturally explicated with reference to the authority in question, as in:

(61)  If, *as you say*, he has treated you like a slave, why don't you leave him?

It is quite clear why these purposes for introducing a premise for further reasoning are unlikely to be operative in (53) and (54). In (53), the antecedent is not taken on some prior authority; the speaker is the authority in question. In (54), the speaker is likely to be as much of an authority on the antecedent as his audience.[35] In neither case do we get

---

[35]There are apparent counterexamples, where speakers seem to be current authorities on the truth of the antecedent:

(i)      Don't you worry about Tom; he is here now. If he is here, he feels good.

However, the antecedent of the conditional in (i) is not specifically concerned with the situation described in the non-conditional first conjunct, as revealed by the fact that the following seems less natural:

(ii)      Tom is here now. If he is here now, he feels good.

One explanation for why (i) is natural and (ii) less so is that the conditional in the former is understood as expressing a habitual or ceteris paribus generalization:

any reason to think that the speaker is engaged in a *reductio* of the antecedent or is arguing from the point of view of someone else.

Since antecedents can be introduced in contexts without uncertainty as premises for much the same sorts of reasoning that matter in contingency planning, we can expect these conditionals to convey relations of consequence, independence, and relevance, and to be used for conditional speech acts. By contrast, we should not expect them to express speech act requirements.

## 11   Perspective Taking

I will mention one final kind of cognitive context where non-truth-presentational introduction makes sense: contexts where understanding the consequent requires taking some (typically non-actual) perspective.[36] If the antecedent can be seen as indicating such a perspective, this relation to the consequent is likely to be highly salient. The relation would matter greatly for interpretation, and interpretation is highly sensitive to various kinds of perspective. We have already seen

---

   (iii)  Whenever Tom is here (and there are no contravening circumstances), he feels
          good.

Such generalizations have the truth-conditions of REG, that is, $(x)((Ax \wedge Cx) \supset Bx) \wedge Cs$, minus the second conjunct. However, when expressed in contexts where their applicability to the present case is presupposed, such expressions *pragmatically* imply that Cs holds, thus in effect mimicking the content of a regular particular consequence conditional. When "now" is added to the antecedent in (ii), the generalized interpretation is blocked. Conditionals are easily interpreted as generalizations for much the same reason as they are interpreted as expressing consequence relations: our regularity concepts form a core part of our cognition. In the case of generalized conditionals, the antecedent introduces a gappy proposition – one that is only true or false relative to a situation – without presenting it as true.
   Another sort of counterexample involves conjunctions:

   (iv)  Tom is here now, and if he is here now, he feels good.

This is a little bit odd, but not nearly as odd as (ii) or (53). The reason is simply that "and" can indicate exactly that what has just been said should be understood as a premise for what is coming.
   [36]Depending on how we understand perspective taking, this is a wide category containing conditionals expressing very different relations between a perspective introduced by the antecedent and the content expressed by the main clause. Apart from the diversity illustrated by (62) through (68), for example, premise conditionals could arguably fit into this category. However, since the relations made salient by premise conditionals coincide with conditionals for contingency planning, my concern is with a narrower class.

conditionals that invoke perspectives, in (9), (10), (11), and (12), reproduced here as (62), (63), (64), and (65):

(62) If we are only talking about taste, you should order the fried mozzarella sticks.
(63) If you believe Gottfried, everything is fine and dandy.
(64) If you look to your right, the book is on the top shelf.
(65) If you are Lance Armstrong, what do you do next to improve?

Conditionals of this sort have a distinctively unconditional flavor: there is no sense that the consequent follows from the antecedent. (62) indicates that ordering the fried Mozzarella sticks would offer *the best taste experiences*, but does not suggest that this depends on what the interlocutors are talking about.[37] (63) conveys that everything is fine and dandy *as Gottfried sees it*, but does not suggest that this depends on whether one believes Gottfried. (64) says that the book is on the top shelf (the one the addressee can see to the right), but does not suggest that this depends on whether the addressee actually looks there or not. (65) asks for a description of what Lance Armstrong is going to do next to improve (to be given in the generic "you" form: "you train harder and smarter, eat better..."), but does not suggest that this answer depends on any possibility presented in the antecedent.

In other conditionals, however, the antecedent both helps to determine the content of the consequent and presents the antecedent as something from which the consequent follows. We have already seen this phenomenon in (39), reproduced here as (66), where a conditional is embedded in the consequent of another conditional:

(66) If a Republican won the election, then if it wasn't Reagan who won, it was Anderson.

Here the antecedent indicates what consequence relation is expressed by the consequent, but is also presented as something from which the consequent *follows*. Other examples might be provided by advice modals:

(67) All this shooting is just stupid. If the crook wants to escape, he should kill the guard silently, with a knife.

---

[37]The meaning of "X should Y" is famously context dependent, meaning roughly that X's Y-ing would satisfy some relevant standards, standards that are determined by the context of utterance (see Kratzer, 1977). For recent discussion, see Kolodny and MacFarlane (ms), Björnsson and Finlay (2010), and Dowell (ms).

(68) If you want to go to Harlem, you should take the A train.

Reference to what the agent wants – escape, to go to Harlem – suggests that "should" relates the action to the standard of best increasing the agent's chances of doing just that (without unduly undermining his other interests), in which case the truth of the consequent might be independent of the antecedent: whether the crook wants to escape or not, the best way to escape might be to kill the guard silently with a knife. Alternatively, reference to what the agent wants might suggest that "should" relates the action to a standard of best satisfying the agent's preferences and interests, period. In that case, the consequent is likely to be understood as following from the antecedent: it serves your interests best to take the A train if you want to go to Harlem, otherwise not.[38]

Conditionals whose antecedents determine the content of the consequents are likely to provide prima facie counterexamples to modus ponens, since modus ponens involves the detachment of the consequent from the antecedent, which might then be given a different content. Take the conditional in (67), which might seem true enough in the context of watching an action movie:

(69) If the crook wants to escape, he should kill the guard silently, with a knife.
The crook wants to escape.
*Hence*, the crook should kill the guard silently, with a knife.

One might well find the first two premises plausible but want to reject the conclusion; the crook should not kill anyone, but instead take the opportunity to give up his miserable life in crime.[39]

## 12    The Generation of Material Implication

Most theorists concerned with conditionals have argued or assumed that the semantics of conditionals should guarantee the validity of

---

[38]For discussion of advice modals, see von Fintel and Iatridou (2005). On Kratzer's view, unlike the present account, if-clauses do the same restrictive or perspective fixing job in all their interactions with main clauses.

[39]For recent discussion of interactions between "if" and "ought," see Kolodny and MacFarlane (2010) and Finlay (2010). The apparent counterexamples to modus ponens are not limited to conditionals with conditionals or modals in the consequent but also occur with some other perspective taking conditionals, such as (63): (i) If you believe Gottfried, everything is fine and dandy. (ii) You believe Gottfried. (iii) Hence, everything is fine and dandy. The two premises might be true while the consequent false: what follows is only that one (or "you") *believes* that everything is fine and dandy.

modus ponens and modus tollens. Some have defended the material implication analysis of declarative indicatives, since it attributes the weakest truth-conditions that offer such a guarantee. Others have responded to the paradoxes of material implication by supplementing the truth-functional analysis with conventionally given epistemic requirements (Jackson, 1987), by suggesting stronger truth-conditions (Stalnaker, 1981; Nolan, 2003), or by abandoning the idea of providing a truth-conditional analysis, opting instead for a characterization of the speech act performed when uttering a conditional (Barnett, 2006; Edgington, 1995), or for a characterization of the state of mind expressed by conditionals (Adams, 1975; Edgington, 1995; Bennett, 2003).

What we have seen here is how if-clauses' conventional function of introducing a proposition without presenting it as true might be sufficient to explain what is right about the requirement that conditionals satisfy material implication (while allowing for the sort of exceptions briefly discussed in Section 4). We have seen why, among various kinds of neighboring relations, the consequence relation would be most easily accessible as we interpret conditionals, and we have seen why relevance conditionals present their consequents as true. But we can generalize these arguments and provide reason to think that the explanations extend to all if-conditionals: If, on the one hand, the conditional expresses some relation of *dependence* between antecedent and consequent, it will be a consequence conditional, supporting modus ponens (barring exception cases). To make salient probabilistically, modally weakened, or exclusionary relations, we need explicit probabilistic, modal, or negative markers, as the corresponding cognitive representations of the content are more complex. If, on the other hand, the conditional does *not* express a dependence relation, it will present the consequent as true. Again, presenting the consequent as merely probable or possible or as simply false requires explicit markers, as the corresponding cognitive representations are more complex.

## 13　Concluding Remarks

I have hypothesized that the interpretation of conditionals is constrained by the assumption that the relation between antecedent and consequent is relevant to the purpose of non-truth-presentational introduction of the if-clause. This constraint, I have argued, can explain prominent features of the semantics of indicative conditionals. If correct, this gives us reason to think that non-truth-presentational introduction exhausts the semantic contribution of if-clauses, and that a form of relational contextualism is correct: conditionals have no truth-evaluable or intuitively complete content absent some contextually determined salient enough relation between antecedent and consequent.

Obviously, much work remains to be done, on many fronts. The account offered here needs to be extended to counterfactual conditionals. It needs to be integrated in a comprehensive theory about the syntax of conditionals and its interaction with semantics. More needs to be said about how conditionals interact with other expressions, in particular modal and probabilistic expressions. Things need to be said about how regularity concepts figure in reasoning and interact with probabilistic thinking. Popular criticism directed at contextualist theories of conditionals must be answered. And it needs to be shown that other theories of conditionals run into problems that are better handled by relational contextualism.

Some of this work has been done or is under way (Björnsson, 2007, 2008, ms1, ms2; Björnsson and Gregoromichelaki, forthcoming). But the arguments in this chapter should be enough to show that relational contextualism is worth further examination. It offers a unified explanation of a wide variety of contents expressed by conditionals, without assimilating contents that are intuitively quite disparate and without divorcing the analysis of conditionals from the content that we intuitively take them to express. Moreover, it builds this explanation on non-truth-presentational introduction, an assumption about the conventional contribution of if-clauses that holds true on any plausible theory of conditionals. Even if it should fall short of explaining everything there is to explain about conditionals, it provides a minimal base on which further assumptions can be added – if needed.

## Acknowledgments

Early versions and parts of this chapter have been presented at the philosophy departments at Oxford, Stockholm, Lund, Uppsala, and Gothenburg Universities, at CSU Northridge, at ECAP5, Lisbon, UICMII, Brussels, and at the CEU summer school on conditionals in Budapest in 2009. I thank the audiences at all those places for valuable comments. A special thanks goes to Ken Turner for encouraging me to finally ready a portion of my sprawling manuscripts for print, to Josep Macia for pushing me to provide better answers to the question of why a contextualist account would not overgenerate contents (I realize that question has not been fully answered yet), and to Brian Leahy and Eleni Gregoromichelaki for their comments on the penultimate draft and their willingness to discuss some of the ideas finally coming together here at various points. Funding from Åke Wibergs Stiftelse and Magnus Bergvalls Stiftelse made it possible to do some of the work on this chapter in a stimulating intellectual environment in London.

# References

Adams, E. W. 1975. *The Logic of Conditionals.* Dordrecht: Reidel.

Allott, N. and H. Uchida. 2009. Natural language indicative conditionals are classical. *UCL Working Papers in Linguistics* 21:1–17.

Barker, S. J. 1995. Towards a pragmatic theory of 'If'. *Philosophical Studies* 79:185–211.

Barnett, D. 2006. Zif is if. *Mind* 115:519–565.

Bennett, J. 2003. *A Philosophical Guide to Conditionals.* Oxford: Oxford University Press.

Björnsson, G. 2007. Comments on Lycan's 'Conditional-Assertion Theories of Conditionals', *Philosophical Communications, Web Series,* 43. Available at http://www.phil.gu.se/gunnar/Lycan%20Commentary.pdf.

Björnsson, G. 2008. Strawson on 'if' and ⊃. *South African Journal of Philosophy* 27:24–35.

Björnsson, G. ms1. Relevance Conditionals are Not Speech-Act Conditionals. Working paper.

Björnsson, G. ms2. In Defence of a Contextualist Theory of Conditionals. Working paper.

Björnsson, G. and E. Gregoromichelaki. Forthcoming. A Contextualist Account of the Syntax and Semantics of Conditionals. *Grammar and Context: A Festschrift for Ruth Kempson.*

Björnsson, G. and S. Finlay. 2010. Defending metaethical contextualism. *Ethics* 121:7–36.

Davis, W. A. 1983. Weak and strong conditionals. *Pacific Philosophical Quarterly* 64:57–71.

Dowell, J. ms. A Flexible Contextualist Account of 'Ought'. Manuscript.

Edgington, D. 1995. On conditionals. *Mind* 104:235–329.

Edgington, D. 2008. Counterfactuals. *Proceedings of the Aristotelian Society* 108:1–21.

Finlay, S. 2010. What 'ought' probably means, and why you can't detach it'. *Synthese* 177:67–89.

Gibbard, A. 1981. Two recent theories of conditionals. In W. L. Harper, R. Stalnaker, and G. Pearce, eds., *Ifs,* pp. 211–247. Dordrecht: Reidel.

Goodman, N. 1947. The problem of counterfactual conditionals. *Journal of Philosophy* 44:113–128.

Grice, H. P. 1975. Logic and conversation. In P. Cole and J. Morgan, eds., *Syntax and Semantics 3: Speech Acts,* pp. 41–58. New York: Academic Press.

Haegeman, L. 2003. Conditional clauses: External and internal syntax. *Mind and Language* 18:317–339. doi: 10.1111/1468-0017-00230.

Iatridou, S. 1991. *Topics in Conditionals*. Ph.D. thesis, MIT.

Jackson, F. 1987. *Conditionals*. Oxford: Blackwell.

Kolodny, N. and J. MacFarlane. ms. Ought: Between Subjective and Objective. Manuscript.

Kolodny, N. and J. MacFarlane. 2010. Ifs and oughts. *Journal of Philosophy* 107:115–143.

Kratzer, A. 1977. What *must* and *can* must and can mean. *Linguistics and Philosophy* 1:337–355. doi: 10.1007/BF00353453.

Lycan, W. G. 2001. *Real Conditionals*. Oxford: Oxford University Press.

Lycan, W. G. 2006. Conditional-assertion theories of conditionals. In J. Thompson and A. Byrne, eds., *Content and Modality: Themes from the Philosophy of Robert Stalnaker*, Available at http://www.unc.edu/~ujanel/CondAssnThs.htm., pp. 148–164. New York: Oxford University Press.

McGee, V. 1985. A counterexample to modus ponens. *Journal of Philosophy* 82:462–471.

Mele, A. 2009. *Effective Intentions: The Power of Conscious Will*. Oxford: Oxford University Press.

Millikan, R. G. 1984. *Language, Thought, and Other Biological Categories: New Foundations for Realism*. Cambridge, MA: MIT Press.

Millikan, R. G. 2000. *On Clear and Confused Ideas: An Essay about Substance Concepts*. New York: Cambridge University Press.

Millikan, R. G. 2005. *Language: A Biological Model*. Oxford: Clarendon Press.

Morton, A. 2004. Against the Ramsey test. *Analysis* 64:294–299.

Noh, E.-J. 1998. A relevance-theoretic account of metarepresentative uses in conditionals. In V. Rouchota and A. H. Jucker, eds., *Current Issues in Relevance Theory*, pp. 271–304. Amsterdam: John Benjamins.

Nolan, D. 2003. Defending a possible-worlds account of indicative conditionals. *Philosophical Studies* 116:215–269.

Siegel, M. E. A. 2006. Biscuit conditionals: Quantification over potential literal acts. *Linguistics and Philosophy* 29:167–203. doi: 10.1007/S10988-006-0003-2.

Smith, N. and A. Smith. 1988. A relevance-theoretic account of conditionals. In L. M. Hyman and C. N. Li, eds., *Language, Speech and Mind: Essays in Honour of Victoria A. Fromkin*, pp. 322–352. London: Routledge.

Stalnaker, R. 1981. Indicative conditionals. In W. L. Harper, R. Stalnaker, and G. Pearce, eds., *Ifs*, pp. 193–210. Dordrecht: Reidel.

von Fintel, K. and S. Iatridou. 2005. What to Do If You Want to Go to Harlem: Anankastic Conditionals and Related Matters. Manuscript. Available at http://mit.edu/fintel/www/harlem-rutgers.pdf.

Weatherson, B. 2009. Conditionals and indexical relativism. *Synthese* 166:333–357.

Williams, B. 2006. *Ethics and the Limits of Philosophy*. London: Routledge.

# 6

---

# French Relational Words, Context Sensitivity and Implicit Arguments

BRENDAN S. GILLON

## 1 Introduction

The aim of this chapter is to shed new light on an old puzzle by seeing the old puzzle as part of a broader pattern of facts. Since the beginning of the study of grammar in Europe and in India, grammarians have distinguished between transitive and intransitive verbs. Particularly puzzling are verbs which have been characterized as optionally transitive. The verb *manger* (*to eat*) is a well-worn example of such a verb. It appears to be a transitive verb.

(1) Paul a mangé une pomme.
    Paul ate an apple.

The verb *manger* certainly expresses a binary relation, for no one can eat without eating something (*Personne ne peut manger sans manger quelque chose*). Yet, one can use this verb in a simple clause to express this relation, even though only one of the relata is actually mentioned.

(2) Pierre a mangé.
    Peter ate.

Verbs are not the only words which express binary relations: so do nouns, adjectives and prepositions. Nor are verbs the only words which express a relation and permit one of the relata to be unexpressed. As we shall see, prepositions, adjectives and nouns all do. For example, the

*Making Semantics Pragmatic*
Ken Turner (ed.).
Current Research in the Semantics/Pragmatics Interface, Vol. 24.
© 2011 by Emerald Group Publishing Limited. All rights reserved.

preposition *derrière* (*behind*) expresses a relation; no one can be behind without being behind something (*Personne ne peut être derrière sans être derrière quelque chose ou quelqu'un.*) Similarly, no one can be a friend without being a friend of someone; and no one can be faraway without being far away from something. Yet, as the following sentences show, the second relatum need not be expressed. In other words, in each case below, the expression in parentheses can be omitted without disturbing the acceptability of the sentence.

(3.1)   Alice est derrière (la voiture).
        Alice is behind (the car).
(3.2)   Alice est une amie (à nous).
        Alice is a friend (of ours).
(3.3)   Alice est loin (d'ici).
        Alice is faraway (from here).

Thus, like the verb *manger* (*to eat*), they permit the omission of their complements.

     Let us refer to these words as relational words with optional complements. Some of these words behave as though the unexpressed relatum could be expressed by some suitably restricted indefinite noun phrase; while others behave as though the unexpressed relatum could be expressed by some suitably chosen context sensitive expression such as a personal pronoun.

     I begin by setting out some basic ideas regarding context sensitivity. Then, I return to examine each of the four word classes to illustrate the pattern. I conclude with a conjecture as to how these words should be analyzed.

## 2   Background

Before proceeding with the details, let me try to reduce the risk of misunderstanding by settling on how I shall use certain terms. The first set of terms pertains to arguments and the second to context sensitivity.

### 2.1   Arguments and Relata

Consider the pair of verbs *arriver* (*to arrive*) and *atteindre* (*to reach*) in the two sentences below:

(4.1)   Alice est arrivée au sommet.
(4.2)   Alice a atteint le sommet.

As Kent Bach (1994) noticed for their English counterparts, sentences such as these are virtually synonymous: they express the very same relation and the relation relates the very same relata and it relates the relata in the very same way. The lexical entries for the verbs *arriver* and *atteindre* are similar in that each has associated with it two argument places. They are also similar insofar as one argument place corresponds, on the one hand, to the person Alice, and, on the other hand, to the subject noun phrase Alice. They are also similar insofar as the second argument place corresponds to the summit. But they differ insofar as the second argument place for the verb *arriver* corresponds to the prepositional phrase *au sommet*, while the other corresponds to the object noun phrase *le sommet*.

Below, I shall distinguish a relation from its relata, the relational word expressing the relation from the argument places it has corresponding to the relation's relata and the positions in the clause of the relational word and of the constituents corresponding to the relational word's argument places.

Since the argument places of relational words manifest themselves only through the phrases in sentences which make them explicit, it is natural to use the positions of the corresponding phrases to distinguish indirectly the argument places of the relational word. Since, as is well known, such phrases can occur in different positions in the sentence, it is necessary to stipulate a type of sentence for the choice of relational word which fixes the positions of the phrases uniquely. In the case of relational words which are verbs, the type of sentence will be one in which the verb is in the active voice. Thus, the first argument of a verb is made explicit by the subject noun phrase. If the verb has a second argument and it is made explicit, it is made explicit by the first phrase following the verb. Thus, the second argument of the verb *a atteint* is made explicit by the noun phrase following *a atteint* in the sentence in (4.2) and the second argument of the verb *arriver* is made explicit by the prepositional phrase following *est arrivée* in the sentence in (4.1).

Now, recall the sentences in (1) above. We know that the verb *manger* expresses a two-place relation: after all, no one can eat without eating something. We also know that the verb expressing it takes two arguments, since the sentence in (1.1) is idiomatic French. In that sentence, both arguments of the verb *manger* are made explicit. However, in the sentence in (1.2) only the first argument is made explicit; the other argument is left implicit. There is no phrase in the sentence which denotes or quantifies over the relatum corresponding to the second argument.

## 2.2 Context Sensitivity

A feature of natural language which has long been recognized is that the construal of an expression can be sensitive to the circumstances in which it is used. Two kinds of expressions have been clearly identified. One kind I call *endophors* and the other *exophors*. To understand what is meant by endophors, consider these three sentences:

(5.1) Elle est intelligente.
      She is intelligent.
(5.2) Alice est intelligente.
      Alice is intelligent.
(5.3) Marie est intelligente.
      Marie is intelligent.

All three sentences not only are judged complete by native speakers but are also grammatical and syntactically isomorphic. Consider circumstances of evaluation in which the person named by *Alice* is quite bright, whereas the one named by *Marie* is not. With respect to those circumstances, the sentence in (5.2) is true and the one in (5.3) is false. In the absence of any knowledge of the circumstances of utterance, no determination of the truth or falsity of the sentence in (5.1) can be made with respect to those circumstances.

Now consider two more sentences and suppose that they too are true with respect to the same circumstances as those set out above.

(6.1) Alice est avocate.
      Alice is a lawyer.
(6.2) Marie est avocate.
      Marie is a lawyer.

Finally, append the sentence in (5.1) with each of the sentences in (6) to obtain the following sequence of two sentences.

(7.1) Alice est avocate. Elle est intelligente.
      Alice is a lawyer. She is intelligent.
(7.2) Marie est avocate. Elle est intelligente.
      Marie is a lawyer. She is intelligent.

Even without any knowledge of the context of use of these sentences, the sentence in (5.1), when preceded by the sentence in (6.1), can be judged true, while the same sentence in (5.1), when preceded by a different sentence, namely the one in (6.2), can be judged false.

Clearly the interpretation of the sentence in (5.1) may depend on its surrounding text, or its *cotext*. Let us call expressions which require other expressions in their cotext for their full interpretation *endophors*. I shall call the smallest relevant expression in the cotext serving to determine the interpretation of the endophor its *antecedent* expression, or its *antecedent* for short. Thus, in the coordinated sentences above, the antecedent of the third person personal pronoun *elle* is *Alice* in the first case and *Marie* in the second.

I now turn to *exophors*. These are expressions which require, for their full interpretation, knowledge of the circumstances in which they are used. They are the philosophers' indexical expressions and the linguists' deictic expressions. The first sentence below contains an example.

(8.1)  Marco Polo est mort ici.
       Marco Polo died here.
(8.2)  Marco Polo est mort à Venise.
       Marco Polo died in Venice.

The second sentence is true, as anyone with an adequate knowledge of Marco Polo's life can judge, whereas even an expert on the life of Marco Polo cannot judge whether or not the first sentence is true without knowing the circumstances of its utterance. Let us call the circumstances in which a sentence is uttered its *setting*.

One can always test to see whether or not an expression is exophoric. One chooses a sentence liable to be judged as true or false and containing the expression of which one wishes to determine whether or not it is exophoric; then, holding the circumstances of evaluation fixed, one changes the circumstances of utterance and ascertains whether or not one's judgement of its truth has changed. In a similar way, one can test for whether or not an expression is endophoric by holding fixed the circumstances of evaluation and changing the cotext to ascertain whether or not one's judgement of the truth value has changed. As Quine (1960 §27: 131–132) has emphasized, one should not confuse the change in one's judgement of the truth value of a sentence which contains an exophoric expression – or, for that matter, an endophoric expression – with the change in one's judgement of the truth value of a sentence which contains an ambiguous expression. Ambiguity gives rise to sentences which can be judged both true and false, without any change in the circumstances of evaluation or in the setting or in the cotext. (See Gillon, 2004 for detailed discussion on testing for ambiguity and context sensitivity.)

It is important to note that these tests apply to whole clauses. Thus, in the first instance, they indicate only whether or not the clause contains an endophoric or exophoric expression. It is a further step to ascertain precisely which word in the clause is the indexical expression.

A few expressions have only an endophoric usage. Examples include the reflexive pronoun *se*.

(9)  Alice s'est tuée.
     Alice killed herself.

Other expressions such as the first person personal pronoun as well as adverbs such as *maintenant* (*now*) and *ici* (*here*) have typically just an exophoric usage. Many expressions have both usages. These include, but are not limited to, the third person personal pronouns. Below, the third person personal pronoun *elle* (*she*) is used endophorically. The first sentence exhibits what has been traditionally called its anaphoric usage, while the second exhibits what has been traditionally called its cataphoric usage.

(10.1)  Quand Alice étudie la linguistique, elle est aux anges.
        When Alice studies linguistics, she is in heaven.
(10.2)  Quand elle étudie la linguistique, Alice est aux anges.
        When she studies linguistics, Alice is in heaven.

## 3  Relational Words

With these basic notions of context clearly in mind, let me turn to relational words with optional complements. I begin with verbs. Then I turn to prepositions, adjectives and nouns.

### 3.1  Verbs

One of the fundamental problems of contemporary syntactic theory is the status of complements to a verb which are optional. It is universally thought that some verbs require having complements of a certain kind and that others resist having them. For example, the verb *gifler* (*to slap*) requires a noun phrase complement, or direct object.

(11.1)  *Paul a giflé.
        Paul slapped.
(11.2)  Paul a giflé son adversaire.
        Paul slapped his opponent.

But the verb *arriver* (*to arrive*) resists having a noun phrase complement, or direct object, though as we saw above, it may take a prepositional phrase complement.

(12.1)  Paul est arrivé.
      Paul arrived.
(12.2)  *Paul est arrivé sa maison.
      Paul arrived his house.

Some verbs, however, seem neither to resist nor to require a noun phrase complement, as we saw in (1).

As we shall see, verbs which take a noun phrase complement, or direct object, and which also permit its omission are of various sorts. There are causative verbs. They are so called, since their transitive usage can be paraphrased with its intransitive usage in a causative construction. (These verbs have also been called *unaccusative* and *anticausative*.) For example, the verb *bouger* (*to move*) has an intransitive usage, as shown in the first sentence below. It also has a transitive usage, as shown in the second sentence. And the transitive usage in the second sentence can be paraphrased in a causative construction, as shown in the third sentence below.

(13.1)  La chaise a bougé.
      The chair moved.
(13.2)  Paul a bougé la chaise.
      Paul moved the chair.
(13.3)  Paul a fait bouger la chaise.
      Paul made the chair move.

One of the distinctive features of these causative verbs is that any instance of the schema in (14.1) entails a corresponding instance of the schema in (14.2).

(14.1)  $NP_1$ V $NP_2$
(14.2)  $NP_2$ V

Thus, the verb bouger (*to* move) is a causative, for, as one can easily verify, the sentence in (15.1) entails the sentence in (15.2).

(15.1)  $[_{NP_1}$ Paul] $[_{VP}$ a bougé $[_{NP_2}$ la chaise]].
      Paul moved the chair.
(15.2)  $[_{NP_2}$ La chaise ] $[_{VP}$ a bougé].
      The chair moved.

These verbs form a class of verbs distinct from verbs such as *manger* (*to eat*). As shown above, verbs such as *manger* (*to eat*), like verbs such as *bouger* (*to move*), may, but need not, have a direct object. Yet, these verbs are not causative verbs, since they do not satisfy the same entailment schema which the causative verbs do. Thus, one observes, for example, that the sentence in (16.1) does not entail the sentence in (16.2).

(16.1) $[_{NP_1}$ Paul] $[_{VP}$ a mangé $[_{NP_2}$ la pomme]].
       Paul ate the apple.
(16.2) $[_{NP_2}$ La pomme ] $[_{VP}$ a mangé].
       The apple ate.

A simple mono-clausal sentence whose verb is one of these but without an object can be paraphrased to a good first approximation by the same sentence with the indefinite noun phrase supplied as a direct object.

(17.1) Paul a mangé.
       Paul ate.
(17.2) Paul a mangé quelque chose.
       Paul ate something.

(For discussion of the nuances of difference, see Fillmore, 1986.)

Of interest to us is still another class of verbs. Consider the verb *remarquer*. It appears to be a transitive verb, since its appearance without a direct object is usually unacceptable.

(18.1) Alice a remarqué une tache sur sa chemise.
       Alice noticed a stain on her shirt.
(18.2) Alice a remarqué qu'elle avait pris du poids.
       Alice noticed that she had put on some weight.
(18.3) *Alice a remarqué.
       Alice noticed.

However, with a suitable cotext, it need have no direct object.

(19) Paul a mis de l'eau dans son vin. Alice a remarqué.
       Paul put water in his wine. Alice noticed.

It is easy to see that such verbs are not causatives, since not only does the expression in (20.2) not follow from the one in (20.1), the expression in (20.2) is not even an acceptable French sentence.

(20.1) Alice a remarqué que Paul avait mis de l'eau dans son vin.
       Alice noticed that Paul had put water in his wine.
(20.2) *Que Paul avait mis de l'eau dans son vin a remarqué.
       That Paul had put water in his wine noticed.

Verbs such as *remarquer* (*to notice*) are not like verbs such as *manger* (*to eat*) either. Suppose that Paul went out for a walk and was smoking. Suppose further that Alice noticed that Paul had gone out for a walk but she did not notice that he was smoking. Now consider the two pairs of sentences, the second of each pair being the sentence in (18.3).

(21.1)  Paul se promenait. Alice a remarqué.
         Paul was taking a walk. Alice noticed.
(21.2)  Paul fumait. Alice a remarqué.
         Paul was smoking. Alice noticed.

We note that, while the sentence in (18.3) seems defective, when it appears by itself, and hence unable to express a proposition, the very same sentence, when preceded by another sentence, as in (21), manages to express a proposition. Moreover, the proposition it expresses depends on the preceding cotext. Thus, an adequate paraphrase of the sentences in (21) are their counterparts in (22).

(22.1)  Paul se promenait. Alice a remarqué qu'il se promenait.
         Paul was taking a walk. Alice noticed that he was taking a walk.
(22.2)  Paul fumait. Alice a remarqué qu'il fumait.
         Paul was smoking. Alice noticed that he was smoking.

They cannot be paraphrased with the addition of an indefinite noun phrase as a direct object, rather they must be paraphrased with a pronominal clitic. Thus, the second sentence in (23.1), not the second sentence in (23.2), is an adequate paraphrase of the second sentence in (21.1).

(23.1)  Paul se promenait. Alice l'a remarqué.
         Paul was taking a walk. Alice noticed.
(23.2)  Paul se promenait. Alice a remarqué quelque chose.
         Paul was taking a walk. Alice noticed something.

Moreover, the otherwise defective clause *Alice a remarqué* (*Alice noticed*) has different truth value judgements made of it, depending on the preceding clause. When the sentence in (18.3) appears in (22.1), it is judged true with respect to the circumstances stated above; but when it appears in (22.2), it is judged false.

Finally, we observe that what it is that Alice notices remains the same under negation for either sentence in (24).

(24.1)  Paul se promenait. Alice ne l'a pas remarqué.
         Paul was taking a walk. Alice did not notice.

(24.2)  Paul fumait. Alice n'a pas remarqué.
        Paul was smoking. Alice did not notice.

Verbs like *manger* (*to eat*) do not show this invariance under negation. To see this, consider two pairs of sentences.

(25.1)  Paul a préparé une tarte. Alice a mangé.
        Paul prepared a pie. Alice ate.
(25.2)  Paul a préparé un gâteau. Alice a mangé.
        Paul prepared a cake. Alice ate.

To be sure, the clause *Alice a mangé* (*Alice ate*) is compatible, in the case of (25.1), with Alice having eaten some of the pie Paul had prepared, and is compatible, in the case of (25.2), with Alice having eaten some of the cake Paul had prepared. But it is also compatible with Alice having eaten anything else. This is not the case when a pronoun for a direct object is added to the clause.

(26.1)  Paul a préparé une tarte et Alice l'a mangée.
        Paul prepared a pie and Alice ate it.
(26.2)  Paul a préparé un gâteau et Alice l'a mangé.
        Paul prepared a cake and Alice ate it.

In these sentences, what Alice has eaten is specified and identified by the antecedent. Furthermore, the sentences in (25) do not behave as sentences which contain endophors do in the presence of negation, as shown by the minimal pair in (27).

(27.1)  Paul a préparé un gâteau. Alice n'a pas mangé.
        Paul prepared a cake. Alice did not eat.
(27.2)  Paul a préparé un gâteau. Alice ne l'a pas mangé.
        Paul prepared a cake. Alice did not eat it.

The situation is altogether different with verbs such as *remarquer* (*to notice*). First, as we saw above, the interpretation of a clause containing the verb *remarquer* (*to notice*) without any complements is sensitive to its preceding cotext. Second, clauses containing the verb without complements cannot be given an adequate paraphrase with an indefinite noun phrase. Third, verbs such as *remarquer* (*to notice*) pattern, not with the intransitive use of verbs such as *manger* (*to eat*), but with the transitive usage, where the direct object is expressed by a pronominal clitic with an antecedent. This is especially evident when the clause containing the contrasting verbs is negated. The sentences in (28) are not paraphrases of each other; those in (29) are.

(28.1)  Alice a préparé une tarte, mais Paul n'a pas mangé.
        Alice prepared a pie, but Paul did not eat.
(28.1)  Alice a préparé <u>une tarte</u>, mais Paul ne <u>l</u>'a pas mangé.
        Alice prepared <u>a pie</u>, but Paul did not eat <u>it</u>.


(29.1)  Alice a préparé une tarte, mais Paul n'avait pas remarqué.
        Alice prepared a pie, but Paul did not notice.
(29.2)  Alice a préparé une tarte, mais Paul ne l'avait pas remarqué.
        Alice prepared a pie, but Paul did not notice that she had.

Other French verbs which pattern with *remarquer* (*to notice*) are *s'étonner de* (*to be amazed at*), *refuser de* (*to refuse*), *approuver* (*to approve*), *se soumettre à* (*to submit to*), etc.

Not only may the unexpressed relatum of these verbs be determined endophorically, as above, it may also be determined exophorically. Imagine, for example, two people walking together past a scene which each would take to attract the other's attention, say, they both notice that Paul is sitting nude on a park bench. The question in (30) is fully acceptable.

(30)  As-tu remarqué?
      Did you notice?

So far, we have confined our attention to binary relational verbs whose clausal complement may be left unexpressed. But verbs with clausal complements are not the only binary relational verbs whose second argument may be left implicit. Verbs with other kinds of complements permit their second arguments to be left implicit. We saw such a case above. The verb *arriver* (*to arrive*) is a binary relational verb. Its second argument is expressed by a prepositional phrase. But, as we shall see, this prepositional phrase can be omitted. When it is, the value of the second argument may be determined either exophorically or endophorically.

(31.1)  ?Alice est arrivée.
        Alice arrived.
(31.2)  Alice est arrivée au sommet.
        Alice arrived at the summit.


(32.1)  *Alice a atteint.
        Alice reached.

(32.2)   Alice a atteint le sommet.
        Alice reached the summit.

However, with a suitable cotext, the verb *arriver* (*to arrive*) requires no PP complement, whereas the verb atteindre (*to reach*) still requires a complement.

(33.1)   Alice est montée au sommet. Elle est arrivée à midi.
        Alice climbed to the summit. She arrived at noon.
(33.2)   *Alice est montée au sommet. Elle a atteint à midi.
        Alice climbed to the summit. She reached at noon.

Clearly, the argument of the verb *arriver* (*to arrive*) left implicit in (33.1) is construed endophorically, for the value to be associated with the implicit argument is determined by the cotext. Thus, what sentence *elle est arrivée à midi* (*she arrived at noon*) expresses in (33.1) is that Alice arrived at the summit at noon; but what it expresses in (34) below is that she arrived at the office at noon.

(34)   Alice est allée au bureau à pied. Elle est arrivée à midi.
      Alice walked to work. She arrived at noon.

A satisfactory paraphrase of the second sentence in (33) can be obtained with an endophoric expression making explicit the second argument of the verb *arriver* (*to arrive*).

(35)   Alice est montée au sommet. Elle y est arrivée à midi.
      Alice climbed to the summit. She arrived there at noon.

The value of the second argument of the verb *arriver* (*to arrive*) can also be determined exophorically. Consider two circumstances of utterance: in one, the speaker A is at the office and in the other he or she is at a house. If the sentence *Alice est arrivée* (*Alice arrived*) is uttered in the first circumstance of utterance, what is conveyed is that Alice has arrived at the place of the circumstance of utterance, namely, the office. If it is uttered in the second circumstance of utterance, what is conveyed is that Alice has arrived at the place of the other circumstance of utterance, namely, the house. In this case, the correct paraphrase of *Alice est arrivée* (*Alice has arrived*) is given by the first sentence below, not the second.

(36.1)   Alice est arrivée ici.
        Alice has arrived here.

(36.2)  Alice est arrivée quelque part.
   Alice has arrived somewhere.

As noted above, the second argument of the verb *arriver* (*to arrive*), when made explicit, is expressed by a prepositional phrase, and when left implicit, is construed either endophorically or exophorically. However, some arguments, which, when made explicit, are expressed by a prepositional phrase, are, when left implicit, construed as existentially quantified. It is a fact of French that the first argument of any binary relational verb appearing in a finite active form must be made explicit and it must be made explicit by the subject of the verb's clause. However, when the verb appears in the passive voice, it is the second argument which must be made explicit by the subject of the clause. The first argument may be left implicit. Moreover, when it is left implicit, it is construed existentially.

(37.1)  Paul a été giflé.
(37.2)  Paul a été giflé par quelqu'un ou quelque chose.

There are other French verbs with indirect complements, but whose construals are typically neither existential nor exophoric. These verbs have been called in the English literature covert reciprocal verbs. They have also been called converse predicates by Paul Pupier (1973), who furnishes the following examples, among others: *correspondre* (*to correspond*), *cohabiter* (*to cohabit*), *fraterniser* (*to fraternize*), *coïncider* (*to coincide*), *contraster* (*to contrast*) and *concorder* (*to agree*). These verbs, when their second argument is left implicit, are construed reciprocally.

(38.1)  *Alice cohabite.
   Alice lives with.
(38.2)  Alice cohabite avec Paul.
   Alice cohabites with Paul.
(38.3)  Alice et Paul cohabitent.
   Alice and Paul cohabit.

I have not attempted to treat all cases where verbs expressing binary relations permit one relatum to go unexpressed. There is a substantial literature on the topic, including work by Rothemberg (1974), Fónagy (1985), Lajavaara (2000) and Cummins and Roberge (2005). In particular, it has been observed that transitive verbs in coordinated structures permit the omission of their direct objects.

(39) Il lit et il sait.
He reads and he knows.

And, as pointed out to me by Paul Pupier, it is also possible to omit the direct objects in commands.

(40) Allez ! Giflez.
Go ahead! Slap.

Nor have I touched on the omission of complements for reasons of tabooing, as noted in Fónagy (1985: 6). For more details on other cases, the interested reader is referred to the work of Cummins and Roberge (2004, 2005).

## 3.2 Prepositions

I now turn to prepositions. The sentence in (41), by itself, seems incomplete.

(41) *Paul a découpé le salami avec.
Paul cut the salami with.

Yet, when preceded by either of the sentences below, it does not.

(42.1) Alice a pris un couteau.
Alice took a knife.
(42.2) Alice a pris des ciseaux.
Alice took scissors.

Either of the sentences in (42), when preceding the sentence in (41) renders the sentence in (41) complete.

(43.1) Alice a pris un couteau et Paul a découpé le salami avec.
Alice took a knife and Paul cut up the salami with it.
(43.2) Alice a pris des ciseaux et Paul a découpé le salami avec.
Alice took scissors and Paul cut up the salami with them.

The sentence in (41), when preceded by the sentence in (42.1), expresses that Paul cut up the salami with the knife which Alice had taken, and when preceded by the sentence in (42.2), expresses that Paul cut up the salami with the scissors which Alice had taken. The preposition in the sentences in (43) is behaving endophorically. The pattern here is the one observed with respect to verbs such as *remarquer* (*to notice*), not the one observed with respect to the verbs such as *manger* (*to eat*). Moreover, the dependence on an antecedent expression is preserved under negation.

(44.1) Alice a pris un couteau, mais Paul n'a pas découpé le salami avec.
Alice took a knife, but Paul did not cut up the salami with it.

(44.2) Alice a pris des ciseaux, mais Paul n'a pas découpé le salami avec.
Alice took up scissors, but Paul did not cut up the salami with them.

It is also clear that the sentences in (43) cannot be paraphrased with the help of an indefinite noun phrase, as is the case with verbs like *manger* (*to eat*).

(45.1) Alice a pris un couteau et Paul a découpé le salami avec quelque chose.
Alice took a knife and Paul cut up the salami with something.

(45.2) Alice a pris des ciseaux et Paul a découpé le salami avec quelque chose.
Alice took the scissors and Paul cut up the salami with something.

In addition, it is interesting to note that these complementless prepositions give rise to ambiguities of antecedent, just like pronouns.

(46) Alice est montée dans l'ascenseur, mais Paul n'est pas monté avec.
Alice went up in the elevator, but Paul did not go up with her/in it.

The second clause can be judged both to be true and to be false the circumstances in which Paul went up by elevator but did not go up with Alice. This follows directly from the underspecification of antecedent for the endophoric element ensconced in the prepositional constituent.

Further evidence that these prepositions form a constituent which is context sensitive comes from the complementarity of the prepositions *dans* (*in*), *sur* (*on*) and *sous* (*under*) with the words *dedans* (*inside*), *dessus* (*on top*) and *dessous* (*underneath*). The former never permit the omission of their complements and, to express what would result from the felicitous omission of their complements, their adverbial counterparts must be used.

(47.1) *Voyez cette boîte. Paul s'est caché dans.
See that box. Paul hid himself in.

(47.2) Voyez cette boîte. Pierre s'est caché dedans.
See that box. Paul hid himself inside.

(48.1) *Mon bureau est là; mettez ce livre sur.
My desk is over there; put this book on.

(48.2) Mon bureau est la; mettez ce livre dessus.
My desk is over there; put this book on it.

(49.1) *Mon bureau est là; mettez la corbeille sous.
My desk is over there; put this waste paper basket under.

(49.2) Mon bureau est là; mettez la corbeille dessous.
My desk is over there; put this waste paper basket underneath.

Nor are prepositions without complements limited to endophoric usage. Here is another example. A couple gets into their car. The driver is about to back up the car when the passenger, who is the driver's spouse, says:

(50) Attention, les enfants sont derrière.
Careful, the children are behind the car.

Suppose that the children of the two adults are indeed behind them. Should the car have been reoriented by one hundred eighty degrees, the sentence in (50) would be false, since the children, though in the same place, are no longer behind the car. This change in truth value judgement is indicative of the sentence containing an exophoric element.

The exophora is also not confined to spatial construals. They can also have temporal construals, as shown by the sentence in (51.1) below, which is an adaptation of a sentence by Montherland, cited in Grevisse (1964 §901).

(51.1) Avant, nous étions exploités par l'envahisseur.
Before, we had been exploited by the invader.

(51.2) Avant maintenant, nous étions exploités par l'envahisseur.
Before now, we had been exploited by the invader.

Note that the second sentence, though awkward, gives an accurate paraphrase of the first. Moreover, the first sentence, like the second, shows the usual evidence of containing an exophoric element.

These usages of prepositions are well documented in traditional grammar. Grevisse (1964 §901) identifies the following: *après* (*after*), *autour* (*around*), *avant* (*before*), *avec* (*with*), *contre* (*against*), *depuis* (*since*), *derrière* (*behind*), *devant* (*before*), *hors* (*out of*), *outre* (*beyond*), *parmi* (*among*), *pour* (*for*), *proche* (*near*), *sans* (*without*), *selon* (*according to*) and *vers* (*toward*).

### 3.3   Adjectives

Next, I come to adjectives which express relations and, again, we observe that such adjectives permit the omission of their complements and that when they do so, they can behave either as endophors, as shown by the pair of sentences below,

(52.1)  La tour Eiffel est magnifique et Paul habite tout près.
        The Eiffel Tower is magnificent and Paul lives nearby.
(52.2)  La tour Eiffel est magnifique et Paul habite tout près d'elle.
        The Eiffel Tower is magnificent and Paul lives near it.

or as exophors, as shown by the next pair.

(53.1)  Paul habite tout près.
        Paul lives nearby.
(53.2)  Paul habite tout près d'ici.
        Paul lives near here.

As the reader can easily verify for himself or herself, the adjectival phrases without complements behave just like the ones with a well-recognized endophoric or exophoric element such as *elle* (*she*; (*it*)) and *ici* (*here*).

   Just as there are reciprocal verbs, there are reciprocal adjectives (Pupier, 1973: 79–80), which include *contradictoire* (*contradictory*), *différent* (*different*), *distinct* (*distinct*), *égal* (*equal*), *équivalent* (*equivalent*), *opposé* (*opposed*), *parallèle* (*parallel*), *perpendiculaire* (*perpendicular*), *simultané* (*simultaneous*), etc.

(54.0)  *L'explosion était simultanée.
        The explosion was simultaneous.
(54.1)  L'explosion était simultanée à l'arrivée du train.
        The explosion was simultaneous with the arrival of the train.
(54.2)  L'explosion et l'arrivée du train étaient simultanées.
        The explosion and the arrival of the train were simultaneous.

### 3.4   Nouns

Finally, I come to nouns. Consider a relational noun such as *père* (*father*). We know that it is a binary relational noun since no one can be a father and never have had a child. Now, when its second argument is left implicit, it is construed existentially.

(55.1)  Paul est père.
        Paul is a father.

(55.2) Paul n'est pas père.
       Paul is not a father.

This is borne out by the fact that the sentence in (54.2) can be correctly paraphrased as

(56) Paul n'est père de personne.
     Paul is a father of no one.

    The second argument of some relational nouns, when left implicit, can be construed exophorically. Such relational nouns include: *ami* (*friend*), *collègue* (*colleague*), *cousin* (*cousin*), *voisin* (*neighbour*), etc. (see Pupier, 1973: 76–78). Thus, the sentences in (57) can be paraphrasal equivalents.

(57.1) Paul est un ami.
       Paul is a friend.
(57.2) Paul est un ami à moi.
       Paul is a friend of mine.

This observation is borne out by the use of negation.

(58.1) Paul n'est pas un ami.
       Paul is not a friend.
(58.2) Paul n'est pas un ami à moi.
       Paul is not a friend of mine.

    Many binary relational nouns are ones whose second argument, when implicit, receives a reciprocal construal. This construal arises for many of the nouns just alluded to above. The reciprocal construal requires that the subject noun phrase be a plural one and that the second argument remain implicit.

(59.1) Paul et Alice sont amis.
       Paul and Alice are friends.
(59.2) Paul et Alice sont amis l'un de l'autre.
       Paul and Alice are friends of each other.


(60.1) Paul et Alice ne sont pas amis.
       Paul and Alice are not friends.
(60.2) Paul et Alice ne sont pas amis, l'un de l'autre.
       Paul and Alice are not friends of each other.

Before bringing this discussion of relational nouns to an end, I would like to point out one other fact about relational nouns whose second argument, when implicit, receives an existential construal. Above, I stated the well-known fact of French that the first argument of any binary relational verb appearing in a finite active form must be made explicit and it must be made explicit by the subject of the verb's clause. I also pointed out another well-known fact, namely that, when the verb appears in the passive voice, it is the second argument which must be made explicit by the subject of the clause. There is a remarkable parallel with relational nouns. When these nouns are NP complements to the verb, if the verb is the verb *être* (*to be*) the first argument must be made explicit and expressed by the verb's subject, and if the verb is the verb *avoir* (*to have*), the second argument must be made explicit and expressed by the verb's subject. In both cases, the implicit argument is construed existentially.

(61.1) Paul est père.
       Paul is a father.
(61.2) Paul a un père.
       Paul has a father.


(62.1) Paul n'est pas père.
       Paul is not a father.
(62.2) Paul n'a pas de père.
       Paul does not have a father.

# 4 Conclusion

We have surveyed binary relational words in French. They have come from all five major lexical classes: adjectives, adverbs, nouns, prepositions and verbs. In every class, we have found binary relational words which permit one of their arguments to remain implicit. Moreover, we have seen that when such arguments remain implicit, their construals fall within a limited range, essentially the range of endophoric and exophoric expressions as well as that of existentially quantified noun phrases.

What this shows is that arguments of words, even if implicit, are grammatically active, as it were. The foregoing says nothing about whether or not the implicit arguments are represented in the syntactic structure of the sentence. In particular, it says nothing about whether or not these arguments 'project' with phonetically null exophors, endophors or existentially quantified noun phrase. Indeed, the evidence is that they do not, but that is another paper.

## Acknowledgements

This paper has greatly benefitted from my numerous and lengthy discussions with Paul Pupier, who has also generously supplied some of the data. I also wish to thank Yves Roberge for readily providing me with the two papers he wrote with Sarah Cummins. Finally, I would like to thank David Nicolas for his comments and suggestions on the penultimate draft of this chapter. The final preparation of this chapter was supported by a grant (SSHRC 410-2010-1254) from the Canadian *Social Science and Humanities Research Council.*

# References

Anderson, S. and P. Kiparsky. (eds.). 1973. *A Festschrift for Morris Halle.* New York: Holt, Rinehart and Winston, Inc.

Auger, J., J. C. Clements, and B. Vance. (eds.). 2004. *Contemporary Approaches to Romance linguistics.* Amsterdam: John Benjamins.

Bach, K. 1994. Semantic slack: What is said and more. In S. L. Tsohatzidis, ed., *Foundations of Speech Act Theory: Philosophical and Linguistic Perspectives*, pp. 267–291. London: Routledge.

Cummins, S. and Y. Roberge. 2004. Null objects in French and English. In: Auger et al. (2004, pp. 121–138).

Cummins, S. and Y. Roberge. 2005. A modular account of null objects in French. *Syntax* 8(1):44–64.

Fillmore, C. 1986. Pragmatically controlled zero anaphora. *Proceedings of the Annual Meeting of the Berkeley Linguistics Society*, vol. 12, pp. 95–107. Berkeley, California: Berkeley Linguistics Society.

Fónagy, I. 1985. J'aime ? je connais ?: verbes transitifs à objet latent. *Revue romane* 20(1):3–35.

Gillon, B. 2004. Ambiguity, indeterminacy, deixis and vagueness : Evidence and theory. In S. Davis and B. Gillon, eds., *Semantics: A Reader*, pp. 157–187. Oxford: Oxford University Press.

Grevisse, M. 1964. *Le Bon Usage.* 8th edn., Revised, Gembloux, Belgium: Duculot.

Lajavaara, M. 2000. *Présence ou absence de l'objet. Limites du possible en français contemporain.* Helsinki: Academia Scientarum Fennica.

Pupier, P. 1973. Observations sur les prédicats converses. *Cahier de linguistique* (2):63–84.

Quine, W. 1960. *Word and Object.* Cambridge, MA: The MIT Press.

Rothemberg, M. 1974. *Les verbes à la fois transitifs et intransitifs en français contemporain.* The Hague, The Netherlands: Mouton.

# 7

## Mutual Manifestness and the Pragmatic Marker *Ne* in Mandarin Chinese

MARITA LJUNGQVIST

## 1 Introduction: Pragmatic Markers and Procedural Encoding

The study of pragmatic markers has for a long time attracted scholars within the field of pragmatics, in particular in the area of experimental pragmatics. Pragmatic markers are interesting for several reasons. Not only are they often perceived by speakers as having vague meanings that are hard to pin down in words but one marker also often seems to contribute in different ways to the explicit or implicit message that the speaker wants to convey depending on the context in which it occurs. The term 'pragmatic marker' is somewhat wider than that of 'discourse marker' and I support Andersen and Fretheim's (2000) arguments for a distinction between pragmatic markers and discourse markers on the basis of Fraser's (1996) definition of discourse markers as a subtype of pragmatic markers – more associated with relationships between a message and the foregoing discourse than with propositional attitude, for example. It will be shown that the object of study in the present chapter – the particle *ne* in Mandarin Chinese – can be used both as an attitudinal marker and as a discourse marker. Since the term 'pragmatic marker' encompasses both these functions, I find it to be the most appropriate one for the classification of *ne*. The term 'discourse marker' has, however, often been used in the literature as a universal term for this

*Making Semantics Pragmatic*
Ken Turner (ed.).
Current Research in the Semantics/Pragmatics Interface, Vol. 24.

group of linguistic entities, even if it has been noticed that it seems to consist of subgroups of different kinds. Zavala (2001: 1000–1001) writes:

> For example, discourse markers such as *and* and *or*, whose function is based on their meaning, often indicate semantic relationships between propositions. Thus, they can be considered cohesive devices which create underlying connections between utterances. On the other hand, markers such as *y'know* and *I mean* function in more social and expressive domains and show the speaker's judgment and attitude toward the proposition to be uttered and toward the interlocutor. In addition, there are other markers like *so, then,* and *well* which solve mechanical problems such as the initiating of discourse, turn taking and topic shifts, and interpersonal problems of conversational management such as face saving. Nevertheless, in spite of these separate functions, it must be said that most markers perform several simultaneous functions in discourse.

Pragmatic markers do not seem to encode lexical content but rather act as pointers or indicators for how to interpret conceptual representations. Blakemore (1987), Wilson and Sperber (1993) and other linguists influenced by Relevance Theory (Sperber and Wilson, 1995) such as Bezuidenhout (2004); Carston (1999, 2002); Moeschler et al. (1998); Saussure (2003) and Wharton (2003), to mention just a few, have contributed to the development of the dichotomic terms conceptual and procedural semantics in order to distinguish between those linguistic items that have a lexically encoded meaning and those that contain instructions for carrying out pragmatic inferences. According to Bezuidenhout (2004: 27–28), the role of procedural entities is

> to guide an interaction between something that belongs to the language system (lexical concepts) and something that lies outside that system (encyclopedic and other non-linguistic knowledge).

Procedural content is a coded element that points the addressee to a certain direction in his/her interpretational process. It is a set of instructions that constrain the inferential processes involved in identifying the explicatures – developments of conceptual representations – or implicatures – intended contextual assumptions or implications – of an utterance. Discourse connectives such as *so* and *after all* in English exercise constraints on implicatures (as shown by, among others, Blakemore, 1987). Other discourse connectives, such as indexicals and tense markers, exercise constraints on explicatures (see, for example, papers in Moeschler et al., 1998 and Saussure, 2003). Illocutionary particles and attitudinal particles encode constraints on higher-level explicatures (Carston, 1999; Andersen and Fretheim, 2000) – embeddings of propositional forms under a higher-level description such as descriptions of propositional attitude. A procedural expression does not encode a concept that can be translated. According to the relevance-theoretic description of the comprehension process, the addressee will follow the path of least effort in computing the contextual effects of an utterance. Procedural expressions such as pragmatic markers constrain or direct the inferential phase of comprehension and thus save the hearer effort when interpreting an utterance. Syntactical considerations, contextual assumptions, recently processed information, world knowledge, etc. will naturally also play a part in deriving these pragmatic inferences. Pragmatic markers act as constraining devices on different levels of utterance meaning, contributing to the derivation of explicatures, higher-level explicatures or implicatures. Some markers act on more than one of these levels. As I will show, the pragmatic marker *ne* in Mandarin Chinese is a case in point.

In this chapter, I will examine the Mandarin particle *ne* in Mandarin Chinese using a relevance-theoretic framework. I will argue that *ne* encodes a procedure that instructs the addressee to search for mutually manifest assumptions that support either the propositional content of the utterance – thereby reminding her of something that she should already know – or a topic shift in the form of a declarative or a question. Basing my discussion on primarily empirical data from the CALLHOME Mandarin Chinese speech corpus,[1] I will demonstrate that *ne* is a procedural marker of mutual manifestness that constrains the derivation of higher-level explicatures and implicatures.

## 2   *Ne*: A Proposal for a Relevance-Theoretic Account

### 2.1   Background

What uses of *ne* does a thorough analysis have to account for? Earlier studies suggest that *ne* has a semantic content, that it communicates a conceptual structure. Some scholars have tried to give a comprehensive list of all the functions of *ne* (Chao, 1968; Chu, 1984). Chu (1984, 1985), for example, lists four functions of *ne:* it signals that there is some understanding between addresser and addressee, a relation with the previous part of the conversation, puzzlement and politeness. He does

---

[1]The Linguistic Data Consortium CALLHOME Mandarin Chinese speech corpus (Canavan and Zipperlen, 1996) consists of 120 telephone conversations between Mandarin Chinese speakers and transcripts (Wheatley, 1996) covering between 5 and 10 minutes of these conversations.

not say anything about how *ne* communicates these conceptual structures, which is something that I will return to later in this chapter. Others have attempted to unify all uses of *ne* under one core meaning or function such as "unexpectedness" (Shifu, 1985) "reminding" (Shao, 1989) or "highlighting or evaluating certain portions of background information in the discourse and bringing them to the attention of the hearer in the speaker/hearer world" (King, 1986). Shi and Zhang (1995) argue that *ne* acts as a factive marker. According to Li and Thompson (1981: 300) *ne* has

> the semantic function of pointing out to the hearer that the information conveyed by the sentence is the speaker's response to some claim, expectation, or belief on the part of the hearer.

It should also be mentioned here that some linguists have discussed whether or not *ne* is a question particle (Hu, 1988; Shao, 1989; Shi and Zhang, 1995; Hsieh, 2001 – all of which agree that it is not).
Consider (1)-(5):

(1)
Ta    haishi yi   ge   xiao  haizi ne
s/he  still  one CL$^2$ small child NE
(Li and Thompson, 1981: 304)
'S/He's still a child, you know'


(2)
Waibian  xia  zhe  Xue    ne
Outside  fall PM   Snow   NE
'(But) it is still snowing outside'

---

$^2$List of abbreviations:

| | |
|---|---|
| CL | Classifier |
| DE | 1) Nominalising/genitive/associative marker *de* |
| | 2) Adverbialising marker *de* |
| | 3) Complex stative construction marker *de*, referring either to manner or extent |
| NEG | Negation markers *bu* or *mei* |
| NEG IMP | Imperative negation marker *bie* |
| NE | Sentence-final marker *ne* |
| PM | Other pragmatic marker |

(3)

| Jieguo | ne, | Wo | jiu | kaoshang | Beijing | Daxue | le |
|--------|-----|----|----|----------|---------|-------|-----|
| result | NE | I | then | take exam-arrive | Beijing | University | PM |

'And as a result, I passed the entrance examination for Beijing University'

(4)

| Ta | yao | Chi | shenme | ne? |
|----|-----|-----|--------|-----|
| s/he | want | Eat | what | NE |

(Li and Thompson, 1981: 305)

'In that case, what does s/he want to eat?'

(5)

| Wo | de | bi | ne? |
|----|----|----|----|
| I | DE | pen | NE |

'Where is that pen of mine, now?'

In (1) and (2), *ne* indicates that there is a contradiction between something which the hearer or the speaker (or someone else) thinks or expects and reality (at least in the speaker's view). In (3), *ne* is used to set off topic from comment. The topic is a subtopic of the overall topic which in this case may be the process involved in getting into the university. (4) and (5) are questions, both bring up subtopics related to the previous context. Questions with *ne* are not used to initiate discourse, claim Li and Thompson (1981). This type of question occurs when there is a mutually manifest context to which the content of the question can be connected. For example, (4) can occur in a setting where the speaker has already asked what other persons want to eat: 'What about you, then, what do you want?', or where the addressee has turned down earlier offers and the speaker is getting frustrated: 'Then (if you don't want this), what do you want?' (5) can occur in a context where perhaps the speaker is asked to sign something, etc. The question concerns an expected subtopic of this context.

## 2.2  *Ne* as a Procedural Marker

According to the proposal that I will put forward here, *ne* contributes to utterance meaning by signalling mutual manifestness of 1) the assumptions communicated by the propositional content or 2) the relevance of a (sub)topic shift/resumption. In the first case, *ne* constrains the higher-level explicatures of the utterance, in the second, it constrains the implicature of the utterance. *Ne* therefore functions as a combined attitudinal and discourse marker. As I will show, these two functions can both be associated with the encoded procedural content of *ne*, which instructs the hearer to search for mutually manifest contextual assumptions that will either support the information expressed in the utterance or justify a resumption of an earlier topic or a topic shift. *Ne* thus acts as a marker of mutual manifestness. An utterance that contains *ne* gives a reminder to the hearer, by strengthening assumptions contained in some of the larger contexts accessible to the participants. *Ne* helps the hearer to identify the propositional attitude of the speaker or to recover contextual effects intended by the speaker to a smaller processing cost than would otherwise be needed.

When *ne* occurs at the end of a declarative sentence or a rhetorical question, it will normally be interpreted as indicating the speaker's attitude towards the proposition expressed. *Ne* reminds the addressee that the information expressed should be manifest to her or someone else (including the speaker), or at least she could have foreseen it, given the mutual cognitive environment. It eliminates assumptions that are implicated by the prior context or that the speaker presumes that the addressee is holding. In these cases, the procedural content of *ne* constrains the higher-level explicatures of an utterance. In its attitudinal use, *ne* is quite similar to the German particle *ja* (Blass, 2000) which can be used both to confirm and eliminate existing assumptions. When, on the other hand, the marker occurs at the end of a question (both full questions and truncated) or after a topic clause, it will normally act as a discourse marker, indicating a (sub)topic shift or the resumption of an earlier topic. Here *ne* constrains the implicatures of an utterance. It instructs the hearer to search for an appropriate mutual background in which to process the utterance that contains it and identify a shift or resumption of (sub)topic that can be related to that background, thereby justifying the shift or resumption. Green (2000: 2) says this about discourse markers in English:

> there are structural discourse markers like the sentence-initial particles *Now, OK, And, But,* which speakers use to indicate a structural boundary, and a hint of how what follows relates to what went before.

Before hearing the utterance with *ne*, the hearer/speaker may have had other expectations and assumptions about either the state of the world or on what would be the next step in the conversation but by this utterance some other assumption should be mutually manifest and the former assumption be eliminated.

What is strengthened as mutually manifest may thus be the information expressed by the propositional content of the utterance (it should be manifest to you – considering our mutual cognitive environment – that you have to eliminate your present assumption about the state of the world) or a turn in the discourse (it should be manifest to you – considering our mutual cognitive environment – that this is a natural topic shift in the conversation).

My proposal also supports King's (1986) suggestion that *ne* indicates a slightly different pragmatic focus depending on its syntactic position. He claims that in the "pause marking position" (King, 1986: 28) – he does not mention questions here – the textual function of *ne* is brought into focus while when it occurs in utterance-final position emphasis is more on the interactional and attitudinal aspects of *ne*. While Chu (1985:73) says that question NP+*ne*? differs from topic NP+*ne* in that the former has a rising intonation, Alleton (1981) argues that questions that consist of NP+*ne* and topic phrases followed by *ne* often have similar intonation. Questions may have a higher intonational level, but it is not obligatory. Shao (1989), too, has observed this phenomenon – although he points out that there seems to exist some disagreement among native speakers when asked whether or not question NP+*ne*? and topic NP+*ne* both can have a non-rising intonation.

The definition of *ne* as a marker of mutual manifestness also explains why it is often used in truncated questions. In questions, *ne* usually functions at the discourse level, indicating that the turn in the discourse should not be unexpected to the hearer (and thus relates to their shared cognitive environment). The fact that truncated questions are often used with *ne* is further evidence that these questions presuppose that the speaker and hearer have a mutual cognitive environment, i.e. the speaker expects the hearer to be able to "fill in the blanks."

## 2.3   An Analysis of Chu's Four Functions of *Ne*

Let's take a look at what this means for Chu's (1984, 1985) account and the four functions he proposes for *ne*. First, Chu (1984: 88) claims that *ne* presupposes that

> there is some previous common understanding, implicit or explicit, between the speaker and the hearer, as in Mäma ne? 'Where's mother?' uttered by a child upon coming home and unexpectedly not finding Mother there [footnote excluded]. The child also supposes that the hearer knows what is expected. A question like

Shü ne? 'Where's the book?' or Xìn ne? 'Where's the letter?' on the same occasion is not appropriate because the speaker and the hearer don't share a common understanding.

At first sight, this seems to contradict my definition of *ne* as a marker that strengthens mutual manifestness, since, if the hearer already knows what is expected, what would be the use of reminding her? In fact, the child's question may have been unexpected to the hearer but the reason for asking it will still, in one way or the other, be considered by the **speaker** as mutually manifest. In other words *ne* only claims that the information expressed by the utterance or the (sub)topic shift or resumption is not far-fetched and that it should in fact be compatible with all that the speaker knows and expects.

Second, Chu (1984: 88) argues that *ne* indicates that "[t]his utterance is related to what has been going on: i.e., what has been going on in the conversation the speaker and the hearer have been engaged in." This function of *ne* is compatible with my definition of *ne* as a marker strengthening mutual manifestness on two levels (higher-level explicatures and implicatures). In these cases, as in the previous example, *ne* strengthens the mutual manifestness of what according to the speaker should be an expected turn in the discourse.

Third, sometimes *ne* seems to hint that the speaker is puzzled by the information expressed, as in

(6)
Ta zhe ge da bendan hai xiang dang zongtong ne.
he this CL big fool still want be president NE
(Chu, 1984: 89)
'(Imagine) a stupid fool like him wants to be the president.'

What is interpreted as "puzzlement" on the part of the speaker is explained if *ne* is redefined as a marker that strengthens mutually manifest assumptions. These assumptions may not always be present prior to the utterance but can be retrieved through perception or deduction. Compare with the use of *ja* in Blass' (2000: 43) example:

reading a letter, a person may say to someone else:

Ich hab ja gewonnen!
I have as-it-is-manifest won!
'What a surprise, I have won!'

That the speaker had won became manifest to her by reading the letter; it became manifest to the hearer also through the speaker's behaviour.

The reason for using *ne* in (6) is simply that the speaker wants to call the hearer's attention to some assumption that should be mutually manifest – that it is absurd that a fool like him wants to be a president – even if it in fact the propositional content is unexpected information for both the hearer and the speaker.

Finally, according to Chu's list, *ne* "involves politeness on the part of the speaker, especially in questions." Alleton (1981) also describes *ne* as a particle without which certain questions may sound rude and more appropriate in situations such as legal interrogations. *Ne* seems to be a weaker indicator of mutual manifestness than for example the German particle *ja* (which sometimes rather seems to correspond to a stronger marker of mutual manifestness in Chinese, *ma*). The fact that it is used to mark a turn in the conversation makes it more polite to use *ne* than not use it, since it signals that the speaker is helping the hearer to follow the conversation.

## 3   Data and Discussion

### 3.1   *Ne* Indicating Speaker's Attitude

First, we will take a look at some examples of declaratives and rhetorical questions, in which *ne* is normally used to express the speaker's attitude towards the information in the utterance (indicating that the information expressed should already be manifest to the hearer or someone else).

(7)

| A: Dui, | | I | na | ge | ai | na | ge | zenmeyang? Na | ge |
| | | | see, | | | | | | |
| | right | I | that | CL | PM | that | CL | how about | that CL |
| | | | see | | | | | | |
| | Lin | Xing | gen na | ge | xiao | hai | hai | hao o? | |
| | Lin | Xing | and that | CL | little | child | still | good PM | |
| B: Hai | keyi | | | | | | | | |
| still | OK | | | | | | | | |
| A: Hai | keyi | | | | | | | | |
| still | OK | | | | | | | | |
| A: Na | ge | ... zenmeyang? | Ni | mama | ting | hao | o? | | |
| that | CL | ... how about | you | mother | very | good | PM | | |
| B: Wo | mama | hai mei | guolai | ne | | | | | |
| I | Mother | still NEG | come- | NE | | | | | |
| | | | over | | | | | | |

(Wheatley, 1996, ma_0029: 329.42 334.00 - 341.31 341.77)

A:    'Right, I see, that what's-her-name – how is she? That Lin Xing and the little baby, are they still fine?'

B:    'They're alright'
A:    'They're alright'
A:    'That ... how is she? Your mother is very good, right?'
B:    '(But) my mother hasn't come over yet'[3]

In (7), *ne* is used to indicate that the information in the answer 'My mother has not come over yet' should be manifest to A. This contrasts with A's previous questions about B's mother: A should know that B's mother hasn't come over, therefore B cannot be expected to know whether his mother's health is very good or not. Alternatively, A's question implicates that he thinks that B's mother is with B, but B's answer with *ne* contradicts that assumption and is marked by *ne* to remind A that he should know that she is not.

(8)

| A: | Xianzai | ni | zhen | Guai | Beibei. | Ayi | xiang, | ai | dou | |
|---|---|---|---|---|---|---|---|---|---|---|
| | now | you | really | Cute | Beibei | aunt | miss | PM | all | |
| | xiang | ni | ne | Beibei. | Zhen | guai | hao | wawa | shi | ma? |
| | miss | you | NE | Beibei | really | cute | good | doll | be | PM |

...

| B: | Ni | shuo | wo | Zai zhe | ((hen)) | kuaile | de, | wo hai | | hui |
|---|---|---|---|---|---|---|---|---|---|---|
| | you | say | I | At here | ((very)) | happy | DE | I also | | know |
| | shuo | yingyu | ne | | | | | | | |
| | speak | English | NE | | | | | | | |

(Wheatley, 1996, ma_0667: 242.40 250.32 - 253.15 256.03)

A:    'You're really cute now Beibei. Aunt misses you, oh misses you so much, Beibei. You're a cute little doll, aren't you?'
B:    'Say: I'm very happy here, I can even speak English (you know)'

(8) is taken from a conversation between three persons, a small child, the child's aunt (A) and the child's mother (B). Two *ne* are used in this passage, one by A and one by B. In the first passage, A is talking emphatically to the child, and says 'Aunt misses you very much'. Here, *ne* is used to indicate that the hearer should already know this information. In the second utterance with *ne*, by the child's mother B, it is used in the same way to express that the information expressed should be mutually manifest. B is urging the child to speak, telling her what to say: 'Say: I am very happy here, I can even speak English'. Also here, *ne* is indicating that the fact that the child can speak English is something that should be manifest to the addressee, if not before, then by the assumptions needed to understand why the speaker is very happy there.

---

[3]The translations of the data found in the CALLHOME transcripts are mine.

(9)

| Mei | guanxi, | bu | yong | zhaoji, | wo | zai | zher | ne |
|-----|---------|-----|------|---------|-----|-----|------|-----|
| NEG | matter | NEG | use | rush | I | at | here | NE |

(Wheatley, 1996, ma_0721: 138.84 141.90)

'It doesn't matter, there's no need to hurry, I'm here, right?'

The setting for (9) is one in which the speaker has called her grandparents and her grandma is trying to wake up her grandfather. The speaker uses *ne* here to calm down her grandmother. *Ne* marks the mutual manifestness of the fact that the speaker is there (and is not going anywhere), so her grandmother needn't hurry.

Sometimes, the presence of *ne* can indicate a slight frustration or impatience, which is natural considering it is used to express that some information or some turn in the conversation should be mutually manifest or expected. In (10), the speaker expresses frustration, here *ne* indicates that the information 'I want to stay at home less and less' should be manifest to the hearer:

(10)

| Zhen | shi | de, | women | jia | xianzai | yi | ge | bi | yi | ge |
|------|-----|-----|-------|-----|---------|-----|-----|----------------|-----|-----|
| really | be | DE | we | family | now | one | CL | compare-to | one | CL |

| piqi | da, | wo | yue lai yue | bu | yuan | zai | jiali | dai | zhe | ne. |
|------|-----|-----|-------------|-----|------|-----|-------|-----|-----|-----|
| temper | big | I | more-and-more | NEG | want | at | home-in | stay | PM | NE |

(Wheatley, 1996, ma_0691: 460.24 464.99)

'Really, in our family now one's temper is worse than the other's, I feel more and more that I don't want to stay here.'

Finally, *ne* is often used in rhetorical questions, in which its function of marking mutual manifestness is perhaps even more obvious. Rhetorical questions are not requests for information but contain information that the addressee is expected to know already. *Ne* instructs the addressee to search for mutually manifest assumptions already included in his/her memory.

(11)

| Bu | he | shui | Zenme | xing | ne? |
|-----|------|-------|-------|------|-----|
| NEG | drink | water | How | ok | NE |

(Wheatley, 1996, ma_1728: 201.80 203.76)

'How can it be good not to drink water? (implying: "of course it's not good")'

## 3.2   *Ne* Indicating (Sub)Topic Shift or Resumption

We turn now to topic phrases and requests for information, where it seems that *ne* is normally used on a discourse level, that is, to indicate a shift to another topic or subtopic or a resumption of a previous topic or subtopic.

(12)

| A: | Wo | tiantian | jiu | shi | shangwu | shangban, | jiu | shi | genzhe |
| | I | everyday | just | be | morning | work | just | be | follow |
| | shi | genzhe | zhuren | a | yiqi | kan | bingren, | | |
| | be | follow | director | PM | together | look-at | patient | | |
| | xiawu | ne,... | | | | | | | |
| | afternoon | NE | | | | | | | |
| B: | A | wo | juede | ting | hao | de, | zhe | bi | dang |
| | PM | I | think | very | good | DE | this | compare-to | work-as |
| | laoshi | hao | duo | le, | ni | xue | yi | dian | juti | de |
| | teacher | good | much | PM | you | study | a | little | concrete | DE |
| | jishu | dao | na | dou | xing | a. | | | |
| | skill | to | where | all | ok | PM | | | |

(Wheatley, 1996, ma_0667: 203.05 207.59 - 206.74 212.06)

A:   'I work every morning, I just see the patients together with the director. As to the afternoon ...'

B:.   'I think that's really good, this is much better than working as a teacher, you learn some real skills, that's good everywhere.'

In (12) A first talks about her duties in the morning and then shifts to talk about her afternoon duties (but is interrupted by B). The subtopic shift is signalled by *ne*.

(13)

| Zheiyang | suoyi | wo | jiu | juede | Xianggang | bijiao | anquan, | Xianggang |
| this way | therefore | I | just | think | Hong Kong | rather | safe | Hong Kong |
| jiu | keyi | suibian | zai | jieshang | zou. | Zhongguo | ne,... | |
| then | can | casually | at | street | walk | China | NE | |

(Wheatley, 1996, ma_0669: 505.61 511.77)

'So I just think that Hong Kong is quite safe, In Hong Kong you can walk the streets carelessly. In China, on the other hand ...'

In (13), the speaker talks about the situation in Hong Kong, that it is safe to walk on the streets there. Then, she shifts to talk about mainland China: 'In China, on the other hand ...' (also here the speaker is interrupted).

(14)

A: Ai,      na   ge   shei  ne,  A Ling sheng     de  shi ge
   PM      that CL   who  NE   A Ling give-birth DE  is  CL
   shenme?
   what

B: O,      ni   gen  ta   shuo ba
   PM      you  with her  talk PM

(Wheatley, 1996, ma_0669: 598.27 600.58 - 601.69 602.80)

A: 'Hey, now that what's-her-name, A Ling, what did she give birth to [a boy or a girl]?'

B: 'Oh, why don't you talk to her ... '

In (14), A brings up a new topic, a person that A and B both know: '(Now) how about what's-her name, A Ling ... '

The background that the speaker relies on when using *ne*, that is, the background that helps him building up a relevant mutual cognitive environment, can consist of previously implicated assumptions.

(15)

A: Ni    Hai   hui  bu    hui      jiang  Chengduhua?
   you   Still can  NEG   can      speak  Chengdu
                                          dialect?

B: Hui
   can

A: Hui   ma?
   know  PM

B: Ng
   PM

A: Ni    Na    ni   yihou zai      nali   shangxue    ne?
   you   So    you  after at       where  go-to-school NE

B: Bu    zhidao, ren  de    anpai
   NEG   Know   people DE   arrangement

(Wheatley, 1996, ma_0717: 284.25 285.66 - 292.28 294.13)

A: 'Can you still speak Chengdu dialect?'

B: 'Yes'

A: 'Can you?'

B: 'U-huh'

A: 'You,... so where will you go to school after this?'

B: 'Don't know, it's their decision.'

In (15), A first asks B if she still can speak Chengdu dialect, which B confirms. Then A continues by asking A where she will go to school later. A indicates, by using *ne*, that the information in this utterance is somehow related to what is implicated by her first question – perhaps that she wants to know whether or not B has lost contact with her roots, if she has become "anglicized" and so forth and thus that this change of topic should come as no surprise to B, that the background to this question should be mutually manifest to both of them.

When the question is about a hypothetical situation, the close relationship between NP+*ne* questions and NP+*ne* topics is apparent:

(16)

| Ta | yao | bu | tongyi | ne? |
|----|-----|-----|--------|-----|
| he | if | NEG | agree | NE |

(Lu, 1993:25)

(And) what if he doesn't agree?[4]

In (16), a comment clause is excluded, for example: ... *zenme ban?* ' ... then what should we do?' The addressee is expected to fill in the comment in her answer: 'Then we should ... '.

## 4    Counterexamples or Not?

It has been claimed (see for example Lu, 2004) that the marker *ne* can be used to express continuative aspect, as in the following passage:

(17)

| A: | Ai, | dan | ta | jiu | benlai, | jihua | jiu | shi | dao | zher | lai | mai | xiangzi |
|----|-----|-----|-----|-----|---------|-------|-----|-----|-----|------|-----|-----|---------|
|    | PM | but | he | just | first | plan | just | be | to | here | come | buy | trunk |
| B: | Zen, | zenme, | xianzai | hai | mei | mai | zhe | a? | | | | | |
|    | how | how | now | still | NEG | buy | PM | PM | | | | | |
| A: | A, | dao | xianzai | hai | mei | huilai | a, | wo | benlai, | wo | benlai | | |
|    | MP | to | now | still | NEG | come-back | PM | I | originally | I | originally | | |
|    | gen | ta | shuohao, | ni | shi'er | dian | yiqian | huilai, | xianzai | shi'er | | | |
|    | with | he | say-good | you | twelve | CL | before | come-back | now | twelve | | | |
|    | dian | yi | ke | le, | hai | mei | huilai | ne | | | | | |
|    | CL | one | quarter | PM | still | NEG | come-back | NE | | | | | |

(Wheatley, 1996, ma_0716: 200.80 204.10 - 207.43 213.46)

A: 'Hey, but his first plan was to come here and buy a trunk'

B: How, how come he still hasn't bought one?'

A: 'Oh, he hasn't come back yet, from the start, from the start I told him: you come back before twelve. Now it's a quarter past but (as you can see) he hasn't come back yet.'

It is the adverb *hai* 'still' that indicates that the situation 'she has not come home' still holds at the reference time, not *ne*. *Ne* marks that

---

[4]My translation.

this information should not come as a surprise to the hearer, that – even if it may be unexpected, considering the speaker has told him to be back by twelve – it should be manifest to both speaker and hearer (considering their cognitive environment, in this case the prior context) that he has not done so. Shi and Zhang (1995) show that in utterances with *ne* that express a continuative situation, there is always some other component that takes on the function of signalling continuative aspect such as the adverb (*zheng*)*zai* or/and the durative aspect marker *zhe*. *Ne* on its own does not express continuative aspect.

In some Chinese dialects, *ne* also occurs – often together with the aspect marker *zhe* – after stative verbs or verb phrases, emphasising a certain fact:

(18)  Tian   hei    zhe   ne!
      sky    black  PM    NE
      'The sky is really dark!'

Even examples such as (18), however, can be explained by the procedural account of *ne* as a marker indicating mutual manifestness presented here. In (18) the expectations being contradicted are of a more universal character – "it is unexpectedly dark outside – but it should be mutually manifest that it is."

## 5  Concluding Remarks

I have argued that the marker *ne* in Mandarin Chinese is a procedural marker indicating mutual manifestness. A procedural marker does not contain a lexical content but an instruction to the addressee on how to process conceptual representations, thereby constraining the recovery of explicitly or implicitly communicated assumptions. *Ne* constrains the addressee's recovery of either the speaker's attitudes towards the propositional content of the utterance or of intended contextual effects. *Ne* saves the addressee some of the effort involved in trying to figure out the speaker's attitude towards the utterance or what kind of process to perform in order to derive the contextual implications of the explicitly communicated proposition. In particular in declaratives and rhetorical questions, *ne* reminds the addressee of the mutual manifestness of the communicated content – it should not come as a surprise to her. In requests for information and after topic phrases, *ne* reminds the addressee of the mutual manifestness of a background in which this is a relevant question or (sub)topic. However, *ne* is not a strong marker of mutual manifestness and is therefore often perceived as indicating politeness. By weakly reminding the addressee of mutual manifestness *ne* helps her to follow the conversation and to draw intended conclusions. This may explain why it is often used to soften interrogatives.

# References

Alleton, V. 1981. Final particles and expressions of modality in modern Chinese. *Journal of Chinese Linguistics* 9:91–115.

Andersen, G. and T. Fretheim. 2000. Introduction. In G. Andersen and T. Fretheim, eds., *Pragmatic Markers and Propositional Attitude*, pp. 1–16. Amsterdam: John Benjamins Publishing Co.

Bezuidenhout, A. 2004. Procedural meaning and the semantics/pragmatics interface. In C. Bianchi, ed., *The Semantics/Pragmatics Distinction*, pp. 101–131. Stanford: CSLI Publications.

Blakemore, D. 1987. *Semantic Constraints on Relevance*. Oxford: Blackwell.

Blass, R. 2000. Particles, propositional attitude and mutual manifestness. In G. Andersen and T. Fretheim, eds., *Pragmatic Markers and Propositional Attitude*, pp. 39–52. Amsterdam: John Benjamins Publishing Co.

Canavan, C. and G. Zipperlen. 1996. *CALLHOME Mandarin Chinese Speech* LDC96S34. CD-ROM. Linguistic Data Consortium, Philadelphia.

Carston, R. 1999. The Semantics/Pragmatics Distinction: A View from Relevance Theory. *UCL Working Papers in Linguistics*, vol. 10, pp. 53–80. London: University College London.

Carston, R. 2002. *Thoughts and Utterances*. Oxford: Blackwell.

Chao, Y-R. 1968. *A Grammar of Spoken Chinese*. Berkeley: University of California Press.

Chu, C. C. 1984. Beef it up with *ne*. *Journal of the Chinese Language Teachers' Association* 19(3):87–91.

Chu, C. C. 1985. How would you like your *ne* cooked? *Journal of the Chinese Language Teachers' Association* 20(3):71–78.

Fraser, B. 1996. Pragmatic markers. *Pragmatics* 6:167–190.

Green, G. 2000. *Discourse Particles in NLP* [online]. Transcript of talk presented at Ohio State University November. Available from: http://www.linguistics.uiuc.edu/g-green/discours.pdf [Accessed 14 February 2006].

Hsieh, M.-L. 2001. *Form and Meaning: Negation and Questions in Chinese*. Ph.D. thesis, University of Southern California, Los Angeles.

Hu, M-Y. 1988. Yuqi zhuci de yuqi yiyi. *Hanyu Xuexi* 6:5–8.

King, B. 1986. *Ne* – A discourse approach. *Journal of Chinese Language Teachers' Association* 21(1):21–46.

Li, C. N. and S. A. Thompson. 1981. *Mandarin Chinese: A Functional Reference Grammar*. Berkeley: University of California Press.

Lu, S-X. 2004. *Xiandai hanyu babai ci.* 3rd edn. Beijing: Shangwu Yinshuguan.

Lu, J-M. 1993. *Lu Jianming zixuanji.* Zhengzhou: Daxiang chubanshe.

Moeschler, J., J. Jayez, M. Kozlowska, J.-M. Luscher, L. de Saussure and B. Sthioul. 1998. *Le temps des événements. Pragmatique de la référence temporelle.* Paris: Kimé.

Saussure, L. de 2003. *Temps et pertinence. Éléments de pragmatique cognitive du temps.* Bruxelles: De Boeck & Larcier.

Shao, J-M. 1989. Yuqici "ne" zai yiwenju zhong de zuoyong. *Zhongguo Yuwen* 3:170–175.

Shi, Y-Z. and P. Zhang. 1995. "Ne" de yufa yiyi ji yu yiwen daici gongxian de tiaojian. *Journal of the Chinese Language Teachers' Association* 30(2):71–83.

Shifu, 1985. We're still cooking *ne* ne! *Journal of Chinese Language Teachers' Association* 20(1):95–97.

Sperber, D. and D. Wilson. 1995. *Relevance: Communication and Cognition.* 2nd edn. Cambridge: Harvard University Press.

Wharton, T. 2003. Interjections, language and the 'showing-saying' continuum. *Pragmatics & Cognition* 11:39–91.

Wheatley, B. 1996. *CALLHOME Mandarin Chinese Transcripts* LDC96T16. Philadelphia: Linguistic Data Consortium.

Wilson, D. and D. Sperber. 1993. Linguistic form and relevance. *Lingua* 90:1–25.

Zavala, V. 2001. Borrowing evidential functions from Quechua: The role of *pues* as a discourse marker in Andean Spanish. *Journal of Pragmatics* 33:999–1023.

# 8

# The Use-Theory of Meaning and the Rules of Our Language Games

JAROSLAV PEREGRIN

While most theoreticians of meaning in the first half of the twentieth century subscribed to a representational theory (viewing meanings as entities *stood for* by the expressions), the second half of the century was marked by the rise of various versions of use-theories of meaning. The roots of this 'pragmatist turn' are detectable in the writings of the later Wittgenstein, the Oxford speech act theorists (Austin, Grice), and the American neopragmatists (Quine, Sellars).

Though it is now rather popular (and sometimes even fashionable) to invoke the use-theory of meaning, it is by far not so popular to inquire what such a theory really is. In this chapter we try to give at least a part of the answer, whereby we find out that the usual conception of such a theory is unsatisfactory. We propose that for an improvement we must, together with Wittgenstein and Sellars, conceive language as a (tool of a) *rule-based activity*, which enables us to replace the concept of *disposition*, usually constituting the backbone of the use-theory, by the concept of *propriety*. The resulting normative version of the use-theory then becomes the investigation of the rules which expressions acquire *vis-à-vis* the rules of the relevant language games – especially of the rules of inference.

## 1   What is (and What is Not) a Use-Theory of Meaning

According to a use-theory of meaning, the meaning of an expression is a matter of the way this expression is put to use by its competent users.

*Making Semantics Pragmatic*
Ken Turner (ed.).
Current Research in the Semantics/Pragmatics Interface, Vol. 24.

In order to understand the nature of such a theory, based on the assumption that

(*)   *the meaning of an* expression *is the way in which the* expression *is employed by the speakers of the relevant community,*

we must distinguish this claim from the claim that

(**)  *any meaning an* expression (i.e., a *sound- or inscription-type*) *has, it has in force of the fact that it is treated in a certain way by the speakers of the relevant community.*

The latter claim is a simple platitude; there is hardly anyone today who would want to defend the contrary: i.e., the claim that meanings are natural properties of expressions not conferred on them by people.[1] However, it is easy to mistake (**) for (*), as it may seem that rendering the two claims identical requires only a broad enough construal of the term "use."

In fact, there are *two* steps which we must make to get from (**) to (*). We need to accept that

(i)  the relevant kind of *treatment* is *use*;

and that

(ii)  if an expression's meaning something is the result of its being used in a certain way, then its meaning is the very use.

What reasons are there to make these steps?

The issue (i) is admittedly largely a terminological one. However, it turns out that it is useful to differentiate between treating something, as it were, *in one's mind*, and treating it *in the outer world*. The term *use* is then plausibly reserved for the *latter* kind of treatment (we may use the term *conceiving of* for the former one). In this way we can contrapose use-theories of meaning to various kinds of semiotic and representational theories which see meaningfulness as a matter of being taken to stand for something else.

---

[1] In his dialogue *Cratylus*, which may be considered as the fountainhead of all philosophy of language, Plato considered two possibilities: either words are *natural* signs of things (and hence each thing has a correct name) or they are *purely conventional* (and hence there are no correct or incorrect names). Since Plato's time, the latter option has prevailed and is now considered the only viable one: linguistic signs are, in de Saussure's (1931) terms, wholly *arbitrary*.

Why should we see meaning as a matter of usage rather than of conception? The first thing is that conception is a private, subjective matter (at least until it becomes manifested by behavior), whereas meaning is essentially intersubjective. Indeed the *point* of meaning is that it can be shared by many: that new people can always enter the realm of a language, learning the meanings of its words and then participating in the language games staged by its means. As Quine (1969: 28) stressed, "each of us, as he learns his language, is a student of his neighbor's behavior" and "the learner has no data to work with, but the overt behavior of other speakers."

But would it not be enough to require that meaning must be *manifested in* use, rather than it being *a matter of* use? The argument against this is that once we have the manifestation, the manifested content of mind becomes, from the viewpoint of language, an 'idle wheel', whose presence or absence is not truly relevant. This is the point of the famous case of the "beetle in the box" of Wittgenstein (1953: §293):[2]

> Angenommen, es hätte Jeder eine Schachtel, darin wäre etwas, was wir "Käfer" nennen. Niemand kann je in die Schachtel des Andern schaun; und Jeder sagt, er wisse nur vom Anblick seines Käfers, was ein Käfer ist. – Da könnte es ja sein, daß Jeder ein anderes Ding in seiner Schachtel hätte. Ja, man könnte sich vorstellen, daß sich ein solches Ding fortwährend veränderte. – Aber wenn nun das Wort "Käfer" dieser Leute doch einen Gebrauch hätte? – So wäre er nicht der der Bezeichnung eines Dings. Das Ding in der Schachtel gehört überhaupt nicht zum Sprachspiel; auch nicht einmal als ein Etwas: denn die Schachtel könnte auch leer sein. – Nein, durch dieses Ding in der Schachtel kann 'gekürzt werden'; es hebt sich weg, was immer es ist.

Note that this is not to indicate that linguistic communication cannot be accompanied by various kinds of mental activities, nor that it is not typically so accompanied, nor that the study of the minds of language users is uninteresting or futile. It is to say that in so far as language and meaning is something essentially intersubjective, the contents of minds of speakers cannot be its *components*.

---

[2]"Suppose everyone had a box with something in it: we call it a 'beetle'. No one can look into anyone else's box, and everyone says he knows what a beetle is only by looking at his beetle. – Here it would be quite possible for everyone to have something different in his box. One might even imagine such a thing constantly changing. – But suppose the word 'beetle' had a use in these people's language? – If so it would not be used as the name of a thing. The thing in the box has no place in the language-game at all; not even as a something: for the box might even be empty. – No, one can 'divide through' by the thing in the box; it cancels out, whatever it is."

Quine (ibid.: 29) comes to a similar conclusion: "There are no meanings, nor likenesses or distinctions in meaning beyond what are implicit in people's dispositions to overt behavior." However, this formulation reveals a snag in this kind of answer: the concept of *disposition*. A disposition is a property the nature of which is more or less unclear and which thus must be characterized in terms of the potential behavior of the entity in question in some special situations (thus, e.g., to say that sugar is soluble in water is to say that in the circumstance of being put into water, we should expect it to dissolve). Moreover, human linguistic dispositions are even much more enigmatic than dispositions such as solubility, for in that case it is essentially problematic to characterize the relevant circumstances.

The concept of disposition comes on board because we cannot simply claim: a sentence $X$ means "lo, a tiger!" if the competent speakers emit it always when there is a tiger around; we know that many people might refrain from commenting on the presence of the beast (preferring, perhaps, to run away – and rightly so!). Thus, to improve on this claim we may want to say that $X$ means "lo, a tiger!" if the speakers *tend to* (*have the disposition to*) emit it always when there is a tiger around. However, how to characterize this disposition? We should be able to say something to the effect that one is disposed to emit $X$ in the presence of a tiger iff one *does* emit it whenever there is a tiger around and some further conditions are fulfilled – but which conditions? That the person in question has no reason to stay silent? That she wants to let others know? That she is not dumb, nor too lazy, nor afraid to talk, etc. (*ad nauseam* ...)? Obviously none of this approaches an accurate characterization of the relevant circumstances.

These obstacles lead us into a true vicious circle: we claim that the meaning of a sentence is a matter of a disposition to utter the sentence; we reduce dispositions to specific behavior in specific situations; but in this case we are unable to specify the relevant circumstances otherwise than as those circumstances in which the relevant sentence is really uttered; hence we say, in effect, that the meaning of a sentence is a matter of uttering the sentence in those situations in which it is really uttered. Of course proponents of the dispositional analysis will claim that there *is* a possibility of characterizing the relevant circumstances explicitly (and that, moreover, the disposition is ultimately a matter of unknown, as yet, physical properties of the brain), but the fact that nobody has been able to progress very far in this direction seems to justify an utter skepticism here.

Hence I doubt that these obstacles can be overcome; it seems to me that the concept of disposition leads us up a blind alley and that we need a fresh start. However, we will abandon the topic for now and return to it later.

## 2   Why Meaning is Not a Represented Entity

We have seen that we may do well to regard the kind of treatment of expressions which grants them their meanings as a matter of the way we use them (rather than the way we conceive of them). Hence we have some arguments in favor of (i) (though, admittedly, they rely on the problematic concept of disposition). Now what about (ii)? Even if we do accept that meaning is determined by our usage rather than by our conception, why go on to say that meaning directly *is* the usage, rather than a thing linked to the expression by its usage? Why exchange the intuitively plausible model – building on the assumption that an expression relates to its meaning analogously to how a proper name relates to its bearer – for the *prima facie* non-intuitive notion of meaning as the 'way of usage'?

The core trouble is that the operation of *naming* and the ensuing notion of *being a name of* or *standing for*, despite appearances, is not something reasonably capable of serving as an 'unexplained explainer'. For what does it mean to be a name of something?

A proper name is usually associated with a person during an act such as christening; it is this act which establishes the relevant link. Hence it seems that we only have to find analogous acts conferring, in a similar way, meanings on other words of natural language. (And indeed this idea seems to underlie the accounts of language and its semantics given by more than one prominent philosopher.[3]) Hence, can we identify the alleged acts which make the types of sounds we emit, or of our inscriptions, into names or representations of certain entities? Preparatory to looking for these acts, we should clarify what generally makes an act into (an analog of) an act *of christening*.

We have put forward, as a paradigmatic act, the christening of a newborn baby; but clearly what makes something into the act relevant to our present search is not a church, a priest, nor any distinguished formula, nor a record in a registry office. Hence what is it? Obviously it is the way the act is 'grasped' by the members of the relevant community – namely the fact that they take it to establish the relevant link so that subsequently they take the sound- or inscription-type in question as standing for the christened entity.

However, what does it mean *to take a sound- or inscription-type as standing for an entity*? To conceive of it in a certain way? But we have already seen that the essentially private act of conception is not capable of grounding the essentially public institution of language. So the *taking*

---

[3]Viz., Charles Morris' (1966) concept of *semiosis*.

relevant here must be a matter of some communal practices. That people of some community mentally associate the name 'Hugo' with a certain person is a fact of their individual psychologies not capable of establishing the fact that 'Hugo' acts as a name of the person within their language – for in order for it to be a name, it is not enough that each of them individually associates it with a person, he/she must also know that the other ones do the same, that he/she can use the name to refer intelligibly to the person in various public circumstances, etc. Hence what is needed aside of the private associations are some public practices that make the link public and shared. And, as we have already seen, once the practices are in place, the private associations become redundant – from the viewpoint of the institution of language (though not from the viewpoint of the psychology of communication) it becomes the idle wheel whose presence or absence is destined to be beyond notice.

This indicates that an explanation of language which rests on the relation of *standing for* cannot be considered as a satisfactory ultimate explanation, but only, at most, as an intermediary step, inviting the subsequent step consisting in the explanation of the very relation of *standing for*. And since resting this last explanation on the facts of conception would not do, we have to proceed to the level of social practices. Hence we must agree with Wittgenstein, who concluded, in the words of Coffa (1991: 267), that "the ultimate explanatory level in semantics is not given by references to unsaturation or to the form of objects or meanings, but by reference to the meaning-giving activity of human beings, of activity embodied in their endorsement of rules."

To quote Wittgenstein (1958: 4) himself:

> Frege ridiculed the formalist conception of mathematics by saying that the formalists confused the unimportant thing, the sign, with the important, the meaning. Surely, one wishes to say, mathematics does not treat of dashes on a bit of paper. Frege's idea could be expressed thus: the propositions of mathematics, if they were just complexes of dashes, would be dead and utterly uninteresting, whereas they obviously have a kind of life. ... And further it seems clear that no adding of inorganic signs can make the proposition live. And the conclusion which one draws from this is that what must be added to the dead signs in order to make a live proposition is something immaterial, with properties different from all mere signs. But, if we had to name anything which is the life of the sign, we should have to say that it was its use. ... The mistake we are liable to make could be expressed thus: We are looking for the use of a sign, but we look for it as though it were an object co-existing with the sign.

## 3   Rules, Rule Following, and Normativity

Wittgenstein's conviction was that the things we do with language are so multifarious that it is helpful to call them games: just as the term "game" covers a huge span from children's chaotic antics to the meticulously orchestrated Football Champions League, our linguistic practices comprise a large span of very different kinds of practices:

> Wieviele Arten der Sätze gibt es aber? Etwa Behauptung, Frage und Befehl? – Es gibt unzählige solcher Arten: unzählige verschiedene Arten der Verwendung alles dessen, was wir "Zeichen", "Worte", "Sätze", nennen. Und diese Mannigfaltigkeit ist nichts Festes, ein für allemal Gegebenes; sondern neue Typen der Sprache, neue Sprachspiele, wie wir sagen können, entstehen und andre veralten und werden vergessen. (Ein ungefähres Bild davon können uns die Wandlungen der Mathematik geben.)[4]

However, his verdict about the heterogeneity of the games we play with language did not make him acquiesce within a linguistic relativism (though he is sometimes read in this way); instead it made him seek out what feature of these games gives language the special status it undoubtedly has. And as indicated within Coffa's characterization, given above, Wittgenstein became immensely interested in the fact that many of the games are *governed by rules*, moreover by rules which appear to be somehow *implicit*.

Why is government by rules so important? Because, as Wittgenstein recognized, it is precisely in this way that an expression can acquire meaning otherwise than by being made to stand for a thing. Meanings may be identified with the *roles* which the expressions play *vis-à-vis* the rules – roles of the kinds of those which make pieces of wood used in chess games into pawns, rooks, or kings.[5]

Why *implicit* rules? Because, as Wittgenstein realized, the rules of language cannot be all explicit – on pain of a vicious circle. We do have explicit rules of chess – we can take a book and read them there. However, to do this, we must know how to interpret the signs in the book – we must know the rules of their interpretation. Perhaps also these rules are somewhere written, but it is clear that the regress must

---

[4]"But how many kinds of sentence are there? Say assertion, question, and command? – There are countless kinds: countless different kinds of use of what we call 'symbols', 'words', 'sentences'. And this multiplicity is not something fixed, given once for all; but new types of language, new language-games, as we may say, come into existence, and others become obsolete and get forgotten. (We can get a rough picture of this from the changes in mathematics.)"

[5]For a detailed discussion of the notion of meaning as a role see Peregrin (2006b).

come to an end and at some point we must be able to follow the rules of interpretation without their being explicit. Elucidation of the nature of the implicit rule-following practices was one of Wittgenstein's principal aims in *Philosophical Investigations* and subsequently became the topic of one of the most heated philosophical debates of the second half of the twentieth century.[6]

What is important is that the realization of the key role of rules enables us to dispose of the troublesome concept of disposition. The point is that, as we can now see, the correct description of the link between a sentence meaning that there is a tiger around and the fact that there is a tiger around is not that the speakers are *disposed* to utter the former in case of the latter, but rather that it is, for them, *correct* (conforming to certain rules of language) to do so. And whereas saying that one is *disposed* to do something amounts to predicting that given suitable conditions one will inevitably do it, to say that one would be correct in doing so does not involve any prediction of this kind.

However, does it not follow that the correctness claim is merely chimerical in that it cannot be confirmed or disconfirmed by anything the speakers of the relevant language actually do? Not really. The acceptance of rules, albeit implicit, *must* be manifested by what they do; but it is manifested "on the metalevel" – namely by what Brandom (1994) calls the competent speakers' *normative attitudes*. We *take* some utterances for correct and we *take* others for incorrect – which may be manifested in various ways, from praising or rebuking our children for the way they talk to granting our fellow speakers various kinds of statuses, from "respected" or "reliable" to "devious" and "untrustworthy."

Of course our linguistic utterances can be classified as correct or incorrect in various senses; and consequently we have, if not entirely a motley of rules, then at least a multiplicity of their layers. An utterance may be correct in that it accords with the grammar of the language in question; it may be correct in that it says that things are in the way they really are; or, it may be correct, say, in that it is not offensive to the audience. The rules directly relevant for semantics are supposed to form one of these layers: namely the one which has to do with, as Aristotle put it, "saying of what is that it is" and which is normally associated with the concept of *truth*. Hence we may say that the relevant sense of "correct" is the one in which we can say that truth amounts to correct assertability.

---

[6]The debate was greatly invigorated in the eighties by Kripke's (1982) book, which was followed by a number of responses – see, e.g., Baker and Hacker (1984), McDowell (1984), or Boghossian (1989).

To avoid misunderstanding: this does not pave the way to the straightforward naturalization of the concept of *truth* and *meaning*. The problem consists in singling out the kind of correctness which amounts to truth without relying on the very concept of truth. Understanding this peculiar kind of correctness is apparently a matter of acquiring a know-how which is explicitly manifested by our usage of the very concept of *truth* – with the result that the specification of the relevant kind of correctness has to rest on the concept of truth rather than vice versa (see Peregrin (2006a) for more detail). Anyway, we may say, the recognition of the normative dimension of language, which is brought about by the realization of the key role of (various kinds of) rules within our language games makes us replace the concept of *disposition* engaged by the non-normative use-theories of meaning by the concept of *propriety*.

## 4   Pattern-Governed Behavior

To sum up: crucial for the Wittgensteinian view of language games is the idea that most of these games have rules (rather like chess or football[7]), and that the rules of at least the most basic of them must not be explicit – on pain of a vicious circle. Hence somewhere between the view that playing language games is a behavior which is merely *regular* (the view which we may call, together with Sellars, *regulism*) and the view that playing them is following rules explicitly (which Brandom dubs *regularism*) there must be room for a third possibility.

This is not the way the problem was addressed by Wittgenstein himself. The philosopher who first pointed it out in roughly these terms was Wilfrid Sellars (whose crucial writings, by the way, predate the publication of *Philosophical Investigations*). Sellars insisted that besides the "merely conforming to rules" and "rule obeying" there is a specific kind of behavior, characteristic of language games, which he called *pattern governed*. His proposal is that "an organism may come to play a language game – that is to move from position to position in a system of moves and positions and to do it 'because of the system' without having to *obey rules* and hence without having to be playing a *meta* language game" (Sellars 1954; 209).

How can a person's behavior become "pattern governed" in this way? Disregarding the possibility of its having been inborn (and it does

---

[7]As Lance (1998) duly points out, it is a *sport* like the latter, rather than a *game* like the former, that is analogous to our linguistic practices. What makes the difference is the extent of *embodiment*. A sport, just like language, is much more inextricably interconnected with our doings within the physical world.

not seem that our linguistic behavior *may* be inborn[8]), the only
possibility left is training. We are, as it were, squeezed into the pattern,
by being encouraged to behave in the right way and corrected if we
deviate from it – in other words, by the fact that our tutors assume
specific attitudes to our behavior. Hence, our tutors treat our behavior
as *right* or as *wrong*, in this way instituting a *rule*.

Sellars also stresses that the pattern is something that we were
taught by our tutors *ought to be*, and hence we take it that we *ought to
do* what would bring this *ought-to-be* about. Thus we reinforce the kind
of behavior of others, and especially of our tutees, which conforms to
the *ought-to-be* and we disapprove of that which does not conform to it.
This creates a circle, which (rather than being *vicious*) promulgates the
pattern of behavior from generation to generation.

It is quite clear that there are many kinds of behavior, to be
encountered across animal species, which would appear to deserve the
label "pattern governed" (the bee dance being one of the popular
examples). However, there is little doubt that these kinds of behavior
*are* inborn, resulting from the pressure of natural selection. Human
linguistic behavior is different in that it requires (besides natural
selection) a *society* with its mutual 'pressure' of its members on each
other. The relevant patterns are forced on us not (directly) by natural
selection, but by the ongoing demands of our peers. From this
viewpoint, a rule is a lever needed to put the exclusively human kind
of forming and maintaining patterns to work.

The rules of the language games, just like the rules of chess or
football, do not tell the players what exactly to do next. They restrict
the spectrum of possibilities – they tell us what the next move, given
the current position, *cannot* be; they always (perhaps with some trivial
exceptions) leave us more than a single option (usually dramatically
more). Of course: it is precisely opening up this space of possibilities out
of which the players must choose which makes a game what it is. This
means that the rules are plausibly seen more as constraints spelling out
what *not* to do than as prescriptions of what to do.

What do the constraints of our language games look like? Consider
assertion (seen by Sellars as a key move of a key language game). By
means of it, a speaker moves to a certain position – "scores," we might
say. However, if this assertion contradicts an assertion already made, it
does not count as "scoring" directly, but only potentially – directly it
counts as a *challenge*: it challenges the assertor of the assertion with

---

[8]Though, of course, many of its predispositions and maybe also some of its 'parts' may be.

which the current one is incompatible to either *defend* her assertion or to *retract* it (i.e., retreat from the position gained by its means). And only if the latter is the case, does the assertor of the current assertion count as "scoring."[9] What is essential from the viewpoint of this rule of "intolerability of incompatibilities" is which pairs (or perhaps greater sets) of utterances are incompatible (and indeed we *need* a nontrivial incompatibility relation to play our usual game of argumentation).

## 5   Playing Language Games, Part I: *Man Against Nature*

Hence, can we now envisage at last a very idealized example of a game we play with language? What does winning and losing in such a game amount to? We saw that Wittgenstein would say that the ways of language are so multifarious that such questions may not have any answer at all. However, it is probable that some of our language games are central, and others only marginal; some are essential and others optional; some are more and others less important. Could we, then, get a grip on the nature of language by pinpointing *the most crucial* language game? But the most crucial in which of all conceivable respects?

As what we are interested in is *semantics*, we should seek a game which is crucial from the viewpoint of the *constitution of meaning*. We have already seen that it is rather problematic to see the constitution of meaning as a matter of naming or christening, or more generally of an explicit convention – hence what is the crucial kind of game? And is there a game *crucial* in respect to the constitution of meaning at all?

It might seem to be natural to turn our attention to logic – for is it not logic that is the 'backbone' of language, and lays the foundations of its semantics? Hence are there some results of logic which can indicate what kind of semantically crucial game(s) we play with language?

An early attempt to represent the basic part of standard logic in game-theoretical terms, and also to account for what Wittgenstein had in mind when speaking about language games, is due to Jaakko Hintikka (from 1973 on).[10] What he did was that with each formula of standard logic (i.e., the first-order predicate calculus) he associated a game of two players, *Me* and *Nature*, so that the formula in question is

---

[9]Thus, this kind of scoring is not quite like scoring in football, where the goals are irrevocable.

[10]See Hintikka and Sandu (1997) for an overview.

valid iff *I* have a winning strategy; and it is contradictory iff *Nature* has a winning strategy. (For a fully interpreted language *My* winning strategy coincides with truth and *Nature's* winning strategy with falsity; in the case of a logical calculus there are, of course, many formulas with no winning strategy for either of us.)

For the first-order predicate calculus, the games, compared with the standard truth-definition, look as follows:

| traditional truth-definition | the associated game |
|---|---|
| $R(i_1, \ldots, i_n)$ is true iff the objects denoted by $i_1, \ldots, i_n$ are in the relation expressed by $R$; otherwise $R(i_1, \ldots, i_n)$ is false | *I* win the game associated with $R(i_1, \ldots, i_n)$ iff the objects denoted by $i_1, \ldots, i_n$ are in the relation expressed by $R$, otherwise *Nature* wins |
| $\neg A$ is true iff $A$ is false | the game associated with $\neg A$ starts with *I* and *Nature* swapping roles and continues as the game associated with $A$ |
| $A \wedge B$ is true iff $A$ is true and $B$ is true | the game associated with $A \wedge B$ starts with *Nature* choosing either $A$ or $B$ and continues as the game associated with the chosen formula |
| $A \vee B$ is true iff $A$ is true or $B$ is true | the game associated with $A \vee B$ starts with *I* choosing either $A$ or $B$ and continues as the game associated with the chosen formula |
| $\forall x A[x]$ is true iff for every element $i$ of the universe $A[x]$ is satisfied by $I$ | the game associated with $\forall x A[x]$ starts with *Nature* choosing an element $i$ of the universe and continues as the game associated with $A[x]$ with $i$ in the role of $x$ |
| $\exists x A[x]$ is true iff there is an element $i$ of the universe such that $A[x]$ is satisfied by $I$ | the game associated with $\exists x A[x]$ starts with *I* choosing an element $i$ of the universe and continues as the game associated with $A[x]$ with $i$ in the role of $x$ |

Let us consider an example: a statement of the form $((A \to B) \to A) \to A$, or, which is the same in classical logic, $A \vee \neg(A \vee \neg(B \vee \neg A))$. How would the associated game proceed? Do $I$ have a winning strategy?

1. As the statement is the disjunction of $A$ and $\neg(A \vee \neg(B \vee \neg A))$, it is *My* move and $I$ must choose one of the disjuncts. Distinguish two cases: If $A$ is true, $I$ may, of course, choose it; and I win. Let us therefore suppose that $A$ is not true – in such a case I choose $\neg(A \vee \neg(B \vee \neg A))$. (Let me remark that of course $I$ do not need to know whether $A$ is, or is not, true, and so $I$ may come to choose wrongly and consequently lose even if there is a winning strategy for *Me*. However, what interests us is not whether $I$ am really able to follow *My* winning strategy, but rather if such a strategy exists.)

2. As now we are facing a statement that is a negation, our roles are swapped and continue with the game associated with $A \vee \neg(B \vee \neg A)$.

3. This is a disjunction again, and hence again $I$ would have to choose one of the disjuncts; but as roles are swapped, it is *Nature* who chooses. *Nature* is thus to choose one of $A$ and $\neg(B \vee \neg A)$. As we have assumed that $A$ is false, if *Nature* chooses it, she loses (she would win if the roles were not swapped, but unfortunately for her, they are), so let us assume that she chooses the second one.

4. The roles are swapped again (so that they are back to normal now) and we continue with the game associated with $B \vee \neg A$.

5. $I$ choose one of $B$ and $\neg A$; and of course $I$ choose the second.

6. The roles are swapped and we continue with the game associated with $A$.

7. It is *Nature*'s turn, and as $A$ is false and the roles are swapped, I win.

---

[11]One of the morals which Hintikka has drawn from these considerations is that the boundaries of standard logic are rather arbitrary. The point is that seen from this game-theoretical perspective, classical logic restricts itself to zero-sum two-player games with complete information. Especially the last restriction seemed unwarranted to Hintikka; and he started to investigate logics whose formulas may amount to games with incomplete information. The result has been his *independence-friendly logic* or *IFL* (see, e.g., Hintikka, 1996). The distinction between IFL and standard logic comes to the surface especially in the case of chained quantifiers: whereas in classical logic all quantifiers must be linearly ordered, IFL allows, in effect, for only a partial ordering: the associated games are such that some of the choices of individuals from the universe, made either by *Me* or by *Nature*, are made, as it were, in parallel rather than in sequence.

Hence we have shown that $I$ have a winning strategy for every $A$ and $B$ – in other words we have shown that the formula $((A \to B) \to A) \to A$ (known as Peirce's law) is a tautology.[11]

In this way we see that the rules of logic can also have an 'interactive' reading – we can read them not as describing the truth or satisfaction conditions for various kinds of statements, but rather as spelling out rules of a language game. In this way, the concept of truth gives way to the concept of *winning strategy*, thus making the assertion of every sentence a game of its own, a game which the assertor wins if she is able to defend the truth of the assertion.

Hintikka's great achievement was that he showed how the logicians' activities of capturing the 'logical backbone' of language could also be seen as describing the most basic kind of language game we play. However, his games are not the kind we were envisaging above – they are duels of a solitary individual against the world, not social games in which people make each other conform to various kinds of patterns. Are we able to do better in this respect?

## 6 Playing Language Games, Part II: *Homo Homini Competitor*

Wrestling with the problem of meaning in mathematics, some philosophers came to the conclusion that what gives a *mathematical* statement its meaning are the ways in which it can be proved, i.e., inferred from axioms; and that meanings of mathematical terms are consequently their contributions to the inferential properties of statements in which they occur. In particular, Michael Dummett (1975, 1976) proposed generalizing this approach beyond the boundaries of mathematics – to see the meaning of a sentence as generally grounded in the ways in which this statement can be justified (plus what role within justification of other statements it may play). Hence could we perhaps see *justification* as underlying the game generally constitutive of meaning?

On first sight, this seems implausible. Outside of mathematics, we use language for many purposes utterly different from justification; justifying may be one of our language games, but, *prima facie*, not one outshining the others. However, we do also use the language of mathematics for many other purposes than proving – e.g., for formulating hypotheses, for storing knowledge, even for making jokes – and this does not seem to contradict the fact that proving is what is crucial for its semantics. So could it be that even with respect to the entire natural language, the activity of justification, though by far not the most frequent language game, and certainly not the most important in all respects, is nevertheless responsible for what we see as meanings? Why should this be so?

The prototypical kind of meaning to be encountered in the context of a distinctively human language is a *concept*, typically the meaning of a common noun, such as "pig" or "philosopher." As already Kant established, concepts are inseparably connected with *judgments* – concepts are, by their very nature, *constituents of judgments*. Hence to have meaning of the kind our usual words have is to be capable of occurring within sentences which are used to make claims. Now a judgment is something which, by *its* nature, exists within a logical space – for nothing is reasonably considered a judgment if it cannot be negated, conjoined with other judgments, inferred from other judgments, etc. – i.e., if it does not constitute, together with other judgments, a complex logical structure. Now the relationships constitutive of this structure can be reduced to the relation of inference – or better of (*correct*) *inerrability*.[12]

Games more closely resembling the actual practices of justifying and arguing about justifiability were presented by Paul Lorenzen and his fellow German logical constructivists. They saw their *dialogic logic* (Lorenzen and Schwemmer, 1975) as predominantly a tool of elucidation of the semantics of logical constants; for their games are devised to capture the most basic semantic operations which characterize the constants. Their approach, however, received very little international attention – until its rediscovery in the course of the recent boom of game-theoretic semantics.

Here the games are not those of *Me* against *Nature*, but games among participants of an argument. Arguments are seen as the putting forward, challenging, and defending of theses. The *Proponent* asserts a statement and the *Opponent* tries to challenge it, by attacking the asserted statement or its parts. He does so by means of asserting other statements, which can in turn be challenged by the *Proponent*. The *Proponent* wins if she deflects all the attacks and if there is no other way for the *Opponent* to attack her.

The rules, specifying what counts as an admissible attack and what as a defense against it are summarized in the following table (note that though *prima facie* one may defend oneself by asserting even

---

[12]Thus a conjunction of $A$ and $B$ can be characterized and the maximal statement from which $A$ and $B$ are inferable, etc. – see Peregrin (2006c) for more detail.

something unwarranted, this would be of no help, for whatever one asserts becomes a legitimate target of a further attack):

| statement | the way(s) of attacking it | the way of defending it against the attack |
|---|---|---|
| $A \wedge B$ | challenging $A$ | asserting $A$ |
|  | challenging $B$ | asserting $B$ |
| $A \vee B$ | challenging | asserting $A$ or asserting $B$ |
| $\neg A$ | asserting $A$ | - |
| $A \rightarrow B$ | asserting $A$ | asserting $B$ |
| $\exists x A[x]$ | challenging | asserting $A[i]$ |
| $\forall x A[x]$ | challenging $A[i]$ | asserting $A[i]$ |

The games within the framework of dialogic logic are then subject to some further restrictions, which do not concern individual types of attack, but the overall structure of the game. Standardly, the following constraints are in force:

(a) The *Proponent* can assert an atomic statement only after it was already asserted by the *Opponent*.
(b) It is possible to defend only the statement lastly attacked.
(c) Only one response to an attack is possible.
(d) An assertion of the *Proponent* may be attacked only once.

The loser of the game is then the player who can make no further legitimate move.

Let us return to our example $((A \rightarrow B) \rightarrow A) \rightarrow A$. (Within this framework, it is *not* equivalent to $A \vee \neg(A \vee \neg(B \vee \neg A))$ – which indicates that we are deviating from classical logic.) The game would now proceed as follows:

1. The *Proponent* asserts $((A \rightarrow B) \rightarrow A) \rightarrow A$.
2. The *Opponent* attacks by asserting $(A \rightarrow B) \rightarrow A$.
3. The *Proponent* cannot defend her assertion against this attack (for she would have to assert the atomic statement $A$, which is forbidden by (a)); however, she may counterattack and challenge the *Opponent*'s assertion. Hence she asserts $A \rightarrow B$.
4. If the *Opponent* were to defend it by asserting $A$, the *Proponent* could use this to repeat this assertion and thereby eventually defend her original assertion; the *Opponent* is thus left with a counter-attack, which, by chance, again amounts to asserting $A$.

5. This is the end of the *Proponent*, for her defense would amount to asserting *B*, which is not possible due to (a). Moreover, she is no longer able to reassert *A* to defend her original statement, for this would break the law (b). The *Proponent* thus has no move left and loses.

In this case, in contrast to the previous one, there is *not* a winning strategy for the *Proponent*. This means that the set of statements for which there is a winning strategy for the *Proponent* within this type of game does not coincide with the set of those in which there is a winning strategy for *Me* within the previous one. What is remarkable is that, as it turns out, this set coincides with the set of statements which are valid within intuitionist logic. (And what is even more remarkable is that we can reach classical logic by canceling some of the above constraints. For example, as we saw, if we cancel (b), then there would be a winning strategy for the *Proponent* in our game.)

Anyway, here we have a *social* rendering of the interactive aspect of the logical backbone of our language – a game consisting in defending one's claim against possible challenges. We are going to see that it is precisely this kind of game which may be seen as the basic building block of our everlasting meaning-conferring games.

# 7   Giving and Asking for Reasons

Hence we have some (very idealized) examples of the (simplest) kind of games which we play with language and which we claim are responsible for the meanings of our words. However, these games are rather like what are called "games" in tennis, i.e., each of them is only a small part of what we perceive as the truly significant game – the whole match consisting of several sets each of them consisting of several games. (It is, however, worth noticing that the distinction between a part of a game and the whole game is often context-dependent: sometimes a single set or perhaps a single tennis game could constitute the whole match; while sometimes even a match could be a part of a bigger venture – such as, in the case of tennis, the Davis Cup.) Hence what is 'the whole match' to which the games envisaged in the previous section add up?

Robert Brandom (1994), elaborating on the proposals of Sellars, suggested that it is our permanent game of "giving and asking for reasons," characteristic of a specific feature of us, humans, as opposed to other kinds of animals. There are many language games we play, some of them closely resembling activities of our animal pals; but, according to Brandom, it is *giving and asking for reasons* which is distinctive of us humans *as rational animals*. To be reasonable is to be able to reason, and to be able to reason is to be able to request and provide reasons.

This is, of course, interconnected with the Kantian observation mentioned above, namely that the *modus vivendi* of the distinctively human kinds of meanings consists in constituting judgments and that judgments need to be situated within a logical space. It is precisely this space which we can also call *the space of reasons* – the space maintained by our ability to reason and by our ensuing activities of requiring and providing reasons.

This brings us to a further distinctive feature of the human way of promulgation of patterns: the promulgation is social in a peculiarly human way. We can surely imagine that a kind of behavior which we would tend to call pattern-governed evolves simply as the result of the pressure of natural selection; and we can even imagine that a similar kind of behavior evolves not because individuals of the species in question have been naturally selected directly for this kind of behavior, but rather for the tendency to force the behavior on their fellow individuals, by somehow 'rewarding' them for behaving in this way and 'penalizing' them for deviations. Though this is imaginable (despite the fact that it might be hard to grasp why natural selection would act in such a roundabout way), this is still *not* the very kind of behavior characteristically instantiated by our language games. The reason is that the kind of patterned-governed behavior represented by them, and especially the game of *giving and asking for reasons*, though surely also underpinned by some mechanisms resulting from natural selection, is promulgated in a still more intrinsically social way.

The point is that in functioning as language tutors, we not only force the relevant patterns on our tutees but also make them do the same with *their* tutees (where the tutor-tutee relation is not a strictly irreflexive one – to a certain extent everybody acts as a tutor of everybody else). And, we may say, what makes this possible is 'normativity': the tutee not only comes to behave in a certain way, but also comes to grasp it as the *ought-to-be*, which makes her become a tutor herself. Thus, in contrast to the previous case, the tendency to force the relevant pattern onto others is not inborn, but rather acquired during the process of tuition in one package with the behavior itself.

Now we may ask: what makes this kind of 'normativity' possible – what makes us able to bind ourselves by rules? And one of the possible answers to this question, the one stressed by Brandom, is that it is our *responsibility*. (Hence another interconnection with Kant.) Rules of this peculiarly human kind, those which "tend to propagate themselves," may obtain because we are able to hold each other responsible for what we do – hence we are able to undertake *commitments* and to be granted *entitlements*. Thus, we take an assertor to be *committed* to defending (i.e., justifying) his assertion if challenged, and only if he is really capable of doing so, we consider him as truly *entitled* to the commitment. On the other hand, the audience of the assertor are *entitled* to adopt his assertion – to reassert it deferring its defense to him.

It is the filigree web of commitments and entitlements which is the normative substrate through which rules can exist without being written down – as "written in flesh and blood, or nerve and sinew, rather than in pen and ink" (Sellars, 1949: 299). It is the attitudes of holding each other responsible for what one does, holding each other committed or entitled to various things, which provides for the fact that what we do, including what we assert and infer, counts as right or wrong. And it is these rules of asserting and inferring which confer meaning on our expressions. In this way, the Brandomian story tries to flesh out the microstructure of the game of *giving and asking for reasons*.

What, then, about the macrostructure of the game, does it have room for something as winning and losing at all? What happens if an assertor does not manage to defend his assertion against challenges? It depends on many other circumstances; but in the majority of cases the consequences are not substantial. However, repetitive losing in this kind of game would mean, in the long run, descending the ladder of trustworthiness to the point of being wholly excluded from the range of people whose assertions (and perhaps other activities too) are to be taken seriously. This indicates that people need to keep track of their peers' victories and defeats – how do they do it? Do we store some mental lists of people around us, with red and black points?

The problem of "scorekeeping in a language game" was probably first explicitly tackled by David Lewis (1979). Brandom's version of the story is based on the assumption that what we keep track of are not directly any points (or victories and defeats) of our fellow language users, but rather their commitments and entitle-ments. If somebody asserts, say, that flat taxation is the way to prosperity, we ascribe to them a commitment to justify this claim (and also a default entitlement to it); and we register the general entitlement to repeat this claim deferring its justification to the assertor. When later somebody else claims that flat taxation is the way to impoverishment, we expect the original assertor to fulfill their commitment, and if they cannot, we retract their entitlement to it, provisionally granting it to the new assertor with the commitment to defend *his* claim.

To sum up: since we humans recognize each other as potentially responsible beings, as potential bearers of commitments and entitlements, we continuously do deals with each other as players of various commitment/entitlement games (social practices), especially of the game of giving and asking for reasons. And this game is inextricably integrated with language – not only that it uses language as its crucial equipment, but it is this very game that makes language into what it is – what provides for its expressions to acquire their meanings.

## 8    Conclusion: A Normative Use-Theory?

We can, finally, return to the original problem of meaning and its use-theories: the normative version of the use-theory we have reached does not literally identify meaning with a *way of usage*, but rather with a *role conferred by rules*. This accounts for meaning as a specifically human matter – but not because a man is the exclusive owner of a mind-stuff whose chunks are able to animate dead signs, but because a man has the exclusive ability of binding himself with rules.

It is, of course, questionable if what we have reached should still count as a species of the use-theory of meaning at all. Maybe not – for what meaning here consists in is not so much the ways of employment of our expressions, but rather the ways of assessment of such employment, the ways we take those employments for right and wrong. It is precisely these takings for right or wrong, these normative attitudes, that provide for the existence of the kind of rules which govern our language games and thus open up the space of reasons in which the expressions may become meaningful. But be this as it may, I am convinced that this theory of meaning is the right one.

## References

Baker, G. P. and P. M. S. Hacker. 1984. *Scepticism, Rules and Language.* Oxford: Blackwell.

Boghossian, P. 1989. The rule-following considerations. *Mind* 98:507–549.

Brandom, R. 1994. *Making It Explicit.* Cambridge, MA: Harvard University Press.

Coffa, A. 1991. *The Semantic Tradition from Kant to Carnap.* Cambridge: Cambridge University Press.

Dummett, M. 1975. What is a theory of meaning? In S. Guttenplan, ed., *Mind and Language.* Oxford: Clarendon Press.

Dummett, M. 1976. What is a theory of meaning? (II). In G. Evans and J. McDowell, eds., *Truth and Meaning,* pp. 67–137. Oxford: Oxford University Press.

Hintikka, J. 1973. *Logic, Language-Games and Information.* Oxford: Clarendon Press.

Hintikka, J. 1996. *The Principles of Mathematics Revisited.* Cambridge: Cambridge University Press.

Hintikka, J. and G. Sandu. 1997. Game-theoretical semantics. In J. van Benthem and A. ter Meulen, eds., *Handbook of Logic and Language,* pp. 361–410. Oxford: Elsevier.

Kripke, S. 1982. *Wittgenstein on Rules and Private Language.* Cambridge, MA: Harvard University Press.

Lance, M. N. 1998. Some reflections on the sport of language. *Philosophical Perspectives* 12:219–240.

Lewis, D. K. 1979. Scorekeeping in a language-game. *Journal of Philosophical Logic* 8:339–359.

Lorenzen, P. and O. Schwemmer. 1975. *Konstruktive Logik, Ethik und Wissenschaftstheorie.* Mannheim: Bibliographisches Institut.

McDowell, J. 1984. Wittgenstein on following a rule. *Synthèse* 58:325–363.

Morris, C. W. 1966. *Foundations of the Theory of Signs (International Encyclopedia of Unified Science 1).* Chicago: University of Chicago Press.

Peregrin, J. 2006a. Brandom and Davidson: What do we need to account for thinking and agency?. *Philosophica* 75:43–59.

Peregrin, J. 2006b. Developing Sellars' semantic legacy: Meaning as a role. In M. Lance and P. Wolf, eds., *The Self-Correcting Enterprise: Essays on Wilfrid Sellars,* pp. 257–274. Amsterdam: Rodopi.

Peregrin, J. 2006c. Semantics as based on inference. In J. van Benthem, G. Heinzmann, M. Rebuschi and H. Visser, eds., *The Age of Alternative Logics,* pp. 25–36. Dordrecht: Kluwer. (The version printed in the book was tampered with in an unauthorized way, so please use the correct version available from my web page at *jarda.peregrin.cz.*)

Quine, W. V. O. 1969. *Ontological Relativity and Other Essays.* New York: Columbia University Press.

Saussure, F. de. 1931. *Cours de linguistique générale.* Paris: Payot. [*Course in General Linguistics.* New York: Philosophical Library, 1959.]

Sellars, W. 1949. Language, rules and behavior. In S. Hook, ed., *John Dewey: Philosopher of Science and Freedom,* pp. 289–315. New York: Dial Press.

Sellars, W. 1954. Some reflections on language games. *Philosophy of Science* 21:204–228.

Wittgenstein, L. 1953. *Philosophische Untersuchungen [Philosophical Investigation]*. Oxford: Blackwell.

Wittgenstein, L. 1958. *The Blue and Brown Books*. Oxford: Blackwell.

# 9

# Say *What?* A Game-Theoretic Approach to the Said/Implicated Distinction

IAN ROSS

**Abstract**

The Games of Partial Information (GPIs) of Parikh (2001) can be used to show that cases of putative implicature in the 'intrusive constructions' of Levinson (2000) are indeed implicatures and *not* part of what is said. In order to reach this conclusion, we must discard reinforceability and cancellability as necessary conditions for conversational implicature. Our game-theoretic model shows that tests of these conditions are sometimes not felicitous as a corollary of interlocuters' utility maximization in sentential contexts. As a result of these arguments and those put forth by Saul (2002), a simpler theory of the semantics/ pragmatics interface can be maintained: one in which ordinary implicatures of sub-sentential constituents do not serve as input to the semantic calculation of the parent sentence.

## 1 Introduction

Where does semantic meaning end and pragmatic meaning (specifically in the form of conversational implicature) begin? Forms contentiously known as *intrusive constructions* (which involve (embedded) implicatures (Levinson, 2000; Recanati, 2003a, b), *free enrichment explicatures* (Carston, 1988) or *implicitures* (Bach, 1994), depending on who you

*Making Semantics Pragmatic*
Ken Turner (ed.).
Current Research in the Semantics/Pragmatics Interface, Vol. 24.

ask) are one class of examples (among many others) that researchers have used to support their respective positions in this larger debate (Recanati, 2003a, b; Bianchi, 2004; Szabo, 2005; Cappelen and Lepore, 2005). While these constructions have so far primarily been used to support Relevance Theory (Carston, 2004) over (neo-)Gricean conceptions of pragmatics, a fresh analysis shows that they need not be a thorn in the neo-Gricean's sides, as they appear to be in Levinson (2000), *inter alia.*

A textbook example of an intrusive construction is shown in (1).

(1) Their parents would prefer it if they got married and had a child, rather than if they had a child and got married.

The puzzle – the example's defining feature – is this: if we interpret *and* as logical conjunction, then the two subclauses, shown in (2a) and (2b), are semantically equivalent. But if this is so, then what is said in (1) is that these parents prefer A to A, which is a contradiction. But (1) does not feel like a contradiction in the slightest. So, the argument goes, perhaps (2a) and (2b) should not be considered semantically equivalent, at least within the context of (1).

All participants in the debate agree that what is communicated (Grice, 1975) by (2a) is (2c) and what is communicated by (2b) is (2d) (with similar content for (1), shown in (2e)), even if they reject Grice's specific terminology. The question, then, is what exactly is said (in the Gricean sense) and what is implicated (if anything) by (1)? Specifically, is the element of temporal succession conveyed by *and* part of what is said or part of what is implicated?

(2) a. They got married and had a child.
    b. They had a child and got married.
    c. They got married and then had a child.
    d. They had a child and then got married.
    e. Their parents would prefer it if they got married and *then* had a child, rather than if they had a child and *then* got married.

This puzzle does not arise in the subclauses of (1) when they are removed from such a context, as they are in (2a) and (2b). Here, there are no contradictions, apparent or otherwise. These sentences have a straightforward neo-Gricean analysis (namely, they contain the generalized conversational implicatures (GCIs) known as I-implicatures, in Levinson's terminology). On the surface at least, (2a) and (2b) are very different beasts than (1). In addition to (1) possibly being a contradiction on the level of what is said and (2a) and (2b) not being so, (1) cannot be felicitously reinforced or cancelled,[1] whereas both (2a) and (2b) can be. Despite all of this, we shall see later that these two cases are not really so different after all. The notion that cancellability is a necessary condition for (at least some) conversational implicatures has recently been challenged by others as well. Weiner (2006) does so on somewhat different grounds than the reasoning presented here, and Huitink and Spenader (2004) do so on more related grounds for particularized conversational implicatures (PCIs).

## 2   The Bigger Picture

The puzzle above is connected to a much larger one: how does conversational implicature projection work? Classical formal implicature theory (Gazdar, 1979) fails for examples like (3) from Sauerland (2004), and only recently have theories been proposed that cover not only the 'base case' but also the inductive step of implicature projection. These are the first comprehensive attempts of demonstrating the compositionality of conversational implicatures.

(3)  Kai had some of the peas or the broccoli last night.

The two leading approaches to implicature projection have been detailed by Sauerland (2004) and Chierchia (2004). Sauerland proposes a minimal extension of Gazdar's implicature projection algorithm ('Gazdar's bucket'), whereas Chierchia proposes a parallel compositional, semantic-style theory that enriches the meaning of scalar implicature triggers (like *some*) as a function of the entailment patterns of the greater context. Sauerland's theory can be thought of as *top-down* while Chierchia's can be thought of as *bottom-up*. Implicatures do not serve as input to larger constituents in Sauerland's theory, while they do in Chierchia's. The theories are empirically distinct and neither's predictions are a subset of the other's (Ross, 2005).

   The basic idea of Sauerland's theory is to generalize Gazdar's approach to sentences with multiple scalar implicature triggers by using Cartesian products. Instead of having a single list of alternatives (that asymmetrically entail the original sentence) that vary in exactly one place, we now have a *product* of alternatives that vary in up to $n$ places, where $n$ is the number of scalar implicature triggers in the original sentence. In cases like (4), this simple generalization (generate

---

[1]Largely held to be the most reliable test for implicatures (Sadock, 1978), with Grice (1989) supporting the latter's felicity being a necessary condition.

the product of asymmetrical entailments and label their negations as implicatures) will yield the correct implicatures (although not without some redundancy), shown in (5)–(7).

(4) Kai had some of the peas and some of the broccoli last night.
(5) ¬Kai had all of the peas and some of the broccoli last night.
(6) ¬Kai had some of the peas and all of the broccoli last night.
(7) ¬Kai had all of the peas and all of the broccoli last night.

Cases like (3), in which one scalar implicature trigger (*some*) is within the scope of another (*or*), require more work. For details, see Sauerland (2004).

The basic idea of Chierchia's theory is to provide a compositional semantics of scalar implicature. Chierchia's semantics is multidimensional: conventional literal meaning is covered by the semantics of what he calls *plain meaning*, while lexicalized (scalar) implicature meaning is covered by the semantics of what he calls *strong meaning*. Just as sentences have asserted and presupposed content, Chierchia argues that they have plain (semantic) and strong (pragmatic) meaning. Whether a scalar implicature trigger gives rise to an implicature is a function of, among other things, whether the local context is downward entailing. For example, *few* is a downward entailing operator, which can be observed by noting that *few people left* entails *few people left early* (the set of people that left early obviously being a subset of the set of people that left).

This same issue that Sauerland and Chierchia are trying to address is present in (1). Do the implicatures get calculated in a bottom-up way and get filtered out (or switched off) by the local context, or are they calculated in a top-down way and discarded if they stand in a particular logical relation to the context sentence on the level of what is said? Sauerland's and Chierchia's theories are only claimed to apply to scalar implicatures (therefore they are inapplicable to the issue presented in (1) as they currently stand), but an analysis of (1) can offer evidence of which broad approach is likely to be more successful. The analysis offered by Carston (2004) (and largely accepted by Levinson (2000)) hews closer to the spirit of Chierchia's theory than Sauerland's; in that implicatures are calculated locally rather than globally. I will argue that, to the contrary, the best analysis of (1) refutes the view of Relevance Theory proponents and that moreover this analysis has more in common with Sauerland's approach (not Chierchia's, which has been argued against by Russell (2004) on more specific grounds), and that GCIs on the whole are more amenable to Sauerland's treatment, rather than Chierchia's.

## 3  Reinforcement and Cancellation Data

Here, we will examine the felicity of reinforcements and cancellations of putative implicatures embedded and unembedded in the problematic context shown in (1), and a number of related ones. There are four parameters which we will examine in detail.

1. Types of GCIs (Q[uantity] vs. M[anner] vs. I[nformativeness] from Levinson)
2. Reinforcement vs. cancellation
3. Tautological vs. contradictory contexts
4. Interior vs. exterior implicature reinforcement/cancellation (disambiguation).

We will examine each parameter in turn.

Parameter 1: (1) is an I implicature (arising from the heuristic 'what is expressed simply is stereotypically exemplified'), (8) is a Q implicature (arising from the heuristic 'what isn't said, isn't') and (9) is an M implicature (arising from the heuristic 'what's said in an abnormal way isn't normal').

(8) I would prefer it if some of the guests accompanied me rather than if all of them did so.
(9) I would prefer being caused to die over being killed.

Parameter 2: (10) is a reinforcement of (2a) and (11) is a cancellation of it.

(10) They got married and had a child ... (in that order/in particular, they got married and *then* had a child).
(11) They got married and had a child ... (but not (necessarily) in that order/but it is not the case that they got married and *then* had a child).

Parameter 3: (1) is a contradictory context – on the level of what is said, *prefer*, which induces a total order on the subclauses it has, causes the matrix clause to be contradictory. (12) is a tautological context – on the level of what is said, *indifferent*, which induces an equivalence class on the subclauses it has, causes the matrix clause to be tautological.

(12) Their parents are indifferent between them getting married and having a child and them having a child and getting married.

Parameter 4: In (10), the implicature is reinforced by what I will call an *exterior* reinforcement – it appears in a new clause subsequent to the one that had the original implicature. In (2c), the implicature is reinforced by what I will call an *interior* reinforcement – it appears in the same clause as the one that had the original implicature (further distinctions along these lines can be made, e.g. 'some but not all dogs ... ' vs. 'some dogs but not all of them ... ', but we will confine ourselves to interior/exterior, which is perhaps the simplest way to illustrate that parameters like these matter).

By allowing these parameters to freely vary, we can gain insight into their relative contributions to (in)felicity. In the following examples (in which '#' denotes infelicity), *i–iii* contain Q, M and I implicatures, respectively and *a* and *b* contain internal and external implicature modifications, respectively. (13) and (14) are reinforcements and (15) and (16) are cancellations, while (13) and (15) are tautological contexts and (14) and (16) are contradictory ones.

(13)  a.  i.   # × 2 I am indifferent between some but not all of the guests accompanying me and all of them doing so.

 ii.  # I am indifferent between being caused to die indirectly and being directly killed.

 iii. # Their parents are indifferent between them getting married and then having a child and them having a child and then getting married.

 b.  i.   # × 3 I am indifferent between some of the guests accompanying me (but not all of them) and all of them doing so.

 ii.  # × 3 I am indifferent between being caused to die and being killed, when the former happens in an indirect manner and the latter happens in a direct one.

 iii. # × 3 Their parents are indifferent between them getting married and having a child and them having a child and getting married, in those respective orders.

(14)  a.  i.   # × 2 I would prefer it if some but not all of the guests accompanied me rather than if all of them did so.

 ii.  # I would prefer being caused to die indirectly over being directly killed.

 iii. # Their parents would prefer it if they got married and then had a child, rather than if they had a child and then got married.

 b.  i.   # × 3 I would prefer it if some of the guests accompanied me (but not all of them) rather than if all of them did so.

     ii.  ♮ × 3 I would prefer being caused to die over being directly, when the former happens in an indirect manner and the latter happens in a direct one.

     iii.  ♮ × 3 Their parents would prefer it if they got married and had a child, rather than if they had a child and got married, in those respective orders.

(15)  a.  i.  ♮ × 4 I am indifferent between some, in fact all, of the guests accompanying me and all of them doing so.

     ii.  ♮ × 3 I am indifferent between being caused to die with a gunshot to the head and being killed in exactly the same manner.

     iii.  ♮ × 4 Their parents are indifferent between them getting married and having a child in no particular order and them having a child and getting married in no particular order.

  b.  i.  ♮ × 5 I am indifferent between some of the guests accompanying me (in fact all of them) and all of them doing so.

     ii.  ♮ × 4 I am indifferent between being caused to die and being killed, presuming both happen in exactly the same manner.

     iii.  ♮ × 5 Their parents are indifferent between them getting married and having a child and them having a child and getting married, neither in any particular order.

(16)  a.  i.  ♮ × 5 I would prefer it if some, in fact all, of the guests accompanied me rather than if all of them did so.

     ii.  ♮ × 4 I would prefer being caused to die with a gunshot to the head over being killed in exactly the same manner.

     iii.  ♮ × 5 Their parents would prefer it if they got married and had a child in no particular order, rather than if they had a child and got married in no particular order.

  b.  i.  ♮ × 6 I would prefer it if some of the guests accompanied me (in fact all of them) rather than if all of them did so.

     ii.  ♮ × 5 I would prefer being caused to die over being killed, presuming both happen in exactly the same manner.

     iii.  ♮ × 6 Their parents would prefer it if they got married and had a child, rather than if they had a child and got married, neither in any particular order.

If the implicature disambiguations (i.e. reinforcements or cancellations) in (13b-iii), (14b-iii), (15b-iii) and (16b-iii) are unclear, they can be replaced by more explicit continuations, like *but not/in fact ... they got married and then had a child ... they had a child and then got married.*

What can we conclude about the above four parameters from the relative felicity of these examples? First let us note why reinforcements and cancellations are to some degree infelicitous in the preceding contexts. Reinforcements are problematic because of their perceived redundancy (which is aggravated by their context here, since it all but forces the unmarked reading even without reinforcement, making it all that much more unnecessary) and cancellations are problematic because in these contexts they result in either a tautology or a contradiction.

For parameter 1, putative Q implicatures appear to be the least amenable to reinforcement (with I and M implicatures being roughly equally amenable) and Q and I implicatures appear to be the least amenable to cancellation, with M implicatures being more amenable. So overall, Q implicatures are the least disambiguable. This is to be expected since Q implicatures are also the least indeterminate. In most, or at least many cases, the scales are more explicit and fixed than their analogues among I and M implicatures which do not have anything as precise as scales accompanying them. As a result, disambiguations of Q implicatures have fewer degrees of freedom (just those corresponding to different items on the relevant scale) than I and M implicatures. For example, the I implicature from A and B could be temporal, causal, teleological (or some set of these) or have its roots in another relation, and M implicatures are often even more 'slippery'. Since I and M implicatures can come in related non-overlapping families of meaning (e.g. causal and temporal), it is difficult to unambiguously reinforce or cancel (all of) them, which is not the case for most Q implicatures. Since the contexts in the examples above indirectly disambiguate the implicature (by way of reinforcement), an explicit reinforcement of a Q implicature would be even more redundant than I or M reinforcements since they are the least indeterminate (they have nothing informative to contribute, whereas the I or M reinforcements could be more easily construed to mean something additional). Similarly, Q cancellations in the above contexts are also more uninterpretable (due to the resultant tautology or contradiction) than I or M cancellations. For example, one could 'save' a sentence like (16a-ii) by interpreting 'killed in exactly the same manner' so as to not be coextensive with 'caused to die with a gunshot to the head'. That 'kill' and 'cause to die' can happen in exactly the same manner but are still somehow different, just as someone might be said to walk and run in exactly the same manner.

For parameter 2, cancellations are far less felicitous than rein-forcements in the above contexts for previously mentioned reasons: the redundancy of reinforcements is not as much a violation of the Cooperative Principle (Grice, 1975) as the tautologies and contradictions that result from cancellations.

For parameter 3, resultant tautologies appear to be somewhat more felicitous than contradictions insofar as (inexplicable) flouts of quality are more serious than those of quantity.

For parameter 4, internal disambiguations appear to be more felicitous than external ones when the phrasing of the continuation is held relatively constant, but when it is not (particularly when internal continuations are more prolix or awkwardly phrased) internal disambiguations may not be more felicitous.

Stepping back a moment, we can see that regardless of how the above parameters are set, putative implicatures in the above contexts are not readily and felicitously reinforceable or cancellable. Insofar as reinforceability or cancellability serves as a test for conversational implicature, examples like (1) seem to indicate that what would otherwise act as an implicature in a different context is in fact not an implicature in the context of (1), and many theorists have accepted as much. However, as we will see, reinforceability or cancellability should not be considered necessary conditions for conversational implicature.

## 4   A Game-Theoretic Solution

Quality (and Quantity) flouts like (1) cannot easily be felicitously cancelled or reinforced, while their simple non-flouting cousins can be ... why? And what are the consequences for pragmatic theory? At the highest level, the distinction between flouting and non-flouting contexts is this: the flouting context itself reinforces the implicature implicitly – reinforcing it again explicitly is needlessly redundant and cancelling it explicitly is contradictory since it has already been (implicitly) reinforced.

Flouts that avert (by way of implicature) tautologies and logical contradictions are far less reinforceable and cancellable than those that merely avert lapses in relevance or the various submaxims of manner. In a sense, these flouts serve as implicature reinforcement of their own kind.

The violations of Quantity and Quality that we have examined so far have been extreme cases (instances of the most extreme cases possible, in fact). There is nothing more blatantly false than a contradiction, and nothing more obviously uninformative than a tautology. Due in part, I believe, to their more non-logical and context-sensitive character, Relevance and Manner do not have such precise extremes. No one is likely to agree on what the most irrelevant statement one could make (even in a particular context) is, nor would people likely be able to agree on the most obscure or ambiguous expressions (although it might be easier to agree on the most non-brief (i.e. infinitely long) and non-orderly expressions).

One can arguably cancel flouts of each maxim, but their plausibility varies widely, as can be seen in (17)–(20), the first two of which are adapted from Grice (1975) ((18) serving as a letter of recommendation for a university faculty position in philosophy).

(17) MANNER: Miss X produced a series of sounds that corresponded closely with the score of 'Home Sweet Home'. In fact, it was as close as a human being has ever come without the use of pitch-shifting software.

(18) RELEVANCE: Mr. X's command of English is excellent, and his attendance at tutorials has been regular. Given how non-fluent and truant the rest of my students are, Mr. X is the only one who meets the minimum standards in these essential areas.

(19) QUANTITY: I am indifferent between some, in fact all, of the guests accompanying me and all of them doing so. Moreover, as a matter of definition, I am indifferent between all equivalent courses of action.

(20) QUALITY: I would prefer it if they got married and had a child in no particular order, rather than if they had a child and got married in no particular order. I am also a very confused person who has trouble making sense.

If successful reinforcement and cancellation tests are necessary conditions for conversational implicature, it is difficult to see how (13)–(16) can be accommodated by a neo-Gricean view like that of Saul (2002). However, we will show that this is in fact possible.

The lens through which we will examine the above puzzles is utility maximization, which is a key component in game and decision theory (Osbourne and Rubinstein, 1994), and is expressed in higher-level terms of description by Grice (1975), and previously in terms of *Speaker's Economy and Auditor's Economy* by Zipf (1949), and further elucidated by Horn (1984) and, more recently, the games of partial information (GPIs) of Parikh (2001). Our aim is to distinguish the cases of rein-forcement and cancellation above from sentences like (21) and (22), in which entailments, not implicatures, are attempted to be reinforced and cancelled, with the effect being incomprehensibility – (21) is redundant and (22) is contradictory. Both types are infelicitous; however, they owe their infelicity to different sources; the previous examples do not reinforce or cancel entailments of what is said – only of what is implicated.

(21) ♯ Most, in fact some, of the guests left early.
(22) ♯ Most, but not some, of the guests left early.

The key question to be answered is why, if sentences like (1) contain conversational implicatures, can they not be felicitously reinforced or cancelled? If this question can be answered satisfactorily, Saul's defense of sentences like (1) as maxim flouts, that counterintuitively or not, have nonsensical content on the level of what is said, can be freed from doubts arising from the contention that reinforceability or cancellability is a necessary condition of conversational implicature and that consequently there is no flout in (1).

The solution will be presented in terms of sketches of GPIs for concreteness, although it is likely amenable to other formalisms involving utility maximization as well. GPIs formalize the tension between utterers (who seek to expend the least resources communicating their intentions) and addressees (who seek to ensure that their interpretation of the utterance is in fact the correct one). These dual tensions are represented in a game in extensive (i.e. sequential) form. These games have a set of players P (each of which has a nonempty set of available actions $A_i$) that take turns executing actions and a preference relation $\geq_i$ on $A = (A_1, \ldots, A_N)$ (i.e. outcomes of every player's actions – each global strategy yields an outcome).

In a GPI, first the utterer chooses a proposition to communicate, and given that proposition, chooses a form to utter, then given that form (but not the proposition), the addressee chooses what (s)he believes to be the intended proposition. A solution to such a game takes the form of a function that maps intended propositions to uttered forms (for the utterer) and maps uttered forms to intended propositions (for the addressee). In Figure 1 is an example featuring the choice between sentences (23)–(25).

(23) Some but not all of the boys smoke.
(24) ♯ Some of the boys, but not all (of them), smoke.
(25) ♯ Some of the boys smoke, but not all do.

In Figure 1, only the utterer has a choice to make (namely, which form to utter, given an intended meaning). *l* is the only action available to the addressee. In this GPI, there are three possible outcomes: one for each

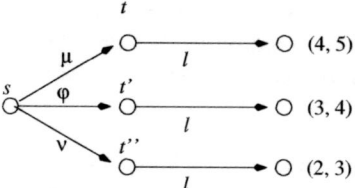

*intentions (utterer)*
*s*: some but not all of the boys smoke

*sentences*
μ: "some but not all of the boys smoke"
φ : "some of the boys, but not all (of them), smoke"
ν : "some of the boys smoke, but not all do"

*situations (addressee)*
*t,t',t''*: speaker utters  φ

*propositions*
*l*: that some but not all of the boys smoke

FIGURE 1    GPI with only one proposition.

possible action of the utterer. Each of these outcomes assigns a payoff
(which is a function of richness of content and complexity of form) to the
utterer and addressee (the first and second coordinates, respectively – the
specific numbers are unimportant here; their significance is in their relation
to the values of other payoffs). A necessary condition for a solution to a GPI
is that it should be a Nash Equilibrium (in this respect, GPIs are similar to
Bidirectional Optimality Theory (Dekker and van Rooy, 2000), which
ensures that neither player (utterer or addressee) can unilaterally deviate
from the solution (by choosing a different individual action) profitably. In
this case, it is easy to select the solution (with payoff (4, 5)) because the
addressee has only one action to choose from. Only the utterer has the
option of deviating (from the action μ), and it would be unprofitable to do
so. (24) and (25) are examples of suboptimal forms, given the intended
meaning *s*. (23)–(25) each contain the same reinforcement and are truth-
conditionally equivalent, but they differ in form (syntactic structure and
length), with some forms being longer (and containing less informational
density/entropy) than others. Since the longer sentences are not any
more clear or unambiguous, the shortest sentence provides the maximal

utility to the interlocuters, *pace* discourse function etc. Aside from discourse function, obviously there may be other reasons for (24) or (25) to be uttered. One large reason relates to the exigencies of online natural language generation. After having already spoken, or at least having begun to speak, the utterer may realize that (s)he wishes to make a different statement, or to ensure that the statement that was made is (more or less) unambiguously understood. In this case, what has already been said can be viewed as a sunk cost, at which point a possibly verbose correction may still be optimal, given the sunk cost.[2]

In Figure 2 a full GPI with multiple propositions is shown, involving both reinforcements and cancellations similar to (10) and (11). The box surrounding both $t$ and $t'$ indicates that these states are indistinguishable to the addressee (although not to the utterer) because the intentions of the utterer are not available to the addressee.

The constituents of the players' payoffs in Figure 2 are shown in Table 1, which is adapted from Parikh (2001). This is currently just a sketch of what payoff components could be (and how their weights could be set). A longer term goal is to recursively tie such components and their weights to forms and meanings. The payoff of an outcome in a GPI with more than one possible intended meaning (which is to say any useful GPI) is determined by multiplying the estimated prior probabilities of each intended proposition (shown as $\rho$ and $\rho'$ in Figure 2) by the payoff that the strategy jointly chosen by the utterer (vocalization) and addressee (interpretation) provides to both players, and summing these products together. The possible outcomes of the game in Figure 2, and their payoffs, are shown in (26).

(26)   a.   $(s \to \varphi, \, s' \to \varphi; \, \varphi \to p)$
       $.8(7, \, 8) + .2(-5, -4) = (4.6, \, 5.6)$
    b.   $(s \to \varphi, \, s' \to \varphi; \, \varphi \to l)$
       $.8(-4, -3) + .2(2, \, 3) = (-2.2, \, -1.2)$
    c.   $(s \to \mu, \, s' \to \varphi; \, \varphi \to p)$
       $.8(6.6, \, 7.8) + .2(-5, \, -4) = (4.28, \, 5.44)$
    d.   $(s \to \mu, \, s' \to \varphi; \, \varphi \to l)$
       $.8(6.6, \, 7.8) + .2(2, \, 3) = (5.68, \, 6.84)$
    e.   $(s \to \varphi, \, s' \to v; \, \varphi \to p)$
       $.8(7, \, 8) + .2(.8, \, 2.4) = (5.76, \, 6.88)$

---

[2]This parallels the solution concept of Subgame Perfect Equilibrium (Osbourne and Rubinstein, 1994), which disallows any global strategy that involves players choosing a non-Nash Equilibrium strategy to the subgame that remains after part of the global game has already been played.

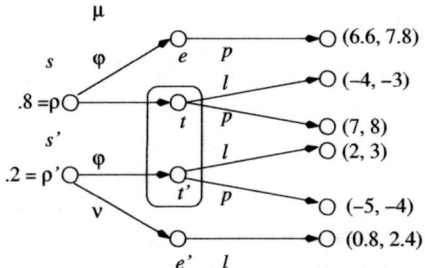

*intentions (speaker)*
s : they got married and then had a child
s': they got married and had a child in no particular order

*sentences*
μ : "they got married and then had a child"
φ : "they got married and had a child"
v : "they got married and had a child in no particular order"

*situations (addressee)*
e: speaker utters  μ
t,t': speaker utters φ
e': speaker utters v

*propositions*
p: that they got married and then had a child
l: that they got married and had a child in no particular order

FIGURE 2    GPI for an I implicature.

f.  $(s \to \varphi, s' \to v; \varphi \to l)$
    $.8(-4, -3) + .2(.8, 2.4) = (-3.04, -1.92)$

g.  $(s \to \mu, s' \to v; \varphi \to p)$
    $.8(6.6, 7.8) + .2(.8, 2.4) = (5.44, 6.72)$

h.  $(s \to \mu, s' \to v; \varphi \to l)$
    $.8(6.6, 7.8) + .2(.8, 2.4) = (5.44, 6.72)$

Observe that (26d) and (26e) are the only Nash Equilibria in (26).

Given (26d), if the addressee deviates to $p$ (the only other choice), the payoff drops to that of (26c). If the utterer deviates to $\varphi$ for both s and $s'$, $\varphi$ and $v$, or $\mu$ and $v$, the payoff would drop to that of (26b), (26f) or (26h), respectively.

For (26e), if the addressee deviates to $l$, the payoff drops to that of (26f). If the utterer deviates to $\varphi$ for both $s$ and $s'$, $\mu$ and $\varphi$, or $\mu$ and $v$, the payoff would drop to that of (26a), (26c) or (26g), respectively.

TABLE 1    Constituents in payoff functions

| Payoff | Players | Explanation |
|---|---|---|
| +4 | A, B | Correct interpretation to *l* |
| +6 | A, B | Correct interpretation to *p* (in addition to the 4 from *l*) |
| −2 | A, B | Incorrect interpretation |
| −1 | A, B | Processing $\varphi$ |
| −1 | A | Producing $\varphi$ |
| −1 | A, B | Additional cost of communicating *p* (over *l*) |
| −.2 | A, B | Additional cost of processing $\mu$ |
| −.2 | A | Additional cost of producing $\mu$ |
| −.6 | A, B | Additional cost of processing $v$ |
| −.6 | A | Additional cost of producing $v$ |

To ensure a unique solution in the above case (but not necessarily in all cases), we can impose an additional criterion on the solution concept: Pareto-dominance. (26e) Pareto-dominates (26d) because both players receive a larger payoff from (26e). If one player received a larger payoff from (26d) and the other received a larger payoff from (26e), neither solution Pareto-dominates the other.

(26d) and (26e) are complements of each other. In (26d), the more informative meaning is assigned an unambiguous (and longer) form and the less informative one is assigned the ambiguous (and shorter) form (to be sure, ambiguity is a matter of degree[3]). In (26e), the case is reversed. In both cases, the unambiguity of one of the forms is used to exploit (and reduce if not eliminate) the ambiguity of the remaining form. The only question is which meaning should be assigned to the shorter, more ambiguous form. In GPIs, this will be a function of the prior probabilities of the intended (and available) propositions and the payoffs associated with each outcome.

As it has been sketched out here, the model is too rough to say exactly what the solution should be with any confidence – the exact solution will depend on the numbers mentioned above, which are just estimates. But by examining the payoffs to the outcomes as a family, we can see the different tiers of payoffs (and outcomes that give rise to them)

---

[3]'A proposition like 'this chair is brown' seems to say something enormously complicated, for if we wanted to express this proposition in such a way that nobody could raise objections to it on grounds of ambiguity, it would have to be infinitely long' (Wittgenstein, 1961: 5e). Thanks to Prashant Parikh for bringing this quote to my attention.

that remain constant through any reasonable tweaking of the payoff constituents or prior probabilities. The first tier, already discussed, is (26d) and (26e). Depending on the numerical details, one of these two forms of outcomes is extremely likely to be the solution to any analogous game. After these two, the strategies (which result in the same outcome here) with the next highest payoff are (26g) and (26h). These are strategies for universal disambiguation: both $s$ and $s'$ are given forms that are longer than $\varphi$ but less ambiguous. Intuitively, the payoffs these yield are suboptimal because the simplicity of form is sacrificed for (partially unnecessary) disambiguation.

Next are (26a) and (26c). In (26a), the same form is chosen for both intended meanings, which introduces a major ambiguity. When $s$ is intended, the addressee interprets it correctly, but when $s'$ is intended (which is far less frequent), the addressee interprets it incorrectly. (26c) runs parallel to (26d) except that $s'$ is misinterpreted as $p$. It is perhaps possible for a strategy like (26a) to yield higher payoffs than strategies like (26d) and (26e) in some circumstances. Namely, when the cost to use a disambiguating form is so high that it is worth absorbing the cost of ensured misinterpretation by using the same form for different intended meanings. However, a strategy like (26c) is unlikely to ever yield an optimal payoff because whatever the payoff constituents are, strategies like (26d) will always be preferred – correct interpretations beat misinterpretations, *ceteris paribus* (a conditions which holds across the comparison of (26c) to (26d)).

Lastly, we have (26b) and (26f), which are the only strategies with negative payoffs for both players. (26b) stands in the same relation to (26a) as (26c) does to (26d). (26f) also stands in this same relation to (26e).

Now consider Figure 3, which shows a GPI corresponding to cases like (1). The material in Figure 2 is embedded in a construction that causes a flout, with payoffs correspondingly changed. Specifically, the correct interpretation of $l$ in this case now has a payoff of 0.

Additionally, the payoffs could be changed so that communicating $l$ is more costly than communicating $p$ (rather than *vice versa*) if one believes that communicating a contradiction is more costly (because it is so nonsensical) than communicating an informative proposition (which, if one takes contradictions as maximally informative and tautologies as minimally so, does not go against the pattern in Table 1 that the more informative the proposition, the more costly it is to communicate it).

If this change is made to the costs of communication, we can observe an interesting property that neither of the previous two games we examined exhibited. Namely, there are two unequal (non-global)

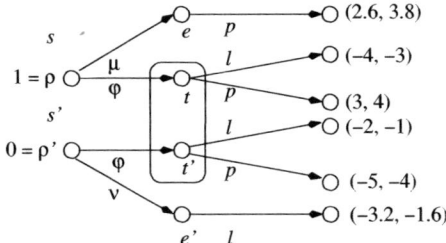

(2.6, 3.8)
(−4, −3)
(3, 4)
(−2, −1)
(−5, −4)
(−3.2, −1.6)

*intentions (speaker)*
s: it is preferred that they get married and then have a child
   rather than have a child and then get married
s': it is preferred that they got married and had a child in no particular
   order rather than have a child and get married in no particular order

*sentences*
μ : "it is preferred that they get married and then have a child
   rather than have a child and then get married"
φ : "it is preferred that they get married and have a child
   rather than have a child and get married"
ν : "it is preferred that they get married and have a child in no particular
   order rather than have a child and get married in no particular order"

*situations (addressee)*
e:   speaker utters     μ
t,t': speaker utters     φ
e':   speaker utters     ν

*propositions*
p: that it is preferred that they get married and then have a child
   rather than have a child and then get married
l: that it is preferred that they got married and had a child in no particular
   order rather than have a child and get married in no particular order

FIGURE 3   GPI for a quality flout.

payoffs neither of which Pareto-dominates the other. The payoff
(unweighted by prior probabilities) for $(s' \to \varphi; \varphi \to p)$ is changed from
$(-5, -4)$ to $(-4, -3)$ and the payoff for $(s' \to \nu; \varphi \to p)$ and $(s' \to \nu; \varphi \to l)$
is changed from $(-3.2, -1.6)$ to $(-4.2, -2.6)$. Note that the utterer's
and addressee's preferences conflict in this case. Given the choice
between these two payoffs, the utterer would prefer uttering φ *and
being misinterpreted* to uttering ν and being understood (although there
is not much to understand in this particular case), while the addressee
would prefer to correctly understand ν rather than misinterpret φ. This

conflict illustrates the tension between the utterer preferring simple forms (since it is (s)he, not the addressee, who must utter them) more than the addressee, sometimes at the cost of correct interpretation (as in this case).

Here, we take the prior probability of the intended meaning being a logical contradiction as 0. Note that there are many reasons for why one would utter a logical contradiction, but there are many fewer reasons (if any) for why one would *intend to communicate* one. If the whole $s'$ branch is weighted by 0, the actions the players choose on it are irrelevant and do not contribute to the total payoff. In this case, $(s \to \varphi; \varphi \to p)$, which yields a payoff of $(3, 4)$, is the solution.

If, however, we perturb the prior probabilities in this game by $\Sigma = .01$, the solution then becomes $(s \to \varphi, s' \to v; \varphi \to p)$, which has a payoff of $(2.938, 3.944)$. For $s$, this solution conforms to our intuition that *and* is interpreted as *and then* (pragmatically, not semantically) in sentences like $\varphi$. For $s'$, however, the sentence $v$ seems somewhat unsatisfactory, perhaps just because $s'$ itself is so unsatisfactory. One option is to add an empty form (call it $\phi$) to the $s'$ branch. That is, the utterer would now have the explicit choice of uttering nothing when intending to communicate $s'$. This may seem to be an odd choice, but depending on the payoff successfully communicating $s'$ yields, it may be the optimal strategy. In the GPI in Figure 3, if the utterer tries to communicate $s'$, both players are guaranteed to receive negative payoffs (i.e. it would be better if the actions that led to this payoff did not happen). One could make a case that $\phi$ would yield higher payoffs for both players than either $\varphi$ or $v$. Specifically, since there is no utterance or interpretation, the payoff for $\phi$ would be $(0, 0)$. On the other hand, one could argue that this degenerate (non-)interpretation is an incorrect one since it is presumably not a contradiction, and should therefore incur a cost of $-2$ for both utterer and addressee (from Table 1). Depending on which of these views one takes, the solution will be the previous one $(s \to \varphi, s' \to v; \varphi \to p)$, or $(s \to \varphi, s' \to \phi; \varphi \to p)$ with a payoff of $(2.97, 3.96)$.

The question we set out to answer in this section was why, if sentences like (1) had implicatures, some implicatures (like that in (2a) could be felicitously cancelled while others (like those in (1)) could not. We now have an answer from game theory, demonstrating that we can maintain the view that (1) contains implicatures (i.e. the temporal meaning of *and* is *not* part of what is said) and that these particular implicatures cannot be felicitously reinforced or cancelled for independent reasons that do not have the *ad hoc* character of Levinson's characterization of intrusive constructions.

Regarding reinforceability, the payoff difference between a reinforced implicature ($\mu$) and an unreinforced but at least nominally ambiguous one ($\varphi$) is smaller in relative and absolute terms (roughly (1.4%, .58%) vs. (13.3%, 5%) and (.08, .04) vs. (.4, .2)) in the game in Figure 2 (roughly corresponding to (2a)) than it is in the game in Figure 3 (roughly corresponding to (1)). That is, reinforcements in sentences like (1) are further from optimal (although both are nonoptimal) than are reinforcements in sentences like (2a), largely because of the differences in prior probabilities between the two types of games. Moreover, the prior probabilities for games like that in Figure 2 are inherently more indeterminate than those like that in Figure 3 because the intended meaning $s'$ in Figure 3 is a contradiction, which under any reasonable assumptions will have at most a negligible prior probability. But $s'$ in Figure 2 is a significant proposition, whose prior probability could have a much wider range under the same assumptions. If its prior probability $\rho'$ increased from .2 to over .25, the winning strategy of the game would change from (26e) to (26d). In this context, reinforcement provides much more value – it is much less certain whether the assumed interpretation is in fact the correct one (the unmarked reading of $\varphi$ in Figure 2 is much less unmarked than the unmarked reading of $\varphi$ in Figure 3).

As for cancellability, the answer is even clearer. The cancellation $v$ in Figure 2 yields positive payoffs for both utterer and addressee, while the cancellation $v$ in Figure 3 yields negative payoffs for both utterer and addressee (because the communicated content, a contradiction, provides no counterbalancing positive payoff in this case). Intuitively, sentences like (16a-iii) are a contradiction on two levels: both on the level of what is said and on the level of what is implicated. By virtue of being a quality flout, it is a contradiction on the level of what is said. But by cancelling the implicature that the flout gives rise to, one is also left with a contradiction on the level of what is implicated. The contradiction on the level of what is said is thus rendered incomprehensible: flouts are used to trigger implicatures but if those implicatures are then immediately cancelled, then the presumed original purpose of the flout is obviated – the original contradiction was for nothing. The result is *worse* than uninformative, if the addressee properly interprets such constructions, they appear irrational, and if (s)he does not, they appear deceptive. Implicatures in such contexts must in fact be true to salvage the coherence of the utterance.

The case of tautologies parallels the case we have sketched out for contradictions, and one could similarly build games to illustrate the difference between Q, M and I implicatures (the M and I games would likely have more possible intended meanings) and internal and external disambiguations (whose relative complexities would affect payoffs). Just like contradictions, tautologies provide no positive payoff for being communicated and their prior probabilities as intended meanings are near if not at 0. The most efficient way to be uninformative is to utter nothing, not to utter a tautology that is intended to be interpreted as such.


## 5   Conclusion

Constructions like (1) present two chief challenges to those who maintain a neo-Gricean conception of what is said. The first of these challenges (mounted by proponents of Relevance Theory and others), that addressees do not consciously interpret sentences like (1) as logical contradictions and therefore no logical contradiction exists on the level of what is said, has been convincingly answered by Saul (2002) – one need not concede that the truth conditions of a sentence like (1) depend on the conversational implicatures of its constituents, and a simpler theory of the semantics/pragmatics interface can be preserved (as Horn (2006) maintains).

The second of these challenges, which this chapter aims to address, is as old as the idea of implicature itself: if a putative implicature cannot be cancelled (or reinforced), it is not an implicature. This second challenge, if successful, has the ability to pre-empt Saul's argument in cases like (1) – by the neo-Griceans' own tests, the putative implicatures are in fact not implicatures so they must be part of what is said and therefore no contradiction ever arises. We have argued, using a game-theoretic model, that both reinforceability and cancellability should not be considered necessary tests for conversational implicature and that differences in felicitous reinforcement and cancellation among implicatures in differing contexts can be accounted for on other grounds (namely, utility maximization). The redundancy of reinforcements of (1) and the incomprehensibility of cancellations of (1) (infelicity in both cases) are corollaries of the GPIs we have built and solved.

Having addressed both of these challenges, one can still maintain that the inference from *and* to *and then* in both (1) and (2a) is not part of what is said, but is one and the same implicature in both cases (*contra* Levinson (2000)), and that this implicature need not serve as input to the compositional semantics of the parent sentence to derive its intuitive meaning (2e).

This line of argumentation removes a large class of constructions that have been held as evidence that the pragmatics (implicature (or explicature or impliciture) in particular) of sub-sentential expressions feeds into semantic computation. This is perhaps suggestive that attempts like Chierchia's, that aim to show that pragmatics serves as the input to semantics and even syntax, may not ultimately be successful.

### Acknowledgements

Thanks to the audience of the 2005 International Pragmatics Association conference's 'Making Semantics Pragmatic' panel, at which many ideas in this chapter were first presented. Thanks also go to Robin Clark and Prashant Parikh for illuminating discussion and thoughtful criticism. All remaining errors are my own.

# References

Bach, K. 1994. Conversational impliciture. *Mind and Language* 9(2):124–162.

Bianchi, C., ed. 2004. *The Semantics/Pragmatics Distinction.* Stanford: CSLI.

Cappelen, H. and E. Lepore. 2005. *Insensitive Semantics: A Defense of Semantic Minimalism and Speech Act Pluralism.* Oxford: Blackwell.

Carston, R. 1988. Implicature, explicature, and truth-theoretic semantics. In R. Kempson, ed., *Mental Representations: The Interface Between Language and Reality*, pp. 155–181. Cambridge: Cambridge University Press.

Carston, R. 2004. Relevance theory and the saying/implicating distinction. In L. Horn and G. Ward, eds., *Handbook of Pragmatics*, pp. 633–656. Oxford: Blackwell.

Chierchia, G. 2004. Scalar implicatures, polarity phenomena, and the syntax/ pragmatics interface. In A. Belletti, ed., *Structures and Beyond: The Cartography of Syntactic Structures*, pp. 39–103. Oxford: Oxford University Press.

Dekker, P. and R. van Rooy. 2000. Bi-directional optimality theory: An application of game theory. *Journal of Semantics* 17(3):217–242.

Gazdar, G. 1979. *Pragmatics: Implicature, Presupposition, and Logical Form.* New York: Academic Press.

Grice, H. P. 1975. Logic and conversation. In P. Cole and J. Morgan, eds., *Syntax and Semantics 3: Speech Acts*, pp. 41–58. New York: Academic Press.

Grice, H. P. 1989. *Studies in the Way of Words.* Cambridge, MA: Harvard University Press.

Horn, L. 1984. Toward a new taxonomy for pragmatic inference: Q-based and R-based implicature. In D. Schiffrin, ed., *Meaning, Form, and Use in Context: Linguistic Applications*, pp. 11–42. Washington, DC: Georgetown University Press.

Horn, L. 2006. The border wars: A neo-Gricean perspective. In K. von Heusinger and K. Turner, eds., *Where Semantics Meets Pragmatics*. Oxford: Elsevier.

Huitink, J. and J. Spenader. 2004. Cancelation resistant PCIs. In R. van der Sandt and B. Geurts, eds., *Proceedings of the ESSLLI 2004 Workshop on Implicature and Conversational Meaning*. Nancy.

Levinson, S. 2000. *Presumptive Meanings: The Theory of Generalized Conversational Implicature*. Cambridge, MA: MIT Press.

Osbourne, M. J. and A. Rubinstein. 1994. *A Course in Game Theory*. Cambridge, MA: MIT Press.

Parikh, P. 2001. *The Use of Language*. Stanford: CSLI.

Recanati, F. 2003a. *Literal Meaning*. Cambridge: Cambridge University Press.

Recanati, F. 2003b. Embedded implicatures. *Philosophical Perspectives* 17(1):299–332.

Ross, I. 2005. Some Implicature Theories Beat Some (Other) Implicature Theories. Second Symposium of the Penn Working Group in Language.

Russell, B. 2004. Against grammatical computation of scalar implicatures. In R. van der Sandt and B. Geurts, eds., *Proceedings of the ESSLLI 2004 Workshop on Implicature and Conversational Meaning*. Nancy.

Sadock, J. 1978. On testing for conversational implicature. In P. Cole, ed., *Syntax and Semantics: Pragmatics*, pp. 281–297. New York: Academic Press.

Sauerland, U. 2004. Scalar implicitures in complex sentences. *Linguistics and Philosophy* 27(3):367–391.

Saul, J. 2002. What is said and psychological reality: Grice's project and relevance theorists' criticisms. *Linguistics and Philosophy* 25(3):347–372.

Szabo, Z., ed. 2005. *Semantics versus Pragmatics*. Oxford: Oxford University Press.

Weiner, M. 2006. Are all conversational implicatures cancelable? *Analysis* 66(2):127–130.

Wittgenstein, L. 1961. *Notebooks 1914–1916*. (Ed. By G. H. von Wright and G. E. M. Anscombe.) Oxford: Blackwell.

Zipf, G. 1949. *Human Behavior and the Principle of Least Effort*. Cambridge: Addison-Wesley.

# Index